COOPERATIVE LEARNING
IN DIVERSE CLASSROOMS

♦

JoAnne Putnam
UNIVERSITY OF MAINE
AT PRESQUE ISLE

Merrill,
an imprint of Prentice Hall
UPPER SADDLE RIVER, NEW JERSEY
COLUMBUS, OHIO

Library of Congress Cataloging-in-Publication Data

Putnam, JoAnne W. (JoAnne Wachholz)
    Cooperative learning in diverse classrooms / JoAnne Putnam.
        p.   cm.
    Includes bibliographical references and index.
    ISBN 0-02-397043-X
    1. Group work in education. 2. Multicultural education. 3. Minorities—
Education.   I. Title.
    LB1032.P88   1997
    371.3'95—dc20

96-22673
CIP

Editor: Debra A. Stollenwerk
Production Editor: Mary Harlan
Photo Researcher: Dawn Garrott
Design Coordinator: Jill E. Bonar
Text Designer: Kip Shaw
Cover photo: © Ed Elberfeld/Uniphoto Picture Agency
Cover Designer: Brian Deep
Production Manager: Deidra M. Schwartz
Electronic Text Management: Marilyn Wilson Phelps, Matthew Williams, Karen L.
    Bretz, Tracey Ward
Illustrations: Berry Bell Graphics

This book was set in Bookman by Prentice Hall/Merrill and was printed and bound
by Book Press, Inc., a Quebecor America Book Group Company. The cover was
printed by Phoenix Color Corp.

© 1997 by Prentice-Hall, Inc.
Simon & Schuster/A Viacom Company
Upper Saddle River, New Jersey 07458

Photo credits: Scott Cunningham/Merrill/Prentice Hall: pp. 4, 37, 54, 101; Anthony
Magnacca/Merrill/Prentice Hall: pp. 13, 64, 98; Barbara Schwartz/Merrill/Prentice
Hall: pp. 109, 143, 190; Anne Vega/Merrill/Prentice Hall: pp. 111, 157, 178; Tom
Watson/Merrill/Prentice Hall: pp. 24, 35, 61, 134; Gordon Wiltsie/AlpenImage Ltd.:
pp. 14, 16; Todd Yarrington/Merrill/Prentice Hall: p. 185. Additional photos
supplied by the author.

Printed in the United States of America

10 9 8 7 6 5 4 3 2 1

ISBN: 0-02-397043-X

Prentice-Hall International (UK) Limited, *London*
Prentice-Hall of Australia Pty. Limited, *Sydney*
Prentice-Hall of Canada, Inc., *Toronto*
Prentice-Hall Hispanoamericana, S. A., *Mexico*
Prentice-Hall of India Private Limited, *New Delhi*
Prentice-Hall of Japan, Inc., *Tokyo*
Simon & Schuster Asia Pte. Ltd., *Singapore*
Editora Prentice-Hall do Brasil, Ltda., *Rio de Janeiro*

To David and Roger Johnson,
who have inspired generations of children
and adults throughout the world to learn
and live more cooperatively.

EX
LIBRIS

SAINT
JOSEPH'S
COLLEGE
RENSSELAER
INDIANA

Gift

PREFACE

◆

Purpose

Cooperative learning has emerged as a powerful method for fostering children's achievement and sociopersonal development in today's heterogeneous classrooms. Our rapidly changing population has created opportunities and challenges for teachers due to the rich diversity in public school classrooms. This diversity includes a mix of students from different cultural, ethnic, and socioeconomic backgrounds as well as students with various cognitive, behavioral, sensory, and physical abilities. Because cooperative learning is highly compatible with the instruction of diverse groups of students, various methods of cooperative learning have been developed and elaborated on, such as Group Investigation, Learning Together, Cooperative Structures, Student Team Learning, and Complex Instruction. More recently, cooperative learning approaches to conflict resolution and peer mediation are gaining in popularity as educators address the disturbing trends in youth violence.

Extensive literature supports cooperative learning as one method of enhancing student achievement and social development. Indeed, it has been said that cooperative learning is one of the most extensively evaluated instructional innovations in the United States. Before undertaking this writing project, I asked myself the inevitable question: Do we really need another book on cooperative learning? Is anything missing from the literature that teachers and future teachers might benefit from? Is there a more creative way to synthesize the literature on the research, theory, and practice of cooperative learning to be more relevant to the issues and problems now confronting teachers?

In reflecting on my own experiences with cooperative learning at the university, and the feedback of my students and public school teachers I have consulted and collaborated with, I concluded that, yes, a book is needed. I identified three major needs which evolved into the purposes that guided the development of this book. First, educators and students preparing to be educators want a book that *presents the various methods of cooperative learning*—not just one method. They want to not only increase their repertoire of cooperative approaches but also understand the circumstances in which each is most useful. Second, students and teachers want a book that specifically *addresses the needs of a greater diversity of learners*, including students from different cultural and ethnic backgrounds as well as those with exceptional needs. They want practical strategies and specific examples of how to modify cooperative activities to respond appropriately to the unique needs of particular students. Finally, they want more ideas about techniques for *assessment and methods for reflective problem solving in cooperative learning*.

It appears, fortunately, that the days of mechanistically implementing pre-established lesson plans are waning in U.S. education. While a point of departure for learning the craft of teaching may be working with ready-made lesson plans that present clear-cut instructions and formulas, the more **learner-focused** (as opposed to lesson-focused) teachers often find these formulas inadequate in meeting the needs of all learners. Successful teachers must be creative in their application of instructional and curricular approaches as they build on the strengths and resources of *all* children. To do so requires that teachers possess a repertoire of instructional strategies, and that they know when to apply them.

Audience and Intended Uses

This book is written for teachers, college students preparing to be teachers, special educators, counselors, school psychologists, paraprofessionals, and administrators who are interested in cooperative learning. The comprehensive and research-based presentation promotes understanding of the circumstances in which cooperative learning most improves student performance. It also offers a wealth of practical ideas for creative cooperative group instruction. The chapter on cooperative behavior management contains information on organizing and managing cooperative classrooms, preventing student misbehaviors, and helping students improve their own behaviors.

Using nontechnical language, this text is intended to be accessible to a broad audience. It will serve as a supplementary text for university methods courses in elementary and secondary education, courses in special education and teaching diverse learners, educational psychology courses, and counseling courses. It is also intended for use by practicing teachers and education professionals who want to expand their conceptual and practical knowledge of cooperative learning. Some reviewers have indicated they would adopt it as a primary methods text due to its comprehensive look at cooperative learning, teaching diverse learners, and classroom management.

Organization

The first section of the book makes a case for using cooperative learning in the classroom. Chapters 1 and 2 provide a foundation for cooperative learning instruction. Chapter 1 describes what is and what is not meant by cooperative learning and presents the context for cooperation in today's classroom and society. The essential components of cooperative learning are identified and distinguished from traditional groupwork. Chapter 2 presents a rationale for using cooperative learning that is grounded in research and theory.

Section 2 provides information on facilitating cooperative learning. Chapter 3 sets forth the practical how to's of cooperative lesson planning. Illustrative vignettes and lesson plans have been incorporated from a variety of grade levels and curricular areas to provide personal, real-life examples of cooperative learning planning and implementation.

Chapter 4 focuses on cooperative behavior management by discussing techniques that prevent or minimize student misbehavior; cooperative classroom management approaches that empower students to take responsibility for their own behaviors; techniques for solving conflicts cooperatively; and specific techniques for helping individual students improve their own behavior during cooperative and other classroom activities.

The final section of the book contains material on extending and evaluating cooperative learning. In an effort to move beyond the basics of cooperative learning to greater breadth of applications and a greater depth of understanding about how we evaluate cooperative group endeavors, Chapters 5 and 6 cover multiple methods and modifications of cooperative learning for diverse and exceptional learners, and assessment and problem solving in cooperative learning.

Chapter 5 presents five popular methods of cooperative learning: Learning Together, The Structural Approach, Student Team Learning, Group Investigation, and Complex Instruction. The second section explores modifications for diverse learners, including students with exceptional needs. Several other topics of current interest are highlighted in this chapter, including educational technology and cooperative grouping, culturally sensitive instructional practices, and involving parents and families in cooperative learning. Guidelines are provided for instructing students in cooperative groups as they take advantage of educational technology, such as using computers for word processing, building databases, graphing, developing multimedia presentations, and using computer networks to seek information (surfing the Internet or the World Wide Web). Suggestions are given for assisting students from various cultural backgrounds by using culturally sensitive instructional practices. Another section on parent/family involvement underscores the importance of taking cooperative learning beyond the boundaries of the classroom and reaching out to parents to promote collaborative partnerships that can make such a difference in student success.

Increasingly, teachers are expanding their repertoires of assessment techniques to include more authentic assessment and portfolio assessment, in addition to more traditional techniques, such as testing. Inevitably, questions arise concerning how assessment techniques apply to cooperative learning. Chapter 6 discusses both traditional and alternative types of assessment in relation to cooperative learning.

The second section of Chapter 6 is devoted to problem solving, with the aim of helping teachers better understand the potential for the unique, various, and sometimes problematic interactions between the cooperative strategies employed and students' reactions to them. The basic assumption is that students may respond in unanticipated and unpredictable ways to cooperative learning interventions. Even though the recommended procedures for a particular cooperative method are followed carefully, students may experience problems and the group may fail to attain the learning objective. Major categories of problems that commonly appear in cooperative groupwork are identified and suggestions are made for solving them. For example, problems can occur when students have difficulty understanding what they are supposed to be doing in their groups; when several group members experience an interpersonal problem; or simply because the instructional task seems boring or irrelevant and thus fails to motivate the students.

Special Features

To assist in understanding and applying the concepts presented, each chapter begins with learning objectives and a vignette, which set the stage for the material that follows. Figures, drawings, photos, and tables are used to illustrate chapter contents, and cooperative lesson plans developed by teachers at different grade levels are included in several chapters. At the close of each chapter, reader reflection is encouraged through the use of discussion questions and suggested activities. Recommended readings are given at the end of each chapter to extend and enrich understanding of the chapter material.

As cooperative learning becomes a more common practice in U.S. education, the need will increase for educators to understand the theoretical foundations and the principles of cooperative learning. The goal of this book is to help you apply these well-validated principles to today's challenging and changing classrooms. Please let me know of your impressions and reactions to this book, if you are so inclined. I would love to hear your personal stories of using cooperative learning in diverse classrooms.

ACKNOWLEDGMENTS

Many thanks to all the people who assisted in writing this book. I am grateful to Ray Glass, my friend and former colleague, who contributed the chapter on cooperative classroom management. For Chapter 6, I am indebted to Richard Tiberius for allowing me to use the problem categories and remedies that he identified in the excellent resource *Small Group Teaching: A Trouble-Shooting Guide,* published by OISE Press, Toronto, 1990. Special appreciation goes to the wonderful teachers and former students in my university courses in Maine, Montana, and Alaska, who provided the lesson plans and the vignettes of cooperative learning instruction in their classrooms. Debbie Stollenwerk's inspiration and expert editorial guidance were ever-present throughout the writing of this book.

I would like to acknowledge the excellent assistance of the reviewers:

- Cynthia G. Kruger, University of Massachusetts, Dartmouth
- Helene T. Mandell, National University
- Nikki L. Murdick, Southeast Missouri State University
- Charleen Peryon, University of Dubuque
- Betty Jo Simmons, Longwood College
- Norma J. Strickland, Rust College
- Barbara Wasson, Moorhead State University
- James E. Watson, Asbury College

Thanks to Sylvia Rosen, who over the decades has encouraged my writing. Finally, thanks to my husband and best friend, David Putnam, who patiently and insightfully discussed the manuscript with me; to our son Aaron, for his artwork and commentary on cooperative learning in his classes; and to our son Ian for allowing me the weekends and evenings required to complete this project.

ABOUT THE AUTHOR

◆

JoAnne Putnam, Ph.D., is Dean of the School of Education and Professional Studies at the University of Maine at Presque Isle. She has taught exceptional learners in special education classes in West Virginia and has been a professor of special education at the University of Montana and the University of Alaska–Anchorage. She has conducted research and written about cooperative learning since her doctoral studies at the University of Minnesota, where she pursued the topic with Drs. David and Roger Johnson. Her more recent writing includes the edited book *Cooperative Learning and Strategies for Inclusion: Celebrating Diversity in the Classroom* and research on future directions in the education of students with disabilities.

Brief Contents

SECTION 1   **The Case for Cooperation**   1

CHAPTER 1   *Cooperative Learning in*
             Diverse Classrooms   3

CHAPTER 2   *Cooperative Learning and*
             Educational Outcomes   23

SECTION 2   **Facilitating Cooperative Learning**   51

CHAPTER 3   *Planning and Conducting*
             Cooperative Activities   53

CHAPTER 4   *Cooperative Classroom Management*   97

SECTION 3   **Extending and Evaluating**
             Cooperative Learning   131

CHAPTER 5   *Multiple Methods and Modifications*
             for Diversity   133

CHAPTER 6   *Assessment and Problem Solving*
             in Cooperative Learning   177

CONTENTS

SECTION 1   *The Case for Cooperation*   1

CHAPTER 1   *Cooperative Learning in Diverse Classrooms*   3

Changing Classrooms   *4*

Learning Cooperatively   *8*

    Learning Alone   *9*

    Learning With Others   *10*

    Competing With Others   *10*

Critical Components of Cooperative Learning   *11*

    Positive Interdependence   *11*

    Individual Accountability   *12*

    Cooperative Skills   *16*

    Face-to-Face Interaction   *17*

    Group Reflection and Goal Setting   *17*

Differentiating Cooperative Group Learning
From Traditional Group Learning   *18*

Conclusion   *18*

Questions and Activities   *20*

Suggested Readings   *21*

References   *22*

CHAPTER 2   *Cooperative Learning and*
Educational Outcomes   23
Rising Expectations for Schools   *24*
Crisis in American Education: Danger, Opportunities,
and Moving Forward   *25*
    Student Diversity   *26*
    The Way Teachers Teach   *29*
Historical Aspects of Cooperative Learning   *30*
Academic Outcomes of Cooperative Learning   *31*
Social Outcomes of Cooperative Learning   *33*
Interpersonal Relations   *35*
    Cross-Ethnic Relations   *35*
    Students With Disabilities   *36*
    Low-Performing Students   *37*
Self-Esteem   *40*
Other Educational Outcomes   *41*
Controversial Issues in Cooperative Learning   *42*
    Gifted Students   *42*
    Students With Disabilities   *44*
Conclusion   *45*
Questions and Activities   *46*
Suggested Readings   *47*
References   *48*

SECTION 2   *Facilitating Cooperative Learning*   **51**

CHAPTER 3   *Planning and Conducting*
Cooperative Activities   53
Structuring Cooperative Groups   *56*
Planning and Setting Up Cooperative Groups   *57*
    Determining the Instructional Objective   *57*
    Forming the Groups   *58*
    Conducting the Lesson   *62*
    Assuring Interdependence   *63*
    Assuring Individual Accountability   *68*
Developing Students' Cooperative Skills   *70*

A Six-Step Process for Teaching
Cooperative Skills   *71*

The "Natural" Approach to Teaching
Cooperative Skills   *76*

Educational Technology and Cooperative Learning   *78*

Global Networking   *80*

Multimedia Presentations   *80*

Lesson Planning   *81*

Conclusion   *94*

Questions and Activities   *94*

Suggested Readings   *95*

References   *95*

CHAPTER 4   *Cooperative Classroom Management*   *97*

Cooperative Classroom Management: An Overview   *99*

Working With Students to Prevent Conflicts   *100*

Develop Clear Rules and Procedures   *100*

Involve Students in the Process of Developing
Rules and Procedures   *103*

Systematically Focus on Positive Behavior   *104*

Working With Students to Develop Conflict
Resolution Skills   *110*

Conducting Classroom Meetings   *111*

Conducting Conflict Resolution Conferences   *113*

Training Students in Conflict Resolution Skills   *114*

Working With Students to Solve Individual
Behavior Problems   *115*

Improving Participation in
Cooperative Groups   *116*

Recognizing Goals of Student Misbehavior   *119*

Developing Constructive Responses to Students
Who Misbehave   *120*

Developing Systematic Feedback Programs   *122*

Rewarding Positive Behavior   *125*

Conclusion   *126*

Questions and Activities   *127*

Suggested Readings   *128*

References   *128*

SECTION 3   *Extending and Evaluating Cooperative Learning*   *131*

CHAPTER 5   *Multiple Methods and Modifications for Diversity*   *133*

Methods of Cooperative Learning   *134*

The Learning Together Model: David Johnson and Roger Johnson   *135*

Features of Learning Together   *136*

The Structural Approach: Spencer Kagan   *139*

Features of the Structural Approach   *140*

Student Team Learning: Robert Slavin   *144*

Features of Student Team Learning (STL)   *145*

Group Investigation: Shlomo Sharan and Yael Sharan   *148*

Features of Group Investigation   *149*

Six Stages of Group Investigation   *150*

Complex Instruction: Elizabeth Cohen   *152*

Similarities and Differences Among the Various Cooperative Methods   *156*

Similar Attributes   *156*

Different Attributes   *156*

Modifications for Diverse Learners   *157*

Modifying Learning Objectives   *158*

Modifying Materials and the Environment   *159*

Providing Tutorials, Study Skills, and Individualized Support   *162*

Cooperative Learning in Inclusive Classrooms   *162*

Culturally Sensitive Instructional Practices   *164*

Creating a Climate of Support and Helpfulness   *168*

Cooperative Learning and Parent/Family Involvement   *168*

Conclusion   *170*

Questions and Activities   *171*

Recommended Readings   *173*

References   *173*

CHAPTER 6   *Assessment and Problem Solving in*
             Cooperative Learning   *177*

    Assessing Cooperative Learning   *179*
        Performance Assessment   *181*
    Assessment Considerations   *181*
        Evaluating Academic Performance   *184*
        Peer Evaluation   *188*
    Problem Solving in Cooperative Groups   *190*
        Problems With Group Learning Objectives   *194*
        Lack of Experience, Cultural Differences, and
        Physical Distance   *198*
        Problems With the Task   *199*
    Conclusion   *203*
    Questions and Activities   *204*
    Suggested Readings   *205*
    References   *205*

INDEX   *209*

SECTION 1

THE CASE FOR COOPERATION

◆

CHAPTER 1   *Cooperative Learning in Diverse Classrooms*

CHAPTER 2   *Cooperative Learning and Educational Outcomes*

CHAPTER 1

COOPERATIVE LEARNING IN DIVERSE CLASSROOMS

◆

This chapter is designed to help you do the following:

- ◆ Identify characteristics of a cooperative classroom.
- ◆ Define cooperative learning by contrasting it to individualistic and competitive learning.
- ◆ Identify five components that are essential to effective cooperative learning.
- ◆ Distinguish among cooperative group learning and more traditional types of group work.
- ◆ Discuss your experiences with learning and working cooperatively, alone, and competitively.

CHANGING CLASSROOMS

Picture in your mind the public school classroom as it was two or three decades ago. Typically, the teacher's desk was at the front of the room and the students' desks were organized in neat rows. The students' primary tools were textbooks, paper, and pencils. Teachers used chalkboards, overhead projectors, movie projectors, and tape recorders.

The primary methods of instruction were teacher presentation to the whole class, teacher-directed discussions, and seatwork. Students were expected to work quietly and on their own for most of the school day. Student performance was evaluated with tests and quarterly report cards. Evaluation was comparative—students were compared with one another in the classroom and with local and national norms.

Most likely, the classroom behavior management approach was authoritarian, with the teacher in control. Students were generally grouped homogeneously according to their age levels and ethnic and cultural backgrounds. Students with learning or behavior problems were instructed in special programs and "pull-out" classrooms. Students with more severe disabilities were not even present in past classrooms; they attended segregated

special schools or, before 1975, they stayed at home. Teachers functioned autonomously in their classrooms and many felt professionally isolated.

As we enter the 21st century, public school classrooms have evolved appreciably from those that characterized the latter half of the 20th century. Rigid uniformity in procedural operation, lock-step curricular approaches, and the homogeneous groupings of students have been abandoned in many classrooms as educators address the needs of a highly diverse and multi-cultural student population. Teachers strive to engage students more actively in learning through instruction that involves discovery, inquiry, and problem solving. They recognize that facilitating learning involves more than imparting factual knowledge and information, especially in light of technologies that provide access to ever-expanding information sources that far exceed the capacity of any human being as a "fountain of knowledge." Many teachers now believe they are most effective when they assume the role of "guide on the side," using a variety of instructional approaches that empower students to shape their own abilities, tap sources of information and knowledge, and reach their own educational goals.

Teachers also recognize that learning is not a solitary activity. Decades of research tell us that students learn the most when they work coopera-tively (Johnson, Johnson, & Maruyama, 1983; Slavin, 1990). The benefits of collaboration extend to teachers, students, parents, support staff, com-munity members, and businesses as they work collectively to enhance stu-dent learning or tackle educational challenges. Consider the following sce-nario depicting a multigrade cooperative classroom in an elementary school in a northwestern city.

Northstar Elementary's Cooperative Classroom

In Northstar Elementary's multigrade classroom No. 5, the seats are arranged in flexible patterns. Students move their desks into rows for a lecture or presentation; they arrange their chairs in a large semicircle for poetry readings; and they move their desks together when working in small groups. The teacher's desk at the side of the room is rarely occupied during instructional periods because Ms. Lopez interacts with students or monitors their work.

Against the east wall of the classroom is a row of computers for student use. The literature area is in a corner with comfortable pillows, soft lighting, and tropical plants. In another corner of the room is a television for viewing instructional programs and for participating in an interactive classroom exchange program with students from a province in Canada, via satellite. Next to the tele-vision is a laser disc player used for interactive instruction in sev-eral subject areas.

Ms. Lopez employs a variety of instructional and curricular approaches in her classroom. At different times, students work independently, in large groups, with peer and adult tutors, with mentors, and in cooperative learning groups. Cooperative learning pervades Northstar's Classroom No. 5. When students arrive in the morning, they meet with their ongoing cooperative base group to take attendance, check in their homework, discuss current events, and, ultimately, provide a base of friendship and support to see them through the school year.

Students engage in cooperative activities for academics, such as peer editing using the classroom computers to produce articles for the school and community newspaper. They might use a cooperative jigsaw for a science unit on pond ecology. In a jigsaw, each student takes responsibility for researching a particular aspect of the topic and then shares the knowledge with other members of their group as the group prepares a paper and presentation. Students also work in cooperative groups for extracurricular activities, including Odyssey of the Mind, planning the class booth for the school carnival, and organizing the class community service activity at the local shelter for homeless children.

Although the classroom is not always quiet, the volume of noise during group work is maintained at a reasonable level for learning, and most conversation is task-related. At times, students work independently and silently. Ms. Lopez recognizes that independent work and cooperative learning are not incompatible. For example, students may work independently with a tutoring program at the computer and later join in on a cooperative project using groupware with students from other locations.

Ms. Lopez's approach to classroom management is cooperative, involving students in developing the class constitution which prescribes student and teacher rights and responsibilities, and the class legal system for handling student and teacher infractions. Ms. Lopez considers herself the class leader and manager, yet she empowers students to monitor their own behaviors and classroom functions. Interestingly, not one case of a student infraction has gone before the class jury during the first three months of school. Perhaps this is due, in part, to a schoolwide peer mediation program that has prepared students to serve in mediator teams to settle the conflicts that inevitably arise between students.

In Northstar school, report cards with grades are no longer issued. Evaluation is a multifaceted activity in which student portfolios are maintained and shared with the student and parents on a quarterly basis. The portfolio contains products related to educational goals and outcomes, samples of the student's work, videos of student performance, curriculum based tests, standardized tests, student self-evaluations, and other work samples. The process of learning is also evaluated on an ongoing basis. Once a week students reflect on and evaluate how well they are accomplishing their personal learning goals. They also meet with their cooperative group to assess how well their group is functioning and to target areas for improvement.

Ms. Lopez's class, like most classrooms, is characterized by student diversity. This diversity is manifested by differences in ethnic and cultural background, socioeconomic group, learning style, and cognitive and physical ability level. The cultural backgrounds represented in this class include African-American, Asian-American, Euro-American, Mexican-American, and Native American students. Several students who were once taught in pull-out special education programs—one with a learning disability and the other with cerebral palsy—are now fully included as members of Ms. Lopez's class. Both students work towards achieving the goals and objectives stated on their Individualized Educational Plans, sometimes with the support of a teaching assistant, a special education consulting teacher, or a peer. They both participate in heterogeneous cooperative activities in academic and nonacademic subject areas.

Ms. Lopez is not the sole adult in this classroom. Often, two or more adults are members of this learning community. The special education consulting teacher spends about eight hours a week in the class, team-teaching with Ms. Lopez. She teaches a study skills unit and provides tutorials for several students. Other specialists, such as the gifted education teacher, the reading specialist, and the speech therapist, also spend time in the classroom. Parents and community members make presentations to the class, tutor students, and help with other classroom functions.

During the spring quarter, the class participates in a four-week unit involving a local enterprise. This year they will form a school-business partnership with the regional hydroelectric power plant to learn how power is generated and delivered to consumers. The class has decided to construct a three-dimensional model grid of the power plant and the pathways connecting power to their school and their houses.

Several times a week, Ms. Lopez meets with a collaborative team of educators from the school to plan lessons, address problems, and make decisions. She also participates on Cooperative Student Support Teams of educators, family members, specialists, and students to address the special learning and behavioral needs of two students in her classroom. Ms. Lopez is never isolated, but truly engaged with other adults and students in both the classroom community and the broader community of learners.

Ms. Lopez sees herself as a facilitator of learning rather than the primary presenter and "knowledge resource" for her students. She teaches through demonstration and modeling, assigning tasks to students, monitoring student performance, and providing feedback on their work. Like all good teachers throughout history, *she works very hard—her motivation an unwavering commitment to fostering the academic achievement, self-esteem, and social skills of all the students she encounters.*

Ms. Lopez is a firm believer in the value of cooperative learning for students and teachers alike. In the following pages and chapters of this text you will explore how cooperative learning is used in today's changing classroom. You will find out what cooperative learning is and what it isn't, why it improves learning and self-esteem, and how to plan cooperative learning activities for student and adult groups.

LEARNING COOPERATIVELY

People learn in numerous ways—from reading, observing, listening, talking with others, and teaching others (see Figure 1.1).

Consider how you learn best. Do the proportions in Figure 1.1 generally ring true for you? Most would agree that we learn the most when we *teach* others. Teaching someone else requires that we first internalize the information and then translate it into our own words before sharing it with others. Mentally rehearsing and then presenting information to others enhances one's own retention of the content. When we actually *apply* information in practical ways, its usefulness and meaning become more apparent, even when the ideas are highly abstract. People are always more motivated to learn material that has relevance to their lives. When we *discuss* ideas with others, opportunities emerge for clarifying information or elaborating on a topic, asking questions, challenging ideas, and taking another's point of view into account.

Well-designed and well-implemented cooperative learning activities result in students who function at the upper ranges of the learning chart. Effective cooperative learning activities engage students in discussions with

FIGURE 1.1
What People Learn
Adapted from Alcorn, Kinder, &
Schunert, 1970.

10% of what they READ
20% of what they READ and HEAR
30% of what they SEE
50% of what they SEE and HEAR
70% of what they SAY*
90% of what they SAY and APPLY in life*
95% when they TEACH others*
*Active behaviors that take place in cooperative group learning.

others, enable students to participate in authentic activities relevant to real life, and encourage students to teach one another.

Just as people learn through various modalities, such as the auditory, kinesthetic, or visual channels, they also learn in a variety of *inter*personal or *intra*personal contexts. Sometimes people learn through interacting with others, sometimes they learn as they compete with others, and sometimes they learn on their own. These three learning structures have been used in U.S. schools, in varying degrees and for various educational purposes. Historically, U.S. schools have been designed predominantly for individualistic learners. In the next section, as you read about and consider each learning structure, try to recall an experience that fits with the particular structure and reflect on how you felt about it at the time.

Learning Alone

Throughout the school day and at home, students work on their own to learn: They read books, write papers, listen to tapes, watch a visual presentation, or work at a computer terminal. Ideally, when learning alone, students are highly focused on the instructional task. They tune out distractions in the environment as they work in their own learning space and with their own materials. Students realize they are responsible for completing the instructional task and that they must depend on their own personal resources and motivation to get the job done.

When students learn alone, the teacher's role is primarily to help the student understand the assignment and plan the activity, and then to provide feedback and performance evaluation when the task is completed. Individualistic learning in schools requires that the teacher and the student interact, although minimally, when the teacher explains the assignment or activity and when feedback is given. Occasionally, teachers and students communicate during the task if the student needs assistance.

Learning alone does not involve other students; the focus is on achieving independently. Consequently, in individualistic learning situations no opportunity exists for learning or practicing social and collaborative skills, such as communication skills or leadership skills.

Many tasks lend themselves to individualistic learning. Analyzing a work of fiction is a learning activity that may begin by reading alone and then reflecting on what has been read. Researching and writing about a self-selected topic is an activity that students often enjoy launching on their own. Memorizing material, such as spelling words, the chemical elements, or math facts, usually requires individual work. Some courses are specifically designed for individualized learning, such as a correspondence course or a computerized self-study course, in which the student takes responsibility for completing the readings and assignments on his or her own.

Teachers should provide opportunities for students to read, write, create, and reflect by themselves. The classroom atmosphere supportive of such activities should be reasonably quiet and calm, enabling students to think without great distraction. Other areas of the school, such as libraries or learning centers, or the home environment can be havens for students seeking a refuge from the hustle and bustle of classrooms.

Learning With Others

Learning is primarily a social act that occurs in the presence of others. We learn by listening to, watching, and talking with others. Many subtle academic and social behaviors are shaped and acquired through observing others. Students may learn how to pronounce a French word, solve an algebra equation, execute a dive, or access information from the Internet by observing a peer.

Social behaviors, of course, are learned primarily through observation. It's fascinating to watch young students learn about body language or the latest styles and trends from one another. Children may pick up on the subtleties of how to *correctly* wear a backpack—with one strap slung over a shoulder, how to *not* tie your shoelaces and tuck them inside your athletic shoes, how to perform the latest dance steps, or simply how to "be cool." They also receive valuable feedback from group participation—if children speak or perform incorrectly, they will certainly learn about it from their peers.

We all have learned in groups from an early age. We learned on the playground, at the swimming pool, in neighborhood gatherings, and in school. Some children participate in and learn from various clubs and organizations, such as Boy Scouts and Girl Scouts, or sports such as basketball, soccer, and softball. These organizations are considered "legitimized" organizations, while others, such as a "dare-devil club," a secret sorority, or a street gang, are not. Social learning occurs in both types of organizations, for better or for worse.

Competing With Others

When students try to outperform one another, they are engaged in competition. In true competition, the goal is to be the best, so there are always winners and losers. Student performance is evaluated by comparison, as with normative evaluation, resulting in a range of outcomes from highest to lowest. It is expected that students will differ in their capacity to learn and perform, and that some will succeed more than others.

A student must compete to win the first chair of violin in the orchestra, students compete in the school spelling bee, and teams of students compete in sports such as tennis, football, track, and skiing. There is a place for healthy competition in our schools and in our society. Competition enables individuals to make comparisons and identify their own strengths and weaknesses, to pinpoint specific errors, and ultimately to improve performance (Perleman, 1992).

Individual competition is not, however, the best way to increase the academic achievement and self-esteem of *all* students, as has been pointed out

by numerous studies comparing competition with cooperative and individualistic learning in our schools. While students should have opportunities to learn by themselves and to compete with others, students master subject matter better and develop greater self-esteem and social skills when they work cooperatively (Johnson, Johnson, & Maruyama, 1983; Slavin, 1990).

CRITICAL COMPONENTS OF COOPERATIVE LEARNING

We have all participated in group activities for learning, work, and play. But not all group activities are cooperative. Therefore, it is important to learn how to distinguish a cooperative group from other types of groups. The following five components are the defining characteristics of cooperative group learning (Johnson, Johnson, & Holubec, 1993):

1. positive interdependence
2. individual accountability
3. cooperative skills
4. face-to-face interaction
5. group reflection and goal setting

Positive Interdependence

The essence of cooperative learning is the requirement that group members work together to accomplish a shared goal. Working together demands a coordination of individual actions through dialogue, planning, decision making, and the give-and-take of negotiation. Each group member has a part to play in the group activity, although the tasks may vary from student to student. The mentality of the group should reflect a "we" rather than "me" type of thinking.

Group members should take interest in and responsibility for the achievement and performance of all group members. Competitive situations are often rewarding to the winning participant when competitors *fail*, because their failure is fundamental to one's success, such as when another student misses a word in the final stages of a spelling bee. On the other hand, the cooperative experience engenders a sense of satisfaction when teammates *succeed*. For example, if students are trying to solve a challenging word problem in mathematics, they are successful only when each person in the group is able to solve the problem and explain how they arrived at the solution. If students in a journalism class are publishing the school newspaper, they are successful only when all have accomplished their assignments, whether it be writing an article, laying out the pages, or editing the final copy.

A number of categories distinguish different types of positive interdependence, such as role interdependence, reward interdependence, and resource interdependence. These and other types of interdependence will be discussed in Chapter 3, along with suggestions for assuring positive interdependence among group members.

Many important life accomplishments can occur only through cooperative effort. Even the accomplishment of personal lifelong dreams involves cooperation with others, for rarely do we succeed in a vacuum. In 1994, for example, Norman Vaughan, age 89, fulfilled a dream to climb a mountain in Antarctica. The mountain had been named after him in a 1928 expedition with Admiral Richard E. Byrd. The story of this remarkable man, now in his tenth decade of life, demonstrates how the principle of positive interdependence made possible the fulfillment of one man's lifelong goal. As described in the boxed feature beginning on page 14, the Mount Vaughan expedition also shows us that, although we may experience unexpected setbacks and disappointments, perseverance is often the key to ultimate success.

Cooperative Learning Logo Devised by the Author to Emphasize Interdependence.

Individual Accountability

Cooperative learning will work only if individual group members assume responsibility for accomplishing the group goal and doing their share of the work. Failure to contribute has resulted in many unsuccessful academic work groups. Almost everyone can recall a group experience in which an individual did not complete his or her work and the other group members had to compensate. By definition, a group in which members are enabled to "coast" or "hitchhike" on the efforts and accomplishments of others is not a true cooperative group.

Another aspect of individual accountability is that each team member must learn the material. Group members should make certain that learning takes place by checking for understanding and quizzing and tutoring one

Tuning Out

another. In truly cooperative classroom and school communities, students develop concern and caring for others. They challenge one another to do their best, and they support one another when assistance and encouragement is needed. The vignette that follows demonstrates the kind of caring relationship that can be cultivated in a cooperative environment.

Cooperation and Caring

Last night Toni, who had been absent from school due to illness, received a call from Adam. The first thing Adam said was that they missed her at school and hoped she was feeling better. Once Adam was assured that Toni was feeling better and that she was planning to attend school the next day, they talked about their cooperative group project. Adam even checked to be certain Toni understood the math word problem the group was solving. According to Toni's mother, no one had called before to see how Toni was feeling. The family had just moved to the area, and knowing that someone cared enough to call meant a lot to Toni. She reviewed the math problem that night and couldn't wait to go to school the next morning.

Mount Vaughan Antarctic Expedition:
A Cooperative Adventure

"Antarctica is a land of towering peaks, raging wind, wild ocean birds, seals, and whales . . . the last true wild place on Earth. Encompassed in mystery and wealth, the vast uninhabited mineral-rich continent surrounding the South Pole protects over 80% of the world's fresh water and Earth's least tainted fisheries and yet, ironically, is the world's largest desert. Antarctica's two-mile thick ice cap hides 10,000 years of atmospheric and climate history . . . and the story of man's expanding impact on this planet."

The Mission

At age 89, Norman D. Vaughan, Carolyn Muegge-Vaughan, Vernon Tejas, and Gordon Wiltsie climbed the mountain named for Vaughan by Admiral Richard E. Byrd back in 1928. The first purpose of the 1994 mission was to demonstrate that age is not a factor in the pursuit of dreams and lofty goals . . . that no challenge is too great at any time in a person's life. The second purpose was to educate people about Antarctica and teach them how important the continent is to global and human survival. The team also wanted to bring attention to the new International Antarctic Treaty and how

Norman Vaughan

that treaty will affect our lives in the future. Through the media and a sophisticated telecommunications network, millions of students were able to study and participate in this dynamic, "live" event, which linked the expedition, environmental experts, and teachers from around the world.

The Mountain

In 1928, Vaughan was chosen by Admiral Richard E. Byrd to be the senior dog handler for Byrd's Antarctic Expedition. During that expedition, Vaughan participated in the first American geological exploration of Antarctica. That exploration proved that Antarctica was actually a continent, not a huge, grounded iceberg. Because of Vaughan's efforts during the expedition, a mountain and glacier were named after him. Mount Vaughan, which reaches 10,302 feet, is 450 miles inland on the Ross Ice Shelf within the Queen Maud Mountains at 85 degrees 55 minutes south, 155 degrees 50 minutes west. On Dec. 16, 1994 (just before his 89th birthday), Vaughan and his expedition team members were the first human beings to set foot on the top of Mount Vaughan—a symbol to the world that courage and dreams never grow old.

The Team

Vaughan's expeditions were cooperative efforts. Carolyn Muegge-Vaughan, Vaughan's wife, is experienced in many wilderness sports and possesses a second degree black belt in judo. Vernon Tejas is a world-class mountaineer who has climbed the highest mountain in each of seven continents, including Mount Everest. Gordon Wiltsie, a mountaineer from Bozeman, Montana, was the photographer for the team. The team was heterogeneous in terms of gender, ages, and talents—each member had a critical role.

Two Expeditions

In December 1993, an expedition team set out with a team of dogs to traverse 550 miles on the snow-covered Ross Ice Sheet to the Queen Maud Mountains and then to Mount Vaughan. But misfortune struck when the expedition's first airplane carrying the dogs, the radio technician and the veterinarian crashed short of the runway. Four dogs were lost, the veterinarian was badly injured, and the costly expedition was brought to a halt. After 16 weeks of trying to wait out the weather, the expedition team returned home.

The failed expedition would have dissuaded most from pursuing the mission, but Norman persevered and a second expedition was planned for the following year. This time, the dogs had to be left at home, and four team members ascended the mountain. The ascent took eight days. On Dec. 16, 1994, three days shy of Vaughan's 89th birthday, the team reached the top of the mountain.

Mount Vaughan Antarctic Expedition Team

The talents and skills of all members made this important but dangerous journey possible. Norman Vaughan could not have made the journey alone, nor would the other team members have had the interest or opportunity to ascend the mountain without him. Perseverance was an essential aspect of the success of this cooperative venture. The Mount Vaughan Antarctic Expedition demonstrates positive interdependence at its best—the success of one depends on the success of all. Vaughn's motto, as given in his speech at the mountain's summit, is *"Dream big and dare to fail."*[1]

Quoted and adapted from "Antarctica: A Man, a Mountain, a Mission," Mount Vaughan Antarctic Expedition brochure, Anchorage, AK, and from "The Old Man and His Mountain" by E. Royte, 1995, *Life,* pp. 78–84.

Cooperative Skills

Cooperative skills are the subset of social skills used in group activities. Cooperative skills are learned and developed throughout a lifetime, and are critical to success in most careers, family life, and community life. An array of interpersonal skills is required to facilitate even the convening of a group. As groups first form, students need to become acquainted with one another, listen to one another, share their ideas about the group goal and expectations, and decide what needs to be done and how to begin.

Cooperative skill expectations differ according to the developmental level of students as well as cultural norms. Staying with the group and taking turns is an important skill for students in the early childhood years. Adolescents should be sharpening their skills in active listening or contributing their ideas to the group, for example. In some cultures, quiet listening is expected, while in others active verbal responding is valued. Interpersonal space expectations also vary according to cultures. For example, Mexican Americans and Asians tend to stand close together while talking, whereas African Americans interact with greater personal distance (Adler, 1993).

Face-to-Face Interaction

Cooperative learning requires that group members interact with one another. Students discuss ideas, make decisions, and often engage in negotiations. While it seems obvious that students should engage in face-to-face interactions in cooperative groups, sometimes teachers mistake "individualistic learning—with talking" for cooperative learning (Johnson & Johnson, 1994). For example, students are asked to complete a set of problems on their own and then share their answers. This activity is not well suited to what Glasser (1986) refers to as a "genuine" cooperative task. If students who are willing to make an effort could learn the material just as easily on their own, and if these students prefer to receive an individual grade, then working individualistically is more appropriate.

Examples of material suited to individualistic learning are fact memorization and practicing a musical instrument. These individually learned skills can be, of course, applied in a context that truly demands cooperation (e.g., taking part in a debate or playing in the orchestra). The requirement of face-to-face interaction does not preclude cooperation at a distance. Effective two-way, interactive communication can occur from faraway places through telecommunications systems, and is becoming more common in American schools.

Group Reflection and Goal Setting

As students engage in cooperative activities, they are encouraged to reflect on how well they are achieving the group goal. They also consider how well they functioned as a team—focusing on their successes as well as areas that need improvement. If the group experiences a problem, members analyze the origin of the problem and propose courses of action to solve it. Goals for subsequent group work are set, preferably in writing, to guide and improve future learning. Teachers also provide students with feedback on the functioning of the groups. Together, students and their teachers build understanding about why groups function well and why they struggle and sometimes fail.

DIFFERENTIATING COOPERATIVE GROUP LEARNING FROM TRADITIONAL GROUP LEARNING

Most teachers employ group learning strategies; however, many forms of group learning do not qualify as cooperative learning. In addition to the five components of cooperative learning discussed previously, the research literature points to the importance of forming *heterogeneous groups* and assuring *equal opportunity for success* for all students (Johnson & Johnson, 1989; Slavin, 1990).

Setting up cooperative learning activities is a systematic process that requires extensive planning, as you will learn in Chapter 3. Selection of group members should not be haphazard, and is rarely a random process. Much thought should go into forming the groups to achieve a mixture of students with respect to cognitive-ability levels; social and behavioral skill levels; gender; cultural, racial, and language characteristics; and socioeconomic status. Often students of differing abilities have complementary talents and learning styles that contribute in unique and positive ways to achievement of the group's goal.

Diversity among learners is the norm rather than the exception in many of today's classrooms. Changes in the school population have resulted in greater numbers than before of students who are immigrants or who have limited English proficiency. More than 70 percent of students qualifying for special education services receive most of their education in regular classrooms. Increasing numbers of students come to school ill-equipped with the skills and resources to profit from traditional approaches, due to disadvantaged backgrounds and changing societal circumstances.

Many of the more traditional education approaches—such as whole class instruction, worksheets, textbooks and ability grouping—are insufficient for handling the range of student differences in classrooms today. In addition, educational trends are moving toward fostering creativity and higher order thinking skills. This greater diversity in our student population, coupled with changing societal conditions calls for more demanding, engaging instruction and the use of innovative educational technologies.

Children learn and develop at different rates and in different ways. As in Ms. Lopez' classroom, described at the beginning of this chapter, students of different abilities are able to engage in cooperative activities, although the expectations for individual students may vary. Slavin (1990) emphasizes the importance of *equal opportunities for success*, which means that students can earn rewards by improving their own past performance or by meeting unique individualized criteria. See Figure 1.2 for a comparison of cooperative and traditional learning groups.

CONCLUSION

Students and teachers alike should realize that the success of cooperative learning depends on many factors. What may contribute to a solution for

Cooperative Learning Groups	Traditional Learning Groups
Positive interdependence	No positive interdependence
Individual accountability	No individual accountability
Cooperative skill instruction	No cooperative skill instruction
Concern for peer learning	Little concern for peer learning
Heterogeneous groups	Homogeneous groups
Teacher selected groups	Student selected groups
Student reflection and goal setting	No student reflection and goal setting
Teacher observation and feedback	No teacher observation and feedback
Equal opportunity for success	Uniform standard for success

FIGURE 1.2

Comparison Between Cooperative Learning Groups and
Traditional Groups

one cooperative group's problem may not apply to problems encountered by other groups. This book is designed to provide you with the basic principles of cooperative learning so you can conduct cooperative activities with a diversity of learners. As a result of reading this book, you should begin to develop a theoretical understanding of why and under what conditions cooperative learning produces high achievement and positive social/psychological outcomes. You should also understand that a complex set of factors contributes to successful or unsuccessful cooperative learning experiences.

It is certainly not unusual for members of cooperative groups to experience difficulties. Moreover, it is not unusual for teachers to make poor decisions about troublesome groups and students. Involving students and adults in cooperative activities can be an adventure into uncharted waters. Structuring cooperative activities involves some risk and you can expect the unexpected. But the more experience you gain, the more your cooperative learning theory base will grow, enabling you to distinguish among groups that function well, marginally, or not at all.

> "I've already had a half-day workshop on cooperative learning. In fact, I organized a cooperative lesson last Friday and it failed miserably. That's the first and the last time I'll ever use cooperative learning in my classroom!"

In the United States, teachers tend to adopt an educational practice just because it is new and different. However, many traditional educational practices have prevailed over the centuries because they are still relevant and result in high achievement. It is not easy to determine which practices are outmoded and ineffective and which are worthy of adoption. Methodologically sound research conducted by universities and teacher practitioners contributes to making these difficult determinations.

A substantive amount of research has demonstrated that cooperative learning produces high achievement and positive social/psychological outcomes, such as higher self-esteem and improvement in social skills, *under certain conditions*. It is imperative to know what these conditions are to maximize the potential benefits of cooperative group learning. The following chapters are designed to help you understand the conditions that contribute to successful cooperative classroom communities. You will encounter a variety of cooperative learning methods and strategies. You also will be challenged to break away from traditional methods of instruction and education that are no longer applicable to a diverse student demography, in the interest of fostering dynamic learning communities in today's schools.

QUESTIONS AND ACTIVITIES

1.   Under what circumstances do you learn the most? Do you agree with the assertion in Figure 1.1 that we learn the most when we teach others? Explain your answer.

2.   Consider Northstar Elementary's classroom No. 5. What characterizes this classroom as cooperative? Are there other ways to infuse cooperation into this environment? What are some barriers to creating such a classroom? Would you rather learn in a cooperative classroom or a more traditional classroom? Explain your responses.

3.   Under what conditions is group learning cooperative? Give an example of a cooperative group and an example of group learning that is *not* cooperative.

4.   *Pairs share.* In pairs, discuss for about three minutes some of the societal changes of the past 50 years. Next, consider for about three minutes how educational institutions have changed during this time period. Is there a discrepancy in the rate of change between the two? Why? (about three minutes) Next, share your answers to the last question with another pair (about three minutes). At the end of this activity, the instructor may select one or two groups of four to summarize their conversations for the class.

5. *Quick jigsaw.* Is there a place for all three learning structures (cooperative, competitive, and individualistic learning) in our schools? In heterogeneous groups of three, assign each person one of the three structures. Each person should independently generate a written rationale and two or three examples of appropriate use of their particular structure (about five minutes). Then, each person should report his or her findings to the group. Next, as a group, determine the percent of time teachers should devote to each structure to achieve an appropriate balance in the daily schedule. Report the group's findings to the class with a rationale.

6. *Round-robin discussion.* Write a brief two-to-three page essay on your experiences working or learning (a) cooperatively, (b) individualistically, and (c) competitively. Try to recall one positive and one negative experience in each of the categories. In class, form a group of four or five to make brief presentations on your essay in round-robin format (three to five minutes per person). In a round robin, each student speaks *without interruption*, moving clockwise around the group. One group member is the timekeeper, signaling when it is time to stop. After everyone has spoken, the group can engage in a brief interactive discussion, summarizing what was stated by individual members.

SUGGESTED READINGS

Books

Johnson, D. W., Johnson, R. T., & Holubec, E. J. (1993). *Circles of learning: Cooperation in the classroom* (4th ed.). Edina, MN: Interaction Books.

Johnson, D. W., & Johnson, R. T. (1994). *Learning together and alone: Cooperative, competitive, and individualistic learning* (4th ed.). Needham Heights, MA: Allyn and Bacon.

Slavin, R. E. (1986). *Using student team learning* (3rd ed.). Baltimore, MD: Johns Hopkins University.

Slavin, R. E. (1991). *Student team learning: A practical guide to cooperative learning.* West Haven, CT: Professional Library, National Education Association.

Magazines

Cooperative Learning: The Magazine for Cooperation in Education. Santa Cruz, CA: International Association for the Study of Cooperation in Education. (Available from the International Association for the Study of Cooperation in Education (IASCE), P.O. Box 1582, Santa Cruz, CA 94061-1582. Phone (408) 335-0408.)

REFERENCES

Adler, S. (1993). *Multicultural communication skills in the classroom.* Needham Heights, MA: Allyn and Bacon.

Alcorn, M. D., Kinder, J. S., & Schunert, J. R. (1970). *Better teaching in secondary schools.* Chicago: Holt, Rinehart and Winston.

Glasser, W. J. (1986). *Control theory in the classroom.* New York: Harper and Row.

Johnson, D. W., & Johnson, R. T. (1989). *Cooperation and competition: Theory and research.* Edina, MN: Interaction Books.

Johnson, D. W., Johnson, R. T. (1994). *Learning together and alone: Cooperative, competitive, and individualistic learning* (4th ed.). Needham Heights, MA: Allyn and Bacon.

Johnson, D. W., Johnson, R. T., & Holubec, E. J. (1993). *Circles of learning: Cooperation in the classroom* (4th ed.). Edina, MN: Interaction Books.

Johnson, D. W., Johnson, R. T., & Maruyama, G. (1983). Interdependence and interpersonal attraction among heterogeneous and homogeneous individuals: A theoretical formulation and a meta-analysis of the research. *Review of Educational Research, 53,* 5–54.

Perleman, L. J. (1992). *School's out.* New York: Avon Books.

Royte, E. (1995, May). The old man and his mountain. *Life,* 78–84.

Slavin, R. E. (1990). *Cooperative learning: Theory, research and practice.* Englewood Cliffs, NJ: Prentice Hall.

CHAPTER 2

COOPERATIVE LEARNING AND EDUCATIONAL OUTCOMES

◆

This chapter is designed to help you do the following:

♦ Consider the need for new educational approaches in light of changing societal conditions and the diversity of students now attending public schools.

♦ Identify the elements of cooperative learning that are associated with high student achievement outcomes.

♦ Identify nonacademic outcomes associated with cooperative learning.

♦ Explain how interethnic group relations can be enhanced by cooperative learning.

♦ Discuss why students with disabilities tend to be more accepted by peers in cooperative situations than in competitive or individualistic learning situations.

♦ Discuss the benefits and the pitfalls of using cooperative learning with students who are gifted or who have disabilities.

RISING EXPECTATIONS FOR SCHOOLS

What teachers and parents want from schools is for students to acquire the knowledge, skills, and attitudes that will enable them to function effectively in our society. Today's students must be prepared to join a work force no longer based on the requirements of the "factory model" of the industrial age, but rather based on the demands of today's service-oriented, technology-based information age. To perform the jobs of the future students will need to be information seekers, technology users, and creative problem solvers. Collaborative skills will continue to be essential for succeeding in most professions and for functioning well in families and communities. Participating in a more diverse, multicultural society will require that students recognize, accept, and affirm human differences related to gender, race, disability, and socioeconomic group (Sleeter & Grant, 1993).

During the past several decades, U.S. schools have been criticized for failing to adequately educate students. In the 1980s, the *Nation At Risk* report published by the National Commission on Excellence in Education (1983) raised serious concerns that schools were producing students who lacked basic mastery of academic and intellectual skills. The commission's recommendations for improving schools were to assign more homework, increase the length of the school day and school year, raise standards for achievement, place greater emphasis on the basics, and improve math and science instruction. Recently, researchers comparing standardized achievement test score results of students from the United States with those from other countries claimed that our student achievement levels had fallen behind. For example, *Newsweek* ("An F," 1992) reported that, out of 15 nations, 13-year-olds in the United States finished 14th in science and 13th in math, based on the results of the Second International Assessment of Educational Progress (IAEP-2). Other researchers, however, have presented data showing that achievement scores are not declining but have remained relatively stable or have even increased somewhat during the past decades. Research by Whittington (1992) concluded that U.S. students actually know as much as or more than students of the past.

Obviously, the causes of poor achievement are a source of controversy. Some place the blame on poor or outmoded instructional methodologies, which have remained relatively static for the past century. They recommend moving away from lock-step curricular approaches, over-reliance on drill and practice activities, passive learning, teaching subject matter in isolation, and teaching students in isolation from one another. Others point to the difficulty of trying to educate children who enter school poorly prepared to learn, noting the decline in our social institutions and the overall decline in our nation's social health (Bracey, 1992). The debates over the condition of public education are likely to continue as we search for reasons and appropriate responses to the perceived crisis in U.S. education.

CRISIS IN AMERICAN EDUCATION: DANGER, OPPORTUNITIES, AND MOVING FORWARD

John F. Kennedy once said, "When written in Chinese, the word 'crisis' is composed of two characters—one represents danger and the other represents opportunity." Dr. Ken Petres, a professor of communication at the University of Maine at Presque Isle, grew up in Chong Qing, China. After surveying a number of native Chinese families, he concurs with those who translate the character for crisis as "moving forward."

The symbolism of these Chinese characters beautifully illustrates the current status of education in the United States. If our schools are, indeed, in crisis, what dangers and opportunities do teachers face in their profession? What dangers or challenges do they face in their classrooms? What opportunities do teachers have to do things differently as we educate students for current and future environments? How are we moving forward to improve learning opportunities for all students?

One of the challenges facing educators today is addressing the needs of today's diversity of learners, including students from different ethnic and cultural backgrounds, students with disabilities, and students who are unprepared to learn because of factors such as socioeconomic disadvantage or problems such as drug and alcohol abuse in the home. Another challenge involves abandoning traditional educational approaches that are no longer effective and adopting newer techniques and technologies to improve learning. These circumstances present both dangers that might impede our success as well as exciting opportunities for improving the way we educate children.

Student Diversity

The U.S. education system is based on the fundamental belief that all children should be afforded an education, regardless of ethnic background, academic ability, socioeconomic status, or geographic location. The task of educating *all* children is indeed formidable, particularly if we attempt to address the learning needs and styles of a wide diversity of children. In many areas of the country, homogeneous classrooms composed of students from similar cultural and ethnic backgrounds have been replaced by heterogeneous classrooms characterized by rich ethnic diversity and varying student learning styles.

Ethnic Minorities.   Today about 25% of school-age children in the United States are ethnic minorities. By the year 2000, it is estimated that 30% of school-age children will be children of color. In our major cities, what was once called the minority population is rapidly becoming the majority. Growth rates show that between 1980 to 1990, the total U.S. population grew by 9.8%. The white, non-Hispanic population increased 6%; the African American population, 13.2%; Native American, 37.9%; Hispanics of all races, 53%; and Asian-Pacific Islanders, 107.8%. Currently minority children constitute 30% of our school population, and projections are that this number will climb to 36% after the year 2000. By 2010, one-third of the nation's youth will reside in four states (New York, Texas, California, and Florida) and more than half of these youth (52%) will be what we currently refer to as "minority." And, the true minority will be non-Hispanic white youth (Hodgkinson, 1993).

Although projections indicate that white, non-Hispanic students will be a minority in our schools within 40 years, the percentage of *teachers* who are nonwhite is projected to be only 19% in California, 15% in Florida and 22% in Texas, based on current enrollments in schools of education today (Hodgkinson, 1992). A critical question that education must address in the future is: *Will white, non-Hispanic teachers be prepared to address the needs of these increasing numbers of culturally diverse students?* Will you?

Exceptional Learners.   Along with increasing ethnic diversity, today's schools and classrooms handle a greater variety of student cognitive, physical and behavioral ability levels. Today, more than 70% of children who require special education services and for whom an individualized educational plan is written are instructed in regular classrooms for 40% or more of the school day. According to the U.S. Department of Education *Sixteenth Annual Report to Congress* (1994), 4,633,674 students, ages 6 through 21, are served by special education and Chapter 1 (through the Individuals with Disabilities Education Act, Part B, and Chapter 1, state-operated or state-supported programs). Of this total, 51.1% have learning disabilities; 21.6% speech or language impairments; 11.5% mental retardation; 8.7% serious emotional disturbance; 2.2% multiple disabilities; 1.3% hearing impairments; 1.1% orthopedic impairments; 1.1% other health impairments; 0.5% visual impairments; 0.3% autism; 0.1% traumatic brain injury; and 0.0% deaf-blindness (total number = 1,425).

Experts expect the number of students with disabilities moving into regular classrooms will continue to increase in the future (Putnam, Spiegel, & Bruininks, 1995). These students require individualized educational plans and support services from special education and related fields. Teachers will be expected to adapt their curriculum and instructional approaches to meet students' individualized learning objectives. Strategies will be needed to foster the social acceptance of students, many of whom were excluded from regular classrooms in the past. New professional roles and relationships will be required as teachers work collaboratively with special educators, specialists from other fields (e.g., social work, the health professions), community members, and families to support students with diverse abilities.

Disadvantaged Children.   In the United States, 23% of all children live below the poverty line (Hodgkinson, 1993). These children tend to be concentrated in certain geographic regions of the country, particularly inner city areas and some rural locations. Unfortunately, America's most underfunded schools tend to be in these same areas, while the most endowed schools are in the suburbs of our 40 largest metropolitan areas.

Students who are most at risk for not achieving their potential in our schools are children and youth in poverty, regardless of their race. Jaeger (1992) examined the nations' scores on the Second International Math Study and found a correlation between low achievement test scores and the percentage of children living in poverty of 99%!

Daunting societal problems plague our nation, as revealed by statistics from the Center for Demographic Policy (Hodgkinson, 1992). Homelessness affects between 20,000 and 200,000 children a night. The number of children from two-parent families is dwindling and it is predicted that 60% of today's children will live with a single parent before they reach the age of

18. Both the "Norman Rockwell" family and the "Leave it to Beaver" two-parent families of the 1960s are becoming relics of the past.

The devastating effects of drug abuse also are beginning to surface in our public awareness. In 1990 alone, about 350,000 children were born to drug-addicted mothers. One only need read the daily newspaper to see that violence and the use of deadly weapons are on the increase in our schools. Sautter (1995) presents some alarming statistics:

> Every two days, guns kill the equivalent of a class of 25 youngsters and injure 60 more, according to the Children's Defense Fund, which has a memorable way of presenting statistics. Adolescents between the ages of 10 and 19 are killed with a gun at a rate of one every three hours. In fact, an American child today is 15 times more likely to be killed by gunfire than was a child in war-ravaged Northern Ireland before the recent peace talks. (p. 2)

Although teachers and public schools certainly cannot be held responsible for all the urgent social problems facing our nation, the reality is that we must educate many students who come to school less predisposed to learn than was the case in the past. Fresh approaches are needed for teaching disadvantaged students who need immediate, extensive, and intensive help (see Kozol, 1991, for a discussion of equity problems in schools today). The most important reforms that need to take place in U.S. education are at the level of the teacher and the classroom—and that is the purpose of this book: to explore cooperative learning as a method that is particularly suited to the education of a diversity of learners.

Nora

Ms. Wilson had 20 years of successful teaching experience when she encountered Nora, a most difficult and perplexing student. Nora joined the fifth-grade classroom in October from another school district in the state. The first week of Nora's attendance, her behavior wavered from extreme withdrawal to outbursts of physical aggression. Nora's hostility was directed at Ms. Wilson as well as her classmates. Her repertoire of foul language shocked even this seasoned and highly regarded teacher who had experience in the nation's toughest inner-city schools as well as in rural Appalachia.

Some days Nora would fall asleep at her desk for long periods, or she would position herself underneath one of the tables in the back of the classroom, refusing to sit at her desk or participate in class activities. Other days, Nora dominated the classroom with her demands and was often physically aggressive toward children both in class and on the playground.

Nora had not received special education services, and apparently did not qualify based on her academic abilities, although she was rapidly falling behind in her studies. Ms. Wilson was directed by the principal to keep a journal on Nora's behavior while school, social welfare, and child protective services person-

nel studied the situation. Many days, Ms. Wilson would remain at the school until late evening, attending meetings with the school counselor and the principal, writing in her journal, and preparing lessons for the 25 students in her classroom. She wished she had a teaching assistant to help with Nora during class time. It wasn't until January that a decision was made to provide Nora intensive therapeutic intervention with a counselor after school. It also became apparent that Nora's family life was the source of many of her problems.

When Nora's home situation was investigated, it was found that the children often stayed up until the early hours of the morning watching television in their disheveled mobile home. Her family had rarely lived in any location for more than a year. When social services personnel came knocking at their door, they simply moved. The father was an alcoholic, and the mother struggled to raise three children on welfare, the youngest a boy with a significant disability.

It was clear that an interdisciplinary team approach was needed to address some of the difficult problems experienced by this family. Ms. Wilson admitted that this year was the most difficult of her teaching career and that it wasn't until after January, when additional support and assistance were provided to Nora and her family, that Ms. Wilson actually got to know the other children in her classroom as individuals.

The Way Teachers Teach

For decades, teachers have approached the practice of classroom instruction in a fairly uniform manner. However, as public concerns have arisen over the poor performance of schools in educating our children, many traditional practices have been called into question. As the educational reform movement gained momentum in the 1980s, researchers began to scrutinize the way teachers teach and manage their classrooms.

What researchers learned about how teachers teach should not be surprising to those who graduated from high school before the 1990s. In an extensive investigation of 1,016 schools, Goodlad (1983) and his colleagues observed that teachers primarily relied on teacher-directed, whole-class instruction with little instructional variability. Mostly, they lectured to their students and led class discussions with few teacher-to-student or student-to-student interactions. Students spent most of their time listening to teacher lectures or engaging in seatwork. Teachers did not provide corrective feedback to students to stimulate concept formation. Goodlad described the classroom atmospheres they observed as "affectless" or "flat." The researchers did, however, observe that more hands-on activities and varied learning occurred in art, physical education, and vocational classes.

Goodlad's descriptions characterized classrooms that were overly regimented and boring, with teachers who employed few instructional approaches, rarely individualized instruction, and rarely engaged students in active learning or group learning. Individualization and adaptation of instructional methods and curriculum were not expected of regular teachers. Teachers were expected to conform to a standardized, lock-step curriculum, with students placed in an age-graded classroom to participate uniformly in the same activities. Students were often forced into the role of passive information receptors, and standardized testing reinforced this role by requiring memorization in the content-oriented core curriculum. Essentially, the curriculum was devoid of experiences that promoted independent and creative thinking, perception, and aesthetic sensitivity (Carter, Steinbrink, & Smiley, 1993).

There were, of course, exceptions to these generalizations about classrooms and teachers. However, the research reports reflected what was typical, and raised the nation's level of concern about the quality of instruction in our public schools. Clearly, the traditional instructional approaches described by Goodlad have outgrown their usefulness, even though they seemed to have served us well during the past century. Given the changes in the types of children who attend school, the changes in society and the goals of education, and recent research concerning how students learn and what motivates them, educators are considering new and alternative educational approaches. One of the approaches educational researchers have focused on is cooperative group learning.

HISTORICAL ASPECTS OF COOPERATIVE LEARNING

For centuries, educators have placed students in small groups or pairs for learning. The idea of cooperative learning was imported from England to a Lancastrian school in New York, where it was championed by Joseph Lancaster and Andrew Bell in the late 1700s. The technique continued to be employed during the Common School Movement in the 1800s. Colonel Francis Parker, superintendent of public schools at Quincy, Massachusetts, from 1875 to 1880, was known for his belief in cooperative learning and a democratic classroom atmosphere where student individuality was valued (Johnson, Johnson, & Holubec, 1993).

Another education philosopher and reformer who promoted cooperative learning and incorporated it into his "project method" of instruction was John Dewey. Dewey (1943) emphasized democratic, egalitarian curriculum measures. He believed education should not stress lectures and the teacher; rather, the focus should be on *experience* and the *student*. Dewey championed the importance of social activities in school and the critical connection between school and home to foster learning (Carter, Steinbrink, & Smiley, 1993).

Following the passage of the Civil Rights Act in 1964, educators became even more interested in cooperative learning as a promising approach to help with the integration of African American students into desegregated schools. By the 1970s, educational researchers began to refine a set of principles to guide teachers in the use of cooperative learning to enhance school performance. They were realizing that too much focus had been placed on the interaction between teachers and individual students in the instructional process to the neglect of student-to-student interactions. In the 1980s, Dr. Maynard Reynolds, a leader in the mainstreaming movement, pointed out the potential of cooperative learning to assist in the education of students with various disabilities who were placed in regular class settings.

During the past 30 years, numerous studies have been conducted on cooperative learning at all grade levels from preschool to college and across curriculum areas such as math, science, social studies, language arts, physical education, art, business education, and music. The number of studies may well surpass those on any other instructional method in U.S. education. This research has been summarized in articles, reviews of research, and books. (See Johnson, Johnson, & Holubec, 1993, and the suggested readings at the end of this chapter for a historical overview and research reviews.) It is important for teachers to understand that the cooperative method of instruction is supported by decades of intensive study. In fact, the research dates back to 1879 with a study by Triplett investigating the effects of the presence of other people on individual performance and has continued for nearly a century (Johnson & Johnson, 1989). While numerous outcomes can result from cooperative learning with children and adolescents, three primary outcome areas—academic achievement, social relationships, and self-esteem—are emphasized in this chapter, due to their importance in public education and the amount of attention they have received in the literature.

ACADEMIC OUTCOMES OF COOPERATIVE LEARNING

Of utmost importance to educators and parents is the influence of an instructional approach on students' academic performance and productivity. When researchers began studying the effects of cooperative learning on achievement, they most often compared cooperative learning with two other types of learning "structures," or methods for organizing learning, predominant in U.S. schools: individualistic learning (learning alone) and competitive learning. Researchers found that students generally achieved better in cooperative situations.

To draw conclusions from the hundreds of studies comparing cooperation to competition and individualistic learning, researchers use special analytical methods. The "best-evidence synthesis" technique was used by Slavin (1990) to examine the effects of 68 studies on cooperative learning and achievement. Slavin found that 49 of the 68 comparisons (72%) were positive, favoring the cooperative learning methods, and only 8 (12%) favored the control groups. This study also looked at different types of cooperative learning methods (for example, cooperative learning with competition among groups, or cooperative learning coupled with individualized instruction), and, as might be expected, it was found that the various cooperative methods had differing results.

From several research reviews, Slavin concludes that three elements are crucial to the success of cooperative learning in enhancing achievement: *group rewards, individual accountability,* and *equal opportunity scoring.* Students in cooperative groups must be rewarded or recognized on the basis of the sum or average of the individual learning performances—*group rewards.* All students must contribute their share of the work and not be "free riders"—*individual accountability.* The purpose of *equal opportunity scoring* is to enable *all* students, regardless of ability level, an equal chance to earn points for improving on their own past performance. These points contribute to their team's score. The goal is for students to surpass their past performance. Individualizing the criteria for success is fundamental to instructing diverse learners in heterogeneous groups—especially when some of those students are gifted or experience academic performance problems.

Requiring all students to work toward the same criteria for success (e.g., 80% on a quiz) poses problems because achieving the criteria might be too easy for some students and too difficult for others. If students are underchallenged, they tend to lose motivation and are not compelled to stretch themselves to achieve to their potential. Less academically able students may fail because they simply cannot perform the tasks or because they have a fear of failure. They also risk being devalued by their group members if they cannot contribute to group success. In either case, the motivation to succeed is diminished and achievement levels are likely to decrease. With equal opportunity scoring, however, all students have an equal chance to positively contribute to the group score, regardless of differing ability levels.

A more recent research review of 99 studies on cooperative learning and achievement adds a new dimension to our understanding of the conditions under which cooperative learning produces positive achievement results: explicit instruction in learning strategies. Slavin (1995) reports that "it is possible to create conditions leading to positive achievement outcomes by directly teaching students structured methods of working with each other (especially in pairs) or teaching them learning strategies closely related to the instructional objective (especially for teaching reading skills)" (p. 45).

Johnson and Johnson (1989) also looked at the research on cooperative learning and achievement using a meta-analysis methodology to analyze the results of 323 studies comparing cooperative learning with individualistic and competitive learning. The data indicate that achievement and productivity are higher when students cooperate than when they work individually or compete. The more methodologically rigorous the study was, the more powerful was the effect of cooperative learning on achievement. More than 50% of the findings were statistically significant in favor of cooperation and only 10% of the findings were statistically significant in favor of competitive or individualistic learning. The researchers found that the average cooperator performed above (about ⅗ a standard deviation) the average person working individually or competitively. Johnson and Johnson (1989) stress that the most positive achievement outcomes are likely to occur when the conditions of positive interdependence, individual accountability, and direct teaching of collaborative skills are ensured. Figure 2.1 identifies important elements of cooperative learning associated with high achievement according to Slavin (1990, 1995) and Johnson and Johnson (1989).

It must be noted, however, that cooperative learning does not *invariably* lead to positive academic outcomes. A few studies have indicated that competition or individualistic efforts lead to higher achievement; these studies involved adults engaged in simple motor tasks or rote learning tasks. Also, gaps exist in the research literature. For example, some researchers complain that investigations on cooperative learning and academic achievement focus too much on learning basic, fundamental skills, such as spelling skills or mathematical procedures. Relatively less research has been conducted on the effects of cooperative methods in helping students solve problems or acquire higher-order skills, particularly in mathematics (Davidson, 1985).

As you read this text you will encounter some of the problematic aspects of cooperative group instruction, such as poor implementation, or examples of lessons in which a variety of factors, such as poor understanding of the group goal, or students' lack of collaborative skills can jeopardize achievement. Chapter 6 discusses major problems that can arise in cooperative learning situations. You will also discover that there are limits to the positive influence of cooperative learning on student achievement and that there are areas that need further exploration by researchers. Nonetheless, the overall conclusions from decades of research are encouraging: When appropriately implemented, cooperative learning enhances student achievement.

SOCIAL OUTCOMES OF COOPERATIVE LEARNING

Learning is a social act. In school, learning involves intellectual, emotional, and social processes simultaneously. An important goal of education is to prepare students to function well in future work, community, and home environments. Success in any of these areas requires a complex set of

FIGURE 2.1
Features of Cooperative Learning Linked to High Achievement

1.   Positive interdependence/group rewards
2.   Individual accountability
3.   Equal opportunity for success
4.   Collaborative skill instruction
5.   Learning strategy instruction

social skills that incorporate interpersonal communication, cooperation, perspective taking, acceptance of differences in others, commitment to helping one another, and conflict resolution. Schooling provides an excellent opportunity for children to learn the social skills that are critical to their future successes in a multitude of life activities.

In today's world, it is not sufficient to graduate from high school having mastered only the basic curriculum or having acquired only one vocational skill. While basic knowledge and vocational skills are important, social and interpersonal skills may be even more fundamental to employability and career success. A survey of businesses, labor unions, and educational institutions by the Center for Public Resources found that of the people who were fired from their first job, 90% of them were let go not because they lacked basic job competence or technical skills, but because they lacked the social skills to work effectively with others (Johnson & Johnson, 1989). Some of the reasons cited were poor job attitudes, poor interpersonal relationships, inappropriate dress, and inappropriate behavior. It is difficult to imagine many occupations that do not require skills of working with colleagues and other professionals. Social and cooperative skills are needed throughout the work force, by entry-level workers, middle managers, and high-level executives alike.

Teachers simply cannot ignore the social aspects of learning and classroom dynamics:

> Classrooms are not socially neutral places. Nonetheless, many teachers ignore the social dimensions of classroom teaching and concentrate exclusively on study tasks. Whatever the teachers' choice of instructional method, it will exert its effects on student relationships. In turn, these relationships will exert their critical influences on students' attitudes toward school and on the way they process learning. (Sharan & Sharan, 1992, p. 149)

Cooperative learning activities are particularly suited to providing opportunities for students to learn and improve their interpersonal skills and to form positive relationships with children, including those who are from different backgrounds. Researchers have explored various ways that cooperative learning might improve social interactions and behaviors. Some of the questions they have posed include the following:

- Does cooperative learning help children from different ethnic groups relate more positively with one another?
- Does cooperative learning improve interactions with and attitudes toward students with disabilities?
- Does cooperative learning improve student self-esteem?

Highlights from the literature that addresses these questions will be presented in the next sections; for a more complete discussion, see the reference list and the suggested reading list at the end of this chapter.

INTERPERSONAL RELATIONS

Simply stated, cooperative learning helps students learn to like one another. In today's diverse classrooms and schools it is extremely important to develop ways to help students to get along with those who have different cultural, ethnic, religious, or socioeconomic backgrounds or who have varying learning, sensory, emotional, or physical abilities.

Cross-Ethnic Relations

When educators and researchers looked for methods for improving the relationships between students in desegregated schools in the 1960s and 1970s, cooperative learning was one method that came to mind. It was already apparent that simply placing students from different ethnic groups into the same schools or classrooms was necessary, but not sufficient, for achieving the goal of positive interpersonal relations. In these schools, students from different racial and ethnic backgrounds tended not to naturally intermingle and form friendships. Ethnic separateness in schools will maintain itself unless systematic interventions are undertaken to reduce it (Gerard & Miller, 1975).

The inclination of groups to segregate themselves is not entirely due to racial or ethnic prejudices; other reasons include differences in the stu-

Cultural Diversity

dents' values, cultural backgrounds, and personal preferences. Often students from different ethnic groups reside in different neighborhoods and have few opportunities to get to know one another or interact outside of school. Also, individuals from different groups form impressions of what persons from another group are like—even before they have met. Quite often, these initial impressions, or stereotypes, are negative, and they usually persist over time.

Four decades ago, Allport (1954) articulated his Contact Theory to explain how prejudice can be decreased among racial groups. Allport believed that by increasing *nonsuperficial contact* among students and having teachers promote the notion of *equal status* among students, interracial relations would improve. Merely sitting in a desk and working individually, comparing test answers with classmates, or engaging in a large group discussion led by the teacher are examples of superficial contact. Examples of nonsuperficial contact are discussing a controversial topic, making decisions, coordinating an activity over a period of time, or helping one another find information. Simply placing students from heterogeneous groups in physical proximity, whether they are from different ethnic groups or have disabling conditions, may actually increase negative interactions and stereotyping. Allport believed the critical factor that determined student relationships was the *nature*, or quality, of the student contact rather than the frequency of the contact.

Cooperative learning is well suited to fulfilling the nonsuperficial contact and equal status requirements of Allport's theory because (1) groups of heterogeneous students are given frequent opportunities for purposeful interactions, (2) all group members are able to achieve equal status as they contribute to the group's progress in the pursuit of common goals, and (3) the teacher can convey his or her full support for interactions between ethnic groups (Slavin, 1990). Most of the research substantiates the idea that cooperative learning enhances interactions among members of different ethnic groups or between students with and without disabilities (Cohen, Lotan, Catanzarite, 1990; Johnson, Johnson, & Maruyama, 1983; Sharan, 1990). According to Johnson and Johnson (1989), a cooperative context is a major determinant of whether cross-ethnic contact results in positive relationships.

Students With Disabilities

Students with disabilities are often judged by their classmates in negative and stereotypic ways. People make unfortunate assumptions that a person with a disability is not capable—even in areas that are unaffected by the disability. For example, a student with cerebral palsy may be highly intelligent, but because she cannot speak clearly and her movements are uncoordinated, it is assumed that she is mentally delayed or functioning at a younger level. Furthermore, students and teachers alike tend to have low expectations for performance of students with disabilities.

Differing Abilities

The research on cooperative learning and the acceptance of students with disabilities is quite positive, indicating that students with disabilities are more accepted by their peers under cooperative conditions (Johnson & Johnson, 1989; Johnson, Johnson, & Maruyama, 1983; Slavin, 1995). In most studies, peer acceptance has been evaluated by asking students in the class to rate other students according to the degree to which they would like to work or play with them, or to numerically rank their friends in the class.

Low-Performing Students

There are often occasions when a student is weak in a particular area or is unable to perform at the same level as the other group members. Most of us have worked with others on a task in which we were the least capable in the group, whether learning a new sport, using new technology, learning a foreign language, or entering a new academic area such as astronomy or art history.

What happens to low-performing students in heterogeneous cooperative groups? Researchers once theorized that individuals in a group who facilitate the attainment of the group goal are liked and accepted, while an individual who frustrates the group's goal attainment with ineffective, or "bumbling," actions will be disliked and rejected (Deutsch, 1949). Although group members will try to compensate for ineffective performance of an individual, they start to resent the person that thwarts their progress. It is interesting that research on cooperative learning and low-performing students suggests that low-achieving individuals are actually *liked more* in cooperative situations than they are in competitive situations, despite the fact that they may not enhance or contribute to the group's goal attainment (Johnson, Johnson, & Scott, 1978). Johnson and Johnson (1989) postulate the following explanations for this tendency:

1.   *Multidimensional perspectives.* Cooperative interactions enable students to perceive one another in multidimensional, as opposed to stereotypic, ways. Individual students are recognized for their abilities, which are revealed over the course of time in sustained activities. For example, a student with a reading disability may display superior abilities or talents in art, mathematics, or in solving "brain teasers" in the context of cooperative activities.

2.   *High effort is valued.* Students also tend to value their low performing peers when they are putting forth high effort, even if they are not as successful as the other students. The student who tries hard will be liked simply for making an honest effort. When a student with a brace on her leg struggles valiantly to complete her segment of a relay at the school's outdoor games, for example, she gains her classmates admiration and applause.

3.   *Helping others is satisfying.* Because there is a norm for helping in our society, individuals feel personally rewarded when they assist one another, and they develop a personal commitment to doing so. The satisfaction gained from the personal commitment to helping another person results in greater liking of that person.

It is now widely recognized that positive peer relationships influence a number of psychological outcomes, such as healthy psychological adjustment in adulthood and positive self-esteem. The improvement in interpersonal relationships that takes place when students with disabilities, low performing students, and students from diverse cultural and ethnic backgrounds participate in high quality heterogeneous cooperative learning groups is encouraging news for educators and families.

The following summary of an investigation of cooperative learning with mixed ability pairs demonstrates the possibilities for enhancing performance of high and low achievers.

Cooperation and Mixed Ability Pairs in Science.   Two researchers from North Carolina (Jones & Carter, 1994) conducted a study of 30 fifth-grade science students who worked in cooperative pairs as they attempted to learn balance concepts by manipulating levers and blocks. To better understand the relationship among students' achievement levels, their interactions with peers, and their approach to knowledge construction, the researchers paired high-achieving students with another high-achieving student or with a low-achieving student. Low-achieving students were paired either with another low-achieving student or with a high-achieving student. High and low achievement was defined as scoring either in the upper or lower quartile (25%) of the school system's student population on the *California Achievement Test*. Average-achieving students who scored in the mid-range (50%) were paired with other average-achieving students.

Through observation and audiotaping, the researchers looked for evidence of concept development while the pairs of students completed three activities related to balance. For example, the first set of activities involved students in exploring the effects of moving a fulcrum on effort force needed and of balancing levers with equal and unequal weights.

At first, as might be expected, the low achieving pairs had difficulty organizing themselves and staying on-task, and they seemed to focus on the irrelevant features of the equipment. Rather than cooperating, they competed for the use of the lab materials, which interfered with the learning of the concepts and accomplishing the task. On the other hand, the high-achieving pairs were organized and efficient in their efforts, and were seldom off-task. They shared equipment and showed initiative and responsibility in performing the task. They also brought to the activities prior experiences and an understanding of the necessary learning strategies.

What is most interesting about this investigation was the performance of the high-low pairs of students. The low-achieving students were better able to accomplish the task and did not impede the performance of the high-achieving students. Each student brought certain behaviors to the task: high-achieving students brought attentiveness, on-task behaviors, prior experiences (e.g., with levers, screwdrivers, fulcrums), and good learning strategies. Low-achieving students brought poor attention skills, a lack of understanding of the task, a focus on irrelevant details, and poor self-regulation skills.

> When the high and low students worked together, they each built successful, but parallel structures. The structures may not have been identical, but each achieved the goal of the builder. . . . The high student modeled learning behaviors, as well as taught the low student. The low student did not necessarily mimic the high student, but used his or her own tools and materials in the learning process. (Jones & Carter, 1994, p. 616)

Jones and Carter emphasize the importance of selecting challenging and multileveled tasks to enable growth at different levels. "It may not be advantageous merely to place high and low students together if the task is not designed for growth at different levels" (p. 618). Their point is worth remembering: *Cooperative learning tasks must contain something for all students.*

SELF-ESTEEM

Self-esteem is defined as a person's own judgment about his or her worth, and is based on that person's perception of how competent and well-liked he or she is.

> Perhaps the most important psychological outcome of cooperative learning methods is their effect on self-esteem. Students' beliefs that they are valuable and important individuals are of critical importance for their ability to withstand the disappointments of life, to be confident decision makers, and ultimately to be happy and productive individuals. (Slavin, 1990, p. 43)

In school-age children, self-esteem is strongly influenced by (1) how well a child is achieving in school and (2) how well liked the child is by his or her peers (Coopersmith, 1967). As has been pointed out, cooperative learning tends to increase student achievement and enhance peer acceptance, therefore it stands to reason that participating in cooperative activities should ultimately lead to improved self-esteem. A child's self-esteem is shaped over a lifetime, so it is unlikely that an instructional intervention is going to alter self-esteem overnight. However, the research does support the idea that cooperative learning can help children raise their self-esteem and sense of self-worth.

While studies on the effects of cooperative learning on self-esteem are not completely consistent, Slavin (1995) found that 11 of 15 studies on cooperative learning and self-esteem resulted in positive effects on some aspect of self-esteem—either general self-esteem, academic self-esteem, or social self-esteem.

Johnson and Johnson (1989) used a meta-analysis methodology to compare the effects of cooperation with competition and individualistic learning on students' self-esteem. Seventy-seven studies were reviewed to compare the effects of cooperation, individualistic, and competitive learning on self-esteem. Results showed that 53% of the findings were statistically significant in favor of cooperation, while only 1% favored competition. The self-esteem of the average cooperator was higher (3/5 of a standard deviation) than the average competitor, and higher (2/5 of a standard deviation) than the average person working individually. When competition and individual learning were compared it was found that working alone results in somewhat higher self-esteem than working competitively.

Researchers believe more studies need to be conducted over the long term to accurately ascertain the effects of cooperative learning on self-esteem, which is influenced by several factors, including a person's ability to function independently as well as compete with others in positive ways. From what we know now, however, it appears that long-lasting and genuine changes in self-esteem could result from sustained use of cooperative learning as a principal instructional methodology in the classroom.

OTHER EDUCATIONAL OUTCOMES

In addition to the effects of cooperative learning on achievement, social relationships, and self-esteem, researchers have found that students participating in cooperative activities respond more favorably to a number of other student and educational outcomes that should be of great interest to teachers. These outcomes are listed in Figure 2.2. Teachers will particularly appreciate the fact that cooperative learning results in increased attendance, increased on-task behavior, less disruptive behavior, greater liking of the subject matter, and greater liking of the teacher!

Based on my own course evaluations and student feedback over the years, I have concluded that students were more satisfied when I incorporated cooperative learning into my instructional methodology. One semester Dr. Ray Glass and I surveyed education majors to find out how they viewed their learning and performance in cooperative activities versus the more standard instructional format of lecture and discussion. Students indicated that they preferred working in cooperative groups, but they also believed there was a place for teacher lecture and large-group discussion in the college classroom (Glass & Putnam, 1989).

FIGURE 2.2
*Cooperative Learning
Outcomes*
Johnson, Johnson, & Holubec,
1990; Slavin, 1991

- Increased academic achievement.
- Improved intergroup relations.
- Improved self-esteem.
- Higher-level reasoning strategies and increased critical reasoning competencies.
- Greater ability to view situations from others' perspectives.
- Greater intrinsic motivation.
- More positive attitudes toward subject areas, learning, and school.
- More positive attitudes toward teachers, principals, and school personnel.
- Less disruptive and more on-task behavior.
- Greater collaborative skills and attitudes necessary for working with others.
- Greater feeling of individual control over one's success in school.
- Increased altruism and supportive behaviors toward others.
- Increased prosocial behavior.
- Improved skills at resolving conflicts.
- Increased attendance.

CONTROVERSIAL ISSUES IN COOPERATIVE LEARNING

As with any instructional approach, teachers need to know when, with whom, and under what circumstances to use cooperative learning. Although we would like to find a panacea for solving all the problems in our schools, it is highly unlikely that any one method will have such broad applications. While educators and researchers marvel at the array of benefits resulting from cooperative learning, questions arise concerning overextension and misapplication of cooperative methods. Two controversial issues surround the use of cooperative learning with gifted students and students with disabilities.

Gifted Students

Following are some questions posed by educators, parents, and students who are not convinced that cooperative learning is beneficial to our brightest students:

- Is cooperative learning truly beneficial to students who are extremely gifted or does it hold them back?

- Should highly gifted students participate in heterogeneous cooperative activities with lower-achieving students, or should they cooperate mostly with other gifted students?

- Will gifted students be relegated to the role of tutor or "junior teacher" for others in their cooperative groups while they are unchallenged in their own work?

- Will the work pace of gifted students be slowed to the pace determined by the group?

- Will gifted students be forced to work on basic skills or material they have already mastered?

- Will funds be diverted from programs for gifted students due to the increasing popularity of cooperative learning and mixed-ability groups?

Proponents of using cooperative learning with gifted students believe the social interaction that occurs in well-structured cooperative activities is invaluable to a child's development. Cooperative activities provide the context in which students can learn the critical skills involved in teamwork. The skills required for communication and coordinating a project with others of various abilities are essential skills required in most jobs. Students also learn a fundamental social skill: To define success in terms of the goals of others as well as one's own goals (Strom, 1983). Conflict resolution skills are also sharpened in cooperative learning activities; they can be applied in family life as well as in the community and workplace. Cooperative learning also provides gifted students with opportunities to learn and perfect leadership skills, which are critically important if one accepts the argument that gifted students should be our future civic leaders (Torrey, 1956).

As noted earlier, those who support cooperative learning in mixed-ability groups for gifted students also believe they will benefit academically (Slavin, 1991). Their rationale is that the students use higher-level reasoning strategies more frequently in cooperative groups and they participate in oral explanations that enhance retention and achievement more than when they simply listen to or read material on their own (Johnson & Johnson, 1991).

Proponents of cooperative learning caution against confusing "ability grouping" and "tracking" of students with cooperative learning. Because the popularity of cooperative learning has coincided with criticisms of ability grouping (Goodlad & Oakes, 1988), professionals in the gifted community worry that cooperative learning, with heterogeneous grouping of mixed-ability students, is a threat to the continuation of gifted and talented programs. It is also feared that in mixed-ability groups, expectations are lowered for gifted students, resulting in lower student achievement levels.

Cooperative learning researchers (Johnson & Johnson, 1991; Slavin, 1991) emphasize that cooperative learning should not be equated with the elimination of ability grouping, and that there is a place for homogeneous grouping of gifted students for cooperative learning as well as for some heterogeneous grouping.

To date, the use of cooperative learning with gifted students has not been well researched. Some researchers report that the achievement of gifted students is usually higher when they work in homogeneous classrooms than in heterogeneous classrooms, particularly in the areas of science and social science (Goldring, 1990). Other researchers have found that gifted students perform better when they work cooperatively rather than individually or competitively and when they work in academically heterogeneous groups rather than academically homogeneous groups (Johnson & Johnson, 1989; Slavin, 1991). Conflicting evidence and opinions abound regarding cooperative learning and grouping strategies, pointing to a need for more study and dialogue among educators to clarify these issues.

Unfortunately, cooperative learning has a history of being misapplied in the classroom, and its use with gifted students is no exception. No student should have to work on material that he or she has already mastered. Teachers should be careful to make informed decisions about which lessons lend themselves to heterogeneous groups and which lend themselves to homogeneous groups. Drill and practice tasks or tasks that focus on basic skills should be avoided and tasks involving higher-order thinking, creativity, critical thinking and problem solving should be planned (Stout, 1993). When gifted students work in mixed-ability cooperative groups, the task should allow for a range of abilities and should challenge all the students. In addition, while students do help and tutor one another in cooperative groups, that role should not be designated solely to the student who is gifted. Gifted students should also experience a range of learning experiences, with opportunities for cooperative groupwork with other gifted students, individual work, or work with an adult mentor.

Students With Disabilities

Students with disabilities can reap many benefits from participating in appropriately organized cooperative learning activities. Substantial research indicates that cooperative learning increases the social acceptance of students with disabilities. However, the question of whether cooperative learning improves the achievement of students with disabilities over other instructional approaches has not been settled. Favorable to the use of cooperative learning to enhance the achievement of students with disabilities are research reviews by Johnson, Maruyama, Johnson, Nelson, and Skon (1981); Johnson and Johnson (1989); and Slavin (1990, 1995). The results indicate that students perform better in cooperative situations than in competitive or individual situations.

On the other hand, Tateyama-Sniezek's (1990) review of 12 selected studies on cooperative learning and students with disabilities found that only about half of them supported cooperative group learning. When Stevens and Slavin (1991) analyzed the 12 studies, they found that four of the studies incorporated group goals and individual accountability, which, you will recall, are essential elements of successful cooperative learning. In looking at just those four studies, the effect size for the achievement of students with disabilities was +0.48. Moreover, some researchers believe that before any conclusions are drawn concerning cooperative learning's value in improving academic achievement of students with disabilities, it should be compared not only with individual and competitive learning, but also with other instructional methods that have well-established records of effectiveness (Lloyd, Crowley, Kohler, & Strain, 1988). Other instructional methods that could be compared with cooperative learning are academic peer tutoring, which involves students directly teaching other children, and teacher-directed tutorials.

It has been found that combining cooperative learning with other instructional approaches, such as individualized instruction, improves the academic achievement of students with mild disabilities (Slavin, 1995). The hallmark of special education is the individualization of instruction to meet a student's unique learning needs. Ultimately, cooperative learning should be used in combination with other approaches, but it has great potential for enhancing achievement because it is particularly well suited to providing opportunities for students to:

- Practice their skills.
- Engage actively in the learning process.
- Apply concepts.
- Observe a variety of useful learning strategies.
- Give and receive explanations.
- Give and receive help from classmates.

Good teachers discover early in their careers that there is no one method of instruction that best suits the needs of all children in all circumstances; the art of teaching requires a repertoire of instructional approaches and the ability and insight to decide when and under what circumstances to use them.

CONCLUSION

U.S. educators are paying serious attention to the criticisms now being levied against public schools for not adequately educating our children and youth. While many are willing to accept at least some of the blame for the problems in our schools, it may be equally reasonable to claim that we are actually doing an outstanding job of teaching our children, given the ever-increasing population of children who come to school ill-prepared to learn. Many of these children have problems associated with alcohol and drug abuse, violence, poor home environments, and poverty.

Whatever the reasons for declining confidence in our schools, many agree that our educational system is in crisis and sorely in need of reform. It is recognized that the factory-model of education and the associated instructional approaches of teacher-directed, whole-class instruction have outgrown their usefulness. It is in this context of perceived educational crisis, with its accompanying dangers and opportunities, that cooperative learning has emerged as a potent approach for enhancing student learning and social development.

The research on cooperative learning is noteworthy in a number of respects: for its long and rich history in U.S. education, its extensiveness, and the breadth of outcomes studied. More than 800 investigations have been conducted on cooperative learning, dating back to the 1800s. This literature is extremely comprehensive in its coverage of curricular areas, age levels, and characteristics of students studied. Researchers have investigated the effects of cooperative learning on a wide array of outcomes, including academic achievement, social/psychological outcomes, and a number of school-related outcomes.

In this chapter, you have learned that cooperative learning can be an effective means for improving student achievement, but only when the conditions of positive interdependence (group goals) and individual accountability are realized. When achievement benefits of cooperative learning are combined with the other positive outcomes, such as improved cross-ethnic relations, peer acceptance of students with disabilities, improved behavior, liking of school and teacher, and increased self-esteem, it becomes apparent that it has advantages over more traditional, strictly noncooperative approaches.

Of course, cooperative learning has not proven superior to other instructional methods in all cases, and teachers should understand that successful cooperative learning is sometimes the result of a complex set of factors that work together to promote student learning and productivity. The challenge for teachers and educational researchers is to learn more about how to effectively design, implement, and evaluate successful cooperative learning activities. As you read on in this text, you will discover how to organize cooperative activities to promote student success.

◆   ◆   ◆

QUESTIONS AND ACTIVITIES

1.   Do you believe a crisis exists in U.S. education? Summarize the points made in the first section of the chapter, and then discuss them with a beginning teacher, an experienced teacher, an educational administrator, and a parent of a student. Write a short paper examining the perspectives of the people you interviewed and your own viewpoint.

2.   To maximize achievement outcomes, cooperative learning activities should incorporate positive interdependence, individual accountability, equal opportunity scoring, learning strategy instruction, and collaborative skill instruction. Recall group activities you have experienced in your education or have observed in schools. Were these aspects incorporated? How do you think their presence or absence influenced your cooperative group experiences?

3.   Identify an occupation and describe how collaborative skills are important to that occupation. Develop a list of collaborative skills (no more than 10) associated with the occupation you have selected. Do you think any of these skills could be introduced and practiced during the school years? Did you learn these skills directly in classrooms? How are they taught in today's schools?

4.   Write a position paper on why students with disabilities should be incorporated into cooperative learning groups in heterogeneous classrooms. Why do students with disabilities tend to be more accepted when they participate in heterogeneous cooperative activities than in individualistic or competitive activities? Orally present your position paper to someone who might be a bit skeptical. After your presentation, summarize the reactions to your talk and discuss how you would modify your talk in the future.

5.   Interview two students from your local school district who have been identified as gifted to ascertain how they feel about working cooperatively in mixed-ability groups and in homogeneous (gifted-only) groups. Summarize their responses and your insights concerning why they feel the way they do.

6.   Review the list of *Outcomes of Cooperative Learning* in Figure 2.2. Which three nonacademic outcomes are the most important to you? Rank them in importance and explain why you chose them.

7.   **Cooperative controversy activity:** In your class discuss whether a crisis exists in U.S. education. Form heterogeneous groups of four, by random assignment. Debate the matter by dividing into two's within your group. One pair will take the extreme position that there is a crisis and the other pair will take the position that there is no crisis. (1) First, each pair develops their arguments or position. (2) Next, each pair presents their position. After the first pair presents its position without interruption or discussion, the other pair will paraphrase the arguments presented. (3) Then, the second pair presents its position, again without interruption or discussion, and the first pair paraphrases what they have said. (4) Finally, everyone discusses the issue as a group and summarizes their major conclusions. Devote about 10 minutes to each of the four steps of the activity.

Discuss the following: Did either group's presentation add anything to your understanding? Did paraphrasing help you understand the other pair's message? Summarize the key points for a brief large-group presentation to the class. Other issues raised in this chapter can be discussed using this group structure—for example, what are the advantages and disadvantages of using cooperative learning with students who are gifted or students with disabilities?

SUGGESTED READINGS

Books

Johnson, D. W., & Johnson, R. T. (1989). *Cooperation and competition: Theory and research*. Edina, MN: Interaction Books.

Slavin, R. E. (1995). *Cooperative learning: Theory, research and practice* (2nd ed.). Boston, MA: Allyn and Bacon.

Magazines

Education Leadership. Alexandria, VA: Association for Supervision and Curriculum Development. This magazine has devoted several issues to cooperative learning and is appropriate for teachers interested in curriculum and instruction. (Information available from the Association for Supervision and Curriculum Development, 1250 N. Pitt St., Alexandria, VA 22314-1403.)

The *Phi Delta Kappan*. Bloomington, IN: Phi Delta Kappa. This magazine contains articles about education research and focuses on current trends and issues in U.S. education. Information available from Phi Delta Kappa Inc., 408 N. Union, P.O. Box 789, Bloomington, IN 47402.

REFERENCES

Allport, G. (1954). *The nature of prejudice.* Cambridge, MA: Addison-Wesley.

An F in World Competition, (February, 1992). *Newsweek, 19,* p. 57.

Bracey, G. W. (1992). The second Bracey report on the condition of public education. *Phi Delta Kappan, 74*(2), 104–117.

Carter, S. A., Steinbrink, J. E., & Smiley, F. M. (1993). Curricular histories— A cooperative learning model: social studies, English, and art. *Education, 113*(2), 263–281.

Coopersmith, S. A. (1967). *The antecedents of self-esteem.* San Francisco: Freeman.

Cohen, E., Lotan, R., & Catanzarite, L. (1990). Treating status problems in the cooperative classroom. In S. Sharan (Ed.), *Cooperative learning: Theory and research* (pp. 203–229). New York: Praeger.

Davidson, N. (1985). Small-group learning and teaching in mathematics: A selective review of the research. In R. Slavin, S. Sharan, S. Kagan, R. Hertz-Lazarowitz, C. Webb, & R. Schmuch (Eds.), *Learning to cooperate, cooperating to learn* (pp. 211–230). New York: Plenum.

Deutsch, M. (1949). A theory of cooperation and competition. *Human Relations, 2,* 199–231.

Dewey, J. (1943). *The school and society.* Chicago: The University of Chicago Press.

Gerard, H. B., & Miller, N. (1975) *School desegregation: A long-range study.* New York: Plenum.

Glass, R. M., & Putnam, J. W. (1989). Cooperative learning in teacher education: A case study. *Action in Teacher Education, 10,* 47–52.

Goldring, E. B. (1990). Assessing the status of information on classroom organizational frameworks for gifted students. *Journal of Educational Research, 83*(6), 313–326.

Goodlad, J. I. (1983). A study of schooling: Some findings and hypotheses. *Phi Delta Kappan, 64,* 462–470.

Goodlad, J. I., & Oakes, J. (1989). We must offer equal access to knowledge. *Educational Leadership, 45*(5), 16–22.

Hodgkinson, H. (1992). *A demographic look at tomorrow.* Institute for Educational Leadership/Center for Demographic Policy, Washington, DC.

Hodgkinson, H. (1993). American Education: The good, the bad, and the task. *Phi Delta Kappan, 74*(8), 619–625.

Jaeger, R. M. (1992). World class standards, choice and privatization: Weak measurement serving presumptive policy. *Phi Delta Kappan, 74*(2), 118–128.

Johnson, D. W., & Johnson, R. T. (1989). *Cooperation and competition: Theory and research.* Edina, MN: Interaction Books.

Johnson, D. W., & Johnson, R. T. (1991). What cooperative learning has to offer the gifted. *Cooperative Learning, 11*(3), 24–27.

Johnson, D. W., Johnson, R. T., & Holubec, E. J. (1993). *Cooperation in the classroom.* (6th ed.). Edina, MN: Interaction Books.

Johnson, D. W., Johnson, R. T., & Maruyama, G. (1983). Interdependence and interpersonal attraction among heterogeneous and homogeneous individuals: A theoretical formulation and a meta-analysis of the research. *Review of Educational Research, 53,* 5–54.

Johnson, D. W., Johnson, R. T., & Scott, L. (1978). The effects of cooperative and individualized instruction on student attitudes and achievement. *The Journal of Social Psychology, 104,* 207–216.

Johnson, D., Maruyama, G., Johnson, R., Nelson, D., & Skon, L. (1981). The effects of cooperative, competitive, and individualistic goal structures on achievement: A meta-analysis. *Psychological Bulletin, 89,* 47–62.

Jones, M. G., & Carter, G. C. (1994). Verbal and nonverbal behavior of ability-grouped dyads. *Journal of Research in Science Teaching, 31*(6), 603–620.

Kaestle, C. F., et al. (1991) *Literacy in the United States: Readers and reading since 1880.* New Haven, CN: Yale University Press.

Kozol, J. (1991). *Savage inequalities.* New York: Crown.

Lloyd, J. W., Crowley, E. P., Kohler, F., & Strain, P. (1988). Redefining the applied research agenda: Cooperative learning, prereferral, teacher consultation, and peer mediated interventions. *Journal of Learning Disabilities, 21,* 43–52.

National Commission on Excellence in Education. (1983). *A nation at risk: The imperative for educational reform.* Washington, DC: U.S. Government Printing Office.

Putnam, J. W., Spiegel, A., Bruininks, R. E. (1995). Future directions in the education of students with disabilities: A Delphi investigation. *Exceptional Children, 61*(6), 553–557.

Sautter, R. C. (1995). Standing up to violence. *Phi Delta Kappan, 95*(5), 1–12.

Sharan, S. (1990). Cooperative learning and helping behavior in the multi-ethnic classroom. In H. Foot, M. Morgan, & R. Shute (Eds.), *Children helping children* (pp. 151–176). London: Wiley.

Sharan, Y., & Sharan, S. (1992). *Expanding cooperative learning through group investigation.* New York: Teachers College Press.

Slavin, R. E. (1990). *Cooperative learning: Theory, research and practice.* Englewood Cliffs, NJ: Prentice Hall.

Slavin, R. E. (1991a). Are cooperative learning and untracking harmful to the gifted? Response to Allan. *Educational Leadership, 48*(6), 68–71.

Slavin, R. E. (1991b). Synthesis of research on cooperative learning. *Educational Leadership, 48*(5), 71–82.

Slavin, R. E. (1995). *Cooperative learning: Theory, research and practice.* (2nd ed.). Boston, MA: Allyn and Bacon.

Sleeter, C. E., & Grant, C. A. (1993). *Making choices for multicultural education.* (2nd ed.). Englewood Cliffs, NJ: Merrill/Prentice Hall.

Stevens, R., & Slavin, R. E. (1991). When cooperative learning improves the achievement of students with mild disabilities: A response to Tateyama-Sniezek. *Exceptional Children, 57,* 276–280.

Stout, J. A. (1993). *The use of cooperative learning with gifted students: A qualitative study.* Lawton, OK: Lawton Public Schools.

Strom, R. D. (1983). Expectations for educating the gifted and talented. *Educational Forum, 47,* 279–303.

Tateyama-Sniezek, K. M. (1990). Cooperative learning: Does it improve the academic achievement of students with handicaps? *Exceptional Children, 56,* 426–437.

Torrey, R. D. (1956). Citizenship education for the gifted adolescent. *Progressive Education, 33,* 78–84.

U.S. Department of Education. (1994). Sixteenth annual report to Congress on the implementation of the Individuals with Disabilities Education Act. Washington, DC: Office of Special Programs.

Whittington, D. (1992, Winter). What have our 17-year-olds known in the past? *American Educational Research Journal,* pp. 776–778.

SECTION 2

FACILITATING
COOPERATIVE LEARNING

CHAPTER 3   Planning and Conducting Cooperative Activities

CHAPTER 4   Cooperative Classroom Management

CHAPTER 3

PLANNING AND CONDUCTING COOPERATIVE ACTIVITIES

◆

This chapter is designed to help you do the following:

- ◆ Consider the practical steps involved in planning a cooperative activity.
- ◆ Identify seven ways to promote positive interdependence among group members.
- ◆ Develop students' cooperative skills through a five-step process.
- ◆ Develop cooperative learning lesson plans.

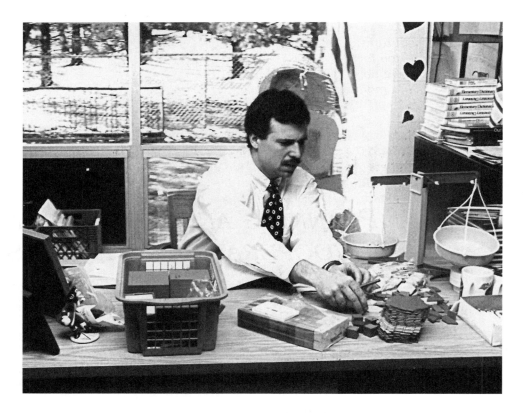

A Cooperative Solution

Substitute teaching can be extremely challenging when the substitute is unfamiliar with the students in the class, the teacher's instructional style, the curriculum, or the classroom management system. This was the situation for David Wright when he assumed responsibility for a sixth-grade class at Eaglewood Middle School. It was a beautiful spring afternoon and the teacher had planned a lesson on percentages. All David had to do was run a laser disc program for the students to view on a TV monitor in the front of the classroom.

"Easy enough," he thought, as he relaxed into what he thought would be an effortless math period.

But as he scanned the room while the program ran, David realized that about 10 students were looking at the television screen and, of these students, only six were following the instructions. He noticed several students passing notes, and two others were starting an argument. So much for active learning and time-on-task! The lesson was clearly degenerating into a social event.

David walked to the front of the room and turned off the TV. He asked the students why they weren't participating or following instructions. The students were quick to respond. Among the litany of complaints and protests were, "I don't get it!" "They go too fast for me." "It's boring." It was evident that something had to be done to capture the interest of the class—so David thought for a moment.

Then he shared a brief story on parts of a whole: "I once had a friend named Frank whose mother asked him if he wanted his pizza cut up into sixths or eighths. Frank answered, 'Just cut it in sixths, I'm not very hungry tonight.' " The students in the class were smiling and attentive now.

"Please form pairs with someone sitting in a different row who was born in the same season of the year as you," David said. Students pushed their desks together to work in twos.

"I will ask you a question about the percentages of a dollar. I want the members of each pair to discuss the question, writing notes or calculations on a scrap piece of paper if you like, and arrive at an answer you both agree with. Write your answer on a piece of paper and initial it if you agree."

David happened to have a pocket full of change from the car wash, so he told the students that the first pair to arrive at a correct answer would receive the amount of change equivalent to the answer. Others who obtained the correct answer later would receive half that amount. He wondered if he was allowed to give money to students, but he knew it wouldn't amount to much. There was no question that now he had the full attention of everyone in the class.

"First question: What's 30 percent of a dollar?" As he proceeded, the questions became more difficult. "What's 80 percent of $1.75?" He required the students to explain how they arrived at their answer: "How did you get $1.40?"

The transformation in student behavior was dramatic. As David looked around the room, he saw students on task, with their heads close together, discussing the problems, writing their answers, raising their hands when they thought they had the correct answer. The 50-minute period flew by. As the students left school that afternoon, David overheard one of the most difficult students telling his classmate, "I learned more math in one day than we usually learn in a week. He's a great teacher!"

Later that evening, David reflected on the students' responses. He discussed the day with his wife, describing the students' inattention and seeming lack of interest in learning about percentages. He recounted the near chaos that erupted in the class and his spontaneous solution. David mused, "What the students didn't realize is that I didn't really teach them—they taught themselves. I just organized an opportunity for them to work together and boosted their motivation a bit."

STRUCTURING COOPERATIVE GROUPS

The initial step in planning an educational activity is to determine *what* the students should gain from the experience. Once the desired learning result is identified, it is translated into an instructional objective, and a method is devised for helping students achieve the objective. Much of the creativity involved in teaching occurs at this early phase of the planning process—the *how* phase—when the instructional method is selected. Although desired learning results and curriculum are often predetermined for classroom teachers through district-mandated curricular sequences, textbooks, or attainment standards, usually some latitude exists in determining the best method for helping students achieve a particular objective. Prepackaged lessons may work beautifully sometimes, but when they fail to achieve the desired goal, teachers are compelled to set aside the textbooks and curriculum guides and use their own skill and creativity in planning a lesson.

A crucial point in the planning process occurs after the instructional objective has been established—Johnson, Johnson and Holubec (1993) refer to this point as "the moment." It is the point when teachers decide how to organize an activity to best facilitate accomplishing the instructional objective. Students may be asked to either work on their own, engage in competition, or work cooperatively. For example, if the learning objective is for students to acquire keyboarding skills, they will likely work individually with computers; if students are involved in a math competition with teams from other schools using the Internet, they will work competitively; if they are involved in a unit to solve problems with recycling at school, they will work in cooperative groups.

When cooperative learning is selected as the preferred method for achieving an instructional objective, the teacher faces a number of lesson-planning decisions. The first section of this chapter discusses the major considerations involved in planning cooperative activities. Next, suggestions are made for incorporating the following three critical components into your cooperative lessons: positive interdependence, individual accountability, and cooperative skill instruction. Finally, a cooperative lesson plan format is presented in the final section and examples of lesson plans from various curricular areas and grade levels are given. But before we delve into the material on planning considerations, let me caution you about the dangers of using a merely technical or "cookbook" approach to delivering instruction. *Facilitating learning through cooperation involves more than following a set of procedures. Good teaching is an art that blends skill and technique with creativity and inventiveness.*

This chapter introduces the key ingredients of the cooperative lesson-planning process. However, simply combining the ingredients according to a particular recipe will not assure successful outcomes. Cooperative learning entails complex interrelationships and interactions among group members, and a multitude of factors may affect the cooperative group process. Just as variations in altitude, kneading method, type of flour, oven temperature, or type of pan affect the baking of bread, there are aspects of the cooperative learning "mix" often not mentioned in simple recipes that will influence the group process and success. Sometimes it takes years of planning and implementing cooperative learning activities before teachers feel confident that they can appropriately apply the many facets of this important technique.

Mastering cooperative learning methodology begins with knowledge of the key ingredients, and progresses to understanding, application, analysis, synthesis, and evaluation. Cooperative group instruction can be a real adventure in teaching—the more you understand it, the less you think you know, and the more you will want to know.

PLANNING AND SETTING UP COOPERATIVE GROUPS

Determining the Instructional Objective

The first question to ask yourself when planning a cooperative activity is, "What is the learning result I am trying to achieve?" The learning result, or **instructional objective,** clarifies what students are to gain from the activity. The purpose of the lesson may be to introduce new information, or impart a new skill, or provide practice for skills that have been previously introduced. Cooperative activities may assist learning at various levels, such as during the initial acquisition of the information or skill, while building fluency of performance, while maintaining the information or skill over time, or when generalizing information to other situations.

It is important to select an instructional objective that is referenced to the appropriate cognitive level for the students and the goal of the lesson. Bloom's taxonomy (Bloom, 1956) includes the following cognitive levels: knowledge, comprehension, analysis, application, synthesis, and evaluation. Cooperatively practicing spelling words, naming the planets, or memorizing the times tables are knowledge-level activities, whereas deliberating about the ethics of assisted suicide or comparing the advantages of various national health plans are evaluative-level activities.

An instructional objective may be either academically or socially oriented, or it may incorporate both dimensions. One of the benefits of cooperative learning is that it lends itself to academic and social skill acquisition simultaneously. For example, students can work cooperatively on an academic objective, such as discriminating between monocot and dicot flowering plants while practicing the social communication skill of listening and paraphrasing others' ideas.

Criteria for Success.   In the process of determining the instructional objective, the teacher should think about ways the student will demonstrate acquisition. To be successful, each student should exhibit specific, predetermined behaviors or accomplishments. Students must be clear about what they plan to accomplish, and for some students it helps to state the objective and criteria for success both orally and in written form, using the chalkboard or overhead projector. The criterion for success in the monocot and dicot lesson, for example, is accurately sorting six plants into their respective categories and naming them.

Forming the Groups

Assigning Students to Groups.   Because group dynamics and student interactions are affected by the composition of the students in each group, teachers need to be thoughtful about how they compose the groups. In most situations, cooperative learning groups should be mixed, or **heterogeneous,** with respect to the ability levels, gender, ethnicity, cultural background, and socioeconomic background of the students. Minority students or students with disabilities generally should not be placed in groups with only students who possess similar characteristics. A number of methods exist for assigning students to groups, including teacher assignment, random assignment, and student self-selection.

1. *Teacher assignment.* When the teacher is familiar with the students in the class, they can be assigned systematically according to academic ability and social skill levels. The teacher should be methodical in making the best assignments by matching students of different ability levels, or students whose interpersonal abilities and styles will complement one another. A student with strong cooperative and social skills would make a good match for a student who is lacking such skills. Students with significant academic problems should be matched with students who have academic strengths. Care must be taken not to assign more than one low achiever, socially unskilled, or behaviorally challenged student to a cooperative group.

2. *Random assignment.* This approach places students into groups without a particular preplanned scheme in mind. Numerous methods exist for randomly assigning students to groups, and students seem to enjoy the more novel approaches. For example, the teacher can ask students to count off according to the number of groups that are desired. If you have 21 students in your class and you desire groups of three, have the students count off by seven. The "ones" will form a group of three, the "twos" will form a group, and so on. Learning to count off in a foreign language, such as Spanish, Japanese, or Russian, can be fun and instructive for students, especially if one of their classmates can teach them to count in his or her native language.

Another method of random assignment is to have students draw group numbers out of a hat or box. I have observed a teacher who cuts photographs into four puzzle pieces, places them in a box, and lets the students pick a piece from the box. Then, students match their pieces with other student's pieces to form a picture and their group at the same time. Another method of assignment is to form groups according to individual characteristics of the students. For example, a four-seasons group can be formed with four people, each of whom was born during a different season of the year. Or students can be randomly assigned to groups according to some attribute related to the lesson, such as a class of 32 counting off by the names of the planets to form groups of four for a lesson on the solar system.

While random assignment typically results in heterogeneous (mixed ability) groups, there is some danger that the assignment will, by chance, result in homogeneous combinations, or otherwise undesirable, combinations of students. A high school English teacher I know formed writing groups of four by random assignment, and it just so happened that several of the groups were composed of one gender, and even more troubling was the fact that the four low achievers all ended up in the same group! Although rarely the case, there are occasions when particular students should not work together because they have a "history" that prevents them from getting along that groupwork alone will not solve. Random assignment will not prevent these unfortunate pairings from occurring, although teacher assignment will. Most students can learn to get along with one another in a group. After one student learned who her group members were to be, she pleaded with the teacher, saying, "Please don't make me work with *him!*" Her teacher aptly responded, "You don't have to marry him and you don't have to bury him. Now, go back and work in your group."

3. *Student self-selection.* Some occasions lend themselves to having students form their own groups. For example, when the teacher assigns a particular activity or topic to each group, it may make sense to allow students to choose the activity or topic they would most like to pursue. The disadvantages of self-selection are evident. Among them are the potential that (1) the high achievers or the low achievers will end up in the same groups; (2) some students will not be chosen by any classmates to be in their group, (3) best friends will gravitate to the same group and socialize or exclude others during the activity. One of the goals of cooperative learning is to encourage students get to know individuals who are unlike themselves. Ideally, students themselves would recognize the importance of working in mixed groups and would make an effort to work with a variety of students in group situations. In practice, however, this tends not to occur without adult intervention.

A teacher from Montana recounted an experience in which a student was paired with a male student she claimed to despise. She protested vehemently to the teacher that the assignment was "not fair!" At the close of the four-week science unit, much to the teacher's surprise, the pair scored 100 percent on the unit test. The next week, the teacher was reassigning students to new groups for the next science unit. The same student came to the teacher's desk to request that her pair be kept intact. When the teacher said no, the student claimed "not fair!"

Group Size.   The size of a cooperative group varies according to a number of factors. For a productive group, the recommended size ranges from two to five students. Groups of six can be unwieldy and, in my experience, tend to naturally split up into two groups of three, or three groups of two.

> Two interactions have to be managed within a pair. Six interactions have to be managed within a group of three. Twelve interactions have to be managed within a group of four. (Johnson, Johnson, & Holubec, 1993)

There are ways to organize the work of larger groups to capitalize on the advantages of pair learning. As Kohn (1987) noted, "It's hard to get left out of a pair." Groups of four lend themselves nicely to initial "pair work" and the subsequent sharing among the two pairs. For example, a pair of students may discuss a response to a teacher's question. Then one member of the pair can paraphrase the ideas of his or her partner and present them to another pair, as they form a group of four. Partners within the pair can be changed during the group activity, enriching and extending the discussions.

The following considerations can help teachers determine appropriate group size:

1. *Task requirements.* Group size can be determined according to the demands of the task. For example, if a research task can be divided into three pieces, assign one to each student in the group, forming groups of three.

2. *Time available.* Larger groups take more time to accomplish a task because they require more interaction and coordination among members than a smaller group. Discussing a poem, for example, will take more time for five students than for three provided that group members actively participate in the discussion.

3. *Complexity of task.* Complex activities requiring more and varied resources lend themselves to larger groups with a more diverse range of student strengths and abilities. An interdisciplinary thematic unit involving writing, reading, drama, and art lends itself more to a larger group. The likelihood of each group possessing someone who is talented in drama or art is greater when more students are involved.

4. *Cooperative skills.* Smaller groups work better with students who lack social or collaborative skills. If students have never engaged in cooperative groupwork, they are likely to perform better with fewer group members as they learn the necessary skills. For example, taking turns talking, critically examining a group member's ideas, or simply sharing materials is easier when there are only a few students, but these skills become more complex and difficult to exercise when groups are composed of four or five students.

Duration of Groups.   Teachers often ask about how long the groups should stay together. There is no magic answer to this question, because the life of a group depends on the nature of the task and on whether the activity is short-term or long-term. In general, groups should stay together long enough to attain a group identity. Students need to get to know group members well enough to work productively with one another and reach the point where they perceive one another in multidimensional ways, as opposed to stereotypic ways. One method for checking whether the groups have congealed is to ask students if they know each other's names, the group name, or possibly the phone numbers of group members if they have been working outside of class or reminding one another to turn in homework. Group members need to work through interpersonal problems that arise—a process that takes time and persistence.

Environmental Considerations.   Students should be in close enough proximity to hear one another and to communicate without disturbing other groups in the class. They should face one another as they communicate. They also need to be able to see the materials, especially if they are sharing one set. In general, closeness fosters cohesiveness. Large tables tend to distance students from one another both physically and psychologically. Round tables with chairs are workable if the tables are not too big. Three student desks placed in a T-shape is an ideal setup. Sometimes students will need particular surfaces or equipment, such as a marker board

Desks Arranged for Interaction

or a computer. Sometimes the group members can sit on the carpet to do their work. The teacher should be able to walk easily among the groups, with access to all parts of the room.

Conducting the Lesson

After the decisions have been made concerning the lesson objective, group assignment and size, and environmental arrangement, the students should be assigned to their groups. When students are unfamiliar with cooperative learning or in the beginning stages of working in cooperative groups, they may need more time to form their groups. When they become more experienced with cooperative learning, they should move fairly quickly into their groups without a lot of discussion or delay.

Introduce the Lesson.   As soon as students have formed their groups, the teacher should explain the *purpose of the lesson*, provide *directions for the activity*, and explain the *criteria for success*. The instructions need to be clear and succinct. Visual instructions are a good supplement to oral instructions and are particularly helpful to students who are better visual learners than auditory learners. Using chart-paper displays or an overhead projector makes the directions visible. To check for understanding, ask one or two students in the class to paraphrase the instructions, or have students paraphrase the instructions within their groups.

Be sure you have captured the students' attention when introducing the lesson. Sometimes when groups are first assembled, students begin to socialize and may fail to attend to the teacher. If the instructions are given at this time, it is likely that students will not listen and will miss crucial information. It is also possible that the noise level will increase to the point where the entire class is out of control. To prevent inattention, the teacher should draw the students' attention to him or her. Directives such as "Everyone look at me," or "Eyes up here," are helpful. Some teachers prefer to use hand signals, such as raising one hand, to signify that students are to put down their materials, stop talking, raise their hands, and listen to the teacher. As students observe others raising their hands, they quickly raise their own hands (Figure 3.1). This visual technique is particularly helpful to students convened in groups, because a portion of the class is invariably facing away from the teacher, but can observe someone raising their hand at the back or side of the room. For fun, the first student to raise his or her hand can be awarded a simple or lighthearted reward, such as three minutes toward extra free time, with the possibility of accumulating extra free time during the quarter.

Students in newly formed groups need an opportunity to get acquainted, and they will benefit from a "warm-up" or "ice-breaker" activity that helps them get to know one another and creates a positive tone in the groups. It is unwise to neglect students' need to socialize during the school day. **Base groups**, which are maintained throughout the academic year, also provide

FIGURE 3.1
The Silence Signal

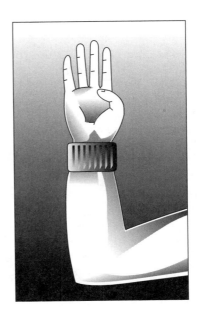

an excellent opportunity for social interaction and support. They can be formed in homerooms at the middle school or high school level, where students do not remain with the same class for the entire day. By planning opportunities for positive interaction in cooperative groups, the need to socialize is addressed and students can be more academically focused when they are working on academic activities. Time provided for building friendships and social bonds is time wisely invested—with payoffs that extend beyond the interpersonal realm and into the realms of achievement and productivity (Johnson & Johnson, 1989).

When teachers give instructions to their class, it is not unusual for one or more students to fail to pay attention or fail to understand the instructions. Rather than repeating the instructions, teachers should direct students to seek clarification from their group members. This saves the teacher and the class valuable time and encourages students to rely on one another. If no one in the group understands the directions, all students should raise their hands simultaneously. This signals the teacher that the instructions were unclear and that further explanation is warranted.

Assuring Interdependence

Strategies are needed for assuring that students work together to accomplish the instructional objective. True cooperative learning requires that students coordinate their actions and develop a "We can do it" rather than a "I can do it on my own" or "You do it" approach to completing the work. Although students may collaborate spontaneously, sometimes interdepen-

Hand Signals

dence will occur only when it is consciously built into a group activity by the teacher. When planning the lesson, the teacher should specify how positive interdependence will be achieved. Seven major categories of positive interdependence, have been identified by Johnson, Johnson, & Holubec (1993) as follows:

1.   *Group goals.* A fundamental aspect of cooperative learning is that students work to attain a shared learning goal. First, all students must achieve the mutual goal, and second, all students must feel a sense of responsibility for group members achieving the goal. For example, a goal might be to produce a replica of a foreign village (e.g., an African, Chinese, or Lapland village). Each group constructs one model village and each student is required to describe the village, presenting facts about the house construction, the foods, agriculture, transportation, etc. One product is required that will be evaluated by the teacher, classmates, and the group members themselves. All cooperative lessons should be organized around a group goal; it is the foundation of cooperative learning. The other types of positive interdependence may or may not be incorporated into a lesson, depending on the aims and requirements of the lesson. Examples of group goals are listed in Figure 3.2.

2.   *Group rewards.* Another way to shape positive interdependence is to offer an incentive for working together. If the goal is for groups to publish a newspaper, students will receive some type of reinforcement for producing a high-quality product (a certificate or a portion of the sales, for exam-

FIGURE 3.2
Examples of Group Goals

One product—writing one report or essay, constructing a miniature village or diorama, or painting a group mural.

Finding a solution to a problem—collectively solving a problem concerning global warming, addressing a problem regarding fund-raising for the class field trip.

Reaching consensus—seeking resolution to a controversy involving differing opinions among group members, such as the pros and cons of capital punishment or euthanasia.

Achieving a group grade—a criterion for success is established for students' spelling achievement, either by averaging the grades in the group, or asking that students all attain a particular score (90% correct).

ple). If students are being graded on an assignment, the teacher can establish a criterion for group success and attach a reward to attaining it. If all students achieve more than 90% on their math test, the group members can receive bonus points, stickers, or certificates. Grades may be averaged or added together and a preset criterion established for receiving a reward, such as requiring that the total score for the group of three be more than 270 points to spend an extra 15 minutes playing a game at the computer.

Sometimes cooperative activities are so motivating for students that no external, or *extrinsic*, reward is necessary to get students to work together. In my experience, an activity that naturally lends itself to positive interdependence is playing traditional music with a group of friends. Simply playing a great tune is *intrinsically* rewarding to most musicians. Have you ever participated in an activity where group members were highly motivated to work together? Unfortunately, not all learning tasks we plan for students at school are intrinsically rewarding. Sometimes an extrinsic reward is needed to encourage students to truly cooperate.

Teachers should be creative about the rewards they give to students. Giving a single group grade should not be overused as a method for achieving positive interdependence. And, in my opinion, lowering an individual's grade on the basis of poor group performance should rarely, if ever, occur. Participating in cooperative learning should not punish students because they happen to be in a group in which one or two students are poorly motivated or difficult to get along with. On the other hand, realizing that the performance of your peers will determine your own success or failure can inspire students to help and encourage one another and to find innovative ways to successfully work together.

I have known teachers who use lighthearted rewards for their students. For example, one high school teacher told me that groups received Tootsie Roll Pops upon the completion of their project. The reward was given for fun and the students really enjoyed it. Another teacher promised her algebra class groups a dollar per member at the end of a three-week unit if they solved a highly complex problem.

3. *Group roles.* When given assigned roles, students in a group assume responsibility for a specific function they must carry out during the cooperative activity. Teachers or students designate in advance which roles are appropriate for the cooperative activity. The responsibilities of the role are explained to the students verbally and sometimes through the use of role cards that describe a specific role for each group member. Roles, which can be task related (reader) or group-process related (encourager), may be assigned randomly to the group members, selected by the students themselves, or assigned by the teacher. Teacher assignment enables the teacher to place particular students in roles that they would especially benefit from. For example, a passive student might be given a role that requires active responding, such as paraphrasing or summarizing the opinions of others in discussions, while an overly talkative student can be given a role requiring more silence, such as being the recorder for the group. Examples of cooperative learning roles and their associated tasks are listed in Figure 3.3.

Sometimes teachers make the mistake of assigning complicated roles before the students have mastered the more basic functions of a cooperative

FIGURE 3.3
Cooperative Group Roles

Recorder   Documents the work of the group, takes notes, writes answers.

Reader   Reads the written material, reads the answer for the group.

Summarizer   Recapitulates what has been decided in the group, summarizes the ideas shared.

Encourager   Reinforces group members for performing well or staying on task, instills a strength of purpose, invites members to participate.

Courier   Brings materials to the group, carries messages or assignments to their destinations, performs errands.

Checker   Makes certain that everyone is on task, agrees with the answer, understands the assignment, discussion, or answer.

Interrogator   Challenges group members to defend their answers and to avoid superficial responses or to explore a matter more deeply.

Manager   Assures that directions are followed, organizes the group process, makes sure the group is ready to report its answer or turn in the work.

Time keeper   Watches the time and keeps the group on task and moving forward.

Voice control technician   Monitors the noise level in the group and indicates when the students need to quiet down.

Equalizer   Makes sure that all group members are treated fairly and courteously, that they have opportunities to participate and derive benefit from the groupwork.

---

group. Only very simple roles are assigned to young children, such as "praiser," "recorder," or "reader." Students unfamiliar with a role may need to practice it before they can enact it in a group setting. Role cards with brief explanations of the responsibilities can help students carry out their particular role.

Not all cooperative activities require assigned roles. Students who are skilled in cooperative learning sometimes spontaneously generate their own roles within the group to accomplish a task, and they can be quite creative in their role designations: "the equalizer," "the vitalizer," "the courier," and "the foreman" are some examples of spontaneous roles created in high schools.

4.   *Sharing materials and resources.* If students are required to share a single set of materials, such as equipment for a science experiment, or one copy of a word problem to be solved, they will need to coordinate their actions and discussion. Several students can share a computer terminal for a cooperative writing or math activity.

The social skill of taking turns is vital for persons of all ages, and can be practiced when only one set or a limited quantity of materials is provided. Most of us have experienced the frustration of gaining access to a library book, computer terminal, or telephone when there are more users than books or equipment. A lack of sensitivity on the part of one person can be irritating to others who need the item. Students learn the conventions of sharing as they work cooperatively with scarce resources. Limiting resources should be done purposefully, because occasions exist when sharing materials detracts from learning and accomplishing the group goal. For example, visual learners may benefit from having their own copy of a poem or essay to follow along with the reader for the group, rather than having to rely solely on the auditory receptive mode.

5.   *Identity interdependence.* Group cohesiveness can be reinforced when students select an identity through a group name, symbol, or motto. We are all familiar with the names of sports teams, such as the Denver Broncos or the Seattle Seahawks, as well as the names students can give their own groups or teams, such as The Eagles, The Mighty Ducks, The Fantastic Four, or The Poison Dart Frogs. Group names may be selected to relate to the academic material, such as cocoon, larva, pupa, or butterfly for a unit on the stages of butterfly development (see the lesson plan on stages of butterfly development in this chapter). Students can produce a banner or flag for their group (Figure 3.4) as well as a group slogan, such as "flying higher" for the Eagles group, or "hopping to success" for the Poison Dart Frogs.

6.   *Task interdependence.* Some tasks lend themselves to a division of labor within the group. For example, to produce a class newspaper, one student will collect articles from classmates, another student may serve as editor and chief of layout, while another student types articles into the computer. Task interdependence requires that each member performs his or her duty, or the task will not get done.

FIGURE 3.4
Sample Group Logo

Poison Dart Frogs

7.   *Interdependence through competition.* A strong degree of interdependence can be achieved when students work together to outperform other groups, or in response to an outside threat. Sports and academic teams, such as basketball, math, or Odyssey of the Mind teams exemplify how group cohesiveness can be built through team competition. Assuring interdependence through such means should be done carefully to avoid a win/lose situation. To depersonalize group competition, the teacher can ask the students to achieve more (e.g., obtain higher scores, read more books, or run faster) than the students from last year's class or a mythical class. When group members perceive that a threat to their performance or functioning exists, they will adhere more closely to one another to thwart that threat. "Outside enemy interdependence" (Johnson, Johnson, & Holubec, 1993) can be observed in international politics, and in nearly all sectors of society—including our schools.

Assuring Individual Accountability

Perhaps one of the most frustrating aspects of working in groups is the group member who does not carry his or her weight in completing the necessary tasks. Often the most responsible member or members of the group will compensate for the weak link in the chain in an effort to accomplish the group goal. However, enabling group members by doing their job does not contribute to the success of a cooperative group in the long run. As was pointed out in Chapter 2, the high achievement and positive social-psychological outcomes associated with cooperative learning require both individual accountability and positive interdependence.

What can be done to avoid the "coasting" or "hitchhiking" of a group member? First, both students and teacher should try to understand *why* a student is not contributing to the group. Is it a lack of skill or a lack of will?

That is, does the student have the ability to accomplish the task? Does the student understand what needs to be done and possess the tools to do it? Or does the student have a lackadaisical attitude or oppositional behavior?

Remedy for a Lack of Skill: Provide Task Assistance.   If a student has a lack of skill, help should be provided through additional explanation and instruction, or through modification of the task to suit the student's abilities. Sometimes additional support outside of class, such as tutoring or preteaching from a peer or teacher, may be helpful. Modifying the task requirements through decreasing the workload, reducing the complexity of the task, or altering the response requirements (such as accepting a verbal response rather than an essay) are common adaptations that will be discussed more fully in Chapter 5.

Remedy for a Lack of Will: Increase Accountability Through Motivational Strategies.   If lack of will appears to be causing the irresponsible behavior, strategies for increasing motivation may help. Hunter (1982) identifies five techniques for increasing motivation, which are highly compatible with cooperative learning:

1.   The first strategy is to influence the students' **level of concern** regarding the importance of completing the work. When introducing the lesson or unit, let students know that an individual test will be given. Tell students you will randomly pick one student in the group to explain their group's answer or findings to the large group.

Engaging students in peer teaching or peer editing activities also may increase level of concern. However, be assured that peer tutors have learned the material themselves before they try to help others. Take care to adjust your demands to the characteristics of individual students, as two students could respond to the same demand with different levels of concern. If the concern level is too high, anxiety is increased; sometimes resulting in dysfunctional responses. If the concern level is too low, the student perceives little reason to produce.

2.   Motivation also increases with a positive **feeling tone** in the classroom atmosphere. Feeling tone refers to the emotional climate in the classroom. Conduct warm-up or social icebreakers to provide students with an opportunity to get to know and appreciate one another at the beginning of the year or when you initiate cooperative learning activities. Find opportunities to praise the class and individuals for their accomplishments and unique abilities. Use a warm voice tone and positive body language. As my youngest son proclaimed before the beginning of school, "I hope I get a teacher who smiles and doesn't like to yell!" Fortunately, he has always had teachers who are calm, collected, and warm. Students in any school can tell you exactly who the "screamers" and the "mean" teachers are. In addition to creating a positive and professional climate, teachers can employ coopera-

tive learning strategies. If the lessons are well organized and conducted appropriately, the feeling tone will likely increase motivation.

3. Increasing the **interest level** through novelty and vividness of the task also enhances motivation. A cooperative task can either be routine and boring or imaginative and engaging. Tasks that are relevant to students' lives and interests are more likely to gain their attention and assure their participation. Activities don't have to rival a trip to Disney World; however, they should be an improvement on the "open your book and answer the 25 questions on page 346." Rote use of cooperative learning strategies for tedious and irrelevant lessons will assure their failure.

4. Provide students with **opportunities for success.** Based on an understanding of the nature of the task and a student's abilities, teachers can determine which tasks and behaviors the student can accomplish. Then, a teacher can build on these accomplishments to introduce more difficult tasks. When possible, assign to an unsure student a role or aspect of the task that he or she will be likely to succeed at in their cooperative groups. Once success has been experienced, the student is more apt to take on the challenge and risk of a more difficult task.

5. Provide students with **feedback on performance.** The feedback should be immediate and descriptive. Teachers who have good rapport with their students are more likely to know when and in what measure a student can handle corrective feedback. For example, a champion soccer player is able to cope with a severe reprimand from a team member or coach and it may inspire him to strive for greater perfection. On the other hand, a beginning player may need a lot of assurance and would not withstand even the most mild criticism. Students themselves can learn the social skill of providing constructive feedback to members in their cooperative groups. Opportunities for self-evaluation should also be incorporated into cooperative activities.

DEVELOPING STUDENTS' COOPERATIVE SKILLS

Working and learning with others involves a complex array of interpersonal and small-group skills. Although some individuals seem to be blessed with what Gardner (1983), in his theory of multiple intelligences, referred to as *interpersonal intelligence*, many others are not. Fortunately, these interpersonal skills can be learned and practiced in the context of cooperative learning activities. Research shows that even with no social skill instruction at all, students working in cooperative learning groups become more caring, helpful, and understanding of one another (Kagan & Kagan, 1994). However, for cooperative group learning to run as smoothly and efficiently as possible, and for students to sharpen their interpersonal skills, it is best if social skills are "taught just as purposefully and precisely as academic skills" (Johnson & Johnson, 1994, p. 59).

Kagan (1991) pointed out that particularly in classrooms for young children, social skills *are* the curriculum. "If in the youngest grades, students learn to support and encourage each other, listen carefully to the ideas of others, and work quietly and efficiently in groups, then they have received instruction in the areas most predictive of future academic and life success" (p. 5). Social skills that are introduced and reinforced throughout the school years provide students with the tools to interact successfully in future work, community, and academic environments.

The subset of social skills that most concern teachers implementing cooperative learning are labeled *cooperative skills*—those skills required for functioning well in small-group activities. Educators determine—with input from students, parents, and others—the specific cooperative skills students need. Although a class as a whole may be working on a sequence of cooperative skills over a period of time (perhaps 3 or 4 skills each quarter), an individual student may also be working on individual cooperative skill objectives. The particular skills to be taught will vary according to the age level of the students and the perceived need for specific social/cooperative skills. Cooperative skills include interpersonal communication, group management, conflict resolution, and leadership skills.

The types of cooperative skills to be directly taught vary according to the developmental level and experience of the students. For example, early elementary level students may need to learn and practice skills such as taking turns, contributing ideas, sharing materials, maintaining an appropriate noise level, and staying with the group. Secondary students might work on active listening, providing constructive criticism, providing social support to group members, working efficiently within tight time lines, and synthesizing diverse perspectives. Figure 3.5 provides a few examples of cooperative skills that can be taught in the context of cooperative groups. The possibilities are numerous, so it is ultimately up to the teacher and students to identify skills that are needed.

A Six-Step Process for Teaching Cooperative Skills

Teachers can support students in gaining cooperative skills through a six-step process (Johnson, Johnson, & Holubec, 1993). These steps are described here and also illustrated in the following vignette, using the example of "encouraging others to participate."

1. *Identify the skill by naming and defining it.* Once the skill to be learned by students is selected, identify and briefly describe the skill. The name of the skill should be easy to remember and appropriate to students' developmental level. A T-chart constructed by the teacher with class participation can be helpful in describing the skill. Place the name of a cooperative skill above two columns, titled "Sounds Like" and "Looks Like." Ask stu-

FIGURE 3.5
Examples of Cooperative Skills

Younger students	Older students
Interpersonal communication skills	
complementing others encouraging others contributing ideas praising others	active listening providing descriptive feedback encouraging others to contribute their ideas criticizing constructively paraphrasing and summarizing
Group management skills	
staying with the group taking turns sharing materials maintaining an appropriate noise level	encouraging equal participation time management skills group observation and feedback skills staying on topic
Conflict resolution skills	
stating a position paraphrasing another's position offering possible solutions	active listening synthesizing diverse perspectives confirming others' personal competence
Leadership skills	
explaining what needs to be done keeping group members on task making sure the materials are available being a liaison with other groups or the teacher	providing direction to the group keeping group members on task acquiring needed resources for the group agenda/workplan management

dents to give examples of what the cooperative skill sounds like, that is, what words and phrases are associated with the cooperative behavior. Then, to complete the "Looks Like" column, ask students to provide examples of what nonverbal behaviors they believe accompany the skill. If there is a strong feeling dimension to demonstrating the skill or being the recipient of such behavior, another column titled "Feels like" can be constructed with input from students.

2. *Explain why the skill is needed.* Students are more likely to learn a skill or behavior if they know why it will benefit them. The skill to be taught should have relevance to the students' lives in and out of school, and it is up to the teacher to help students make the connections between the need for the skill in and beyond the classroom. A specific explanation is better than a general one. Don't tell students they'll be more cooperative or get along better if they possess the skill, tell them specifically why the skill makes a difference.

3. *Demonstrate the skill.* In the first two steps of cooperative skill instruction, the skill is identified and briefly described, and a rationale is provided for possessing the skill. But the most potent aspect of cooperative skill instruction is providing a demonstration of the skill. Demonstrations can assume a variety of forms: (1) the teacher can model the skill, (2) students can engage in a role play to demonstrate the skill, (3) a videotape can be shown depicting the skill in action, (4) puppets can be used to illustrate the skill, and (5) students can watch others using the skill. Observational learning of social skills can be a powerful tool to promote understanding.

Another technique for sensitizing students to the need for a cooperative skill is to set up a lighthearted simulation or role play in which a cooperative skill is lacking or is misused. Students can observe and then reflect on the ramifications of the social skill deficits in the given situation. Such **negative exemplars,** when carefully planned, can be thought provoking and highly instructive.

4. *Provide opportunities to use and practice the cooperative skill.* Group learning provides excellent opportunities for students to practice their cooperative skills. A cooperative lesson can be designed specifically to focus on a cooperative skill, or a cooperative skill can be practiced in the context of an academically oriented lesson. Instruct students to practice the cooperative skill at every opportunity, even if the exercise seems to be artificial or unspontaneous. Ask students to practice the skill outside of school when suitable occasions arise. Not only do students benefit from learning social skills, but others in the family or the neighborhood can be the beneficiaries of more "cooperative" behavior. It is gratifying to receive feedback from parents who attribute positive behavioral changes in their child and sometimes the entire family to the exposure to cooperative learning and cooperative skill instruction.

5. *Observation and feedback concerning cooperative skills.* An important aspect of learning and motivation is knowing how well you are doing. Teachers can observe cooperative groups or individual students either formally or informally. Formal observations can be made using a checklist or by taking notes. An example of a checklist is shown in Figure 3.6. Teachers can also circulate among the groups for informal observations. Feedback from the teacher about the performance of designated cooperative skills can be given at the cooperative group level or at the class level.

Students need to be reassured that cooperative and social skills are not learned overnight, but during a lifetime. It takes practice, patience, and persistence to develop good cooperative skills. Social situations are diverse, and the same cooperative skill may have differing effects depending on the group membership and the situation. Practicing the skill of active listening with a succinct communicator is a different experience from actively listening to an incessant talker.

Constructively criticizing others' ideas may be effortless when the issue being discussed is of little importance to the group members. However, as

FIGURE 3.6
Sample Observation Form

Skill: Encouraging Others to Participate					
Observer _____					
Names	**Dates**				**Student Totals**
	9/16	9/17	9/18	9/19	
Rhonda	✓✓✓	✓✓✓✓	✓✓	✓	10
Brian	✓	✓	✓✓✓	✓✓	7
Arlita	✓✓		✓✓✓✓	✓✓	8
Group totals	6	5	9	5	25

the content of a discussion takes on greater personal significance, it may become heated and emotional, in which case it may be difficult to refrain from destructive criticism in the form of personal attacks or slights. Have you ever engaged in a discussion concerning politics, religion, or lifestyle that degenerated into a mudslinging battle? Recently I witnessed a group of middle school students who began insulting each other's families in an irrational discussion of which computer was the best—a Macintosh or an IBM!

Students can also observe cooperative skills in their group and provide feedback to group members. Observations can be set up formally with a checklist or an observation form for recording behaviors. In some cases it can be instructive for a group member to be a nonparticipant in the activity while conducting observations. Then, at the end of the activity, the student can report to the group what he or she saw and heard. Outside observers are free from the demands and distractions of groupwork requirements and often obtain a more unbiased and objective view of group behaviors.

6. *Reflection and future goal setting.* At the end of an activity or at an appropriate stopping point, it is important for group members to consider their cooperative behavior and interactions. If a specific skill has been targeted for the week, such as encouraging others' participation, at the end of the week a brief discussion can be scheduled for students to evaluate how well they performed, both individually and collectively. Observation data can be used to guide the discussion, or students can discuss their perceptions of their own performances. It is essential that students reflect on their behaviors and how their actions affect others and the group process, and to consider what they should practice or improve on in the future.

It is sometimes surprising to find out how highly aware students are of their own strengths and weaknesses in interpersonal or cooperative skill areas. It is equally gratifying when students are able to target these areas for future improvement. For a teacher to point out a social or cooperative skill deficit can be difficult and discouraging to the student, whereas recognizing one's own skill needs is not nearly as threatening. Can you identify any cooperative skills that you could work on? It is probably safe to say that we all have cooperative skills that can be improved.

Encouraging Others To Participate

Introduce the Skill

In Roy Gordon's algebra class, the cooperative skill of the week is "encouraging others to participate."

Explain Its Importance

On the walls of his classroom, he displays a poster that defines the skill and provides a brief rationale for using the skill. It is November now, and students are familiar with the six-step process for learning cooperative skills.

Demonstrate the Skill

During the previous week, Roy arranged for four students to plan a role play highlighting the need to encourage others to participate in cooperative group activities. Using a bit of humor and some overdramatization, the group illustrates the skill by showing how a shy student is ignored in a group. Between classes, the shy student, Mario, meets a good friend and shares his frustrations about being left out of the groupwork and the domineering behavior of one of the group members. Eventually, another student discovers how to draw out Mario's ideas and involvement in the groupwork. Ultimately, it is Mario who finds the key to solving the math problem.

Explain the Need

After the role play, Roy leads a class discussion about encouraging others to participate. The students themselves explain the need for the skill by reacting to the role play. How did Mario feel when he was left out of the group? Why was it beneficial for the group to include Mario?

Next, Roy asks the students to help him construct a T-chart, which is displayed on the overhead projector. Students volunteer phrases and words that are used when encouraging others to participate for the "Sounds Like" column of the chart. Then, they describe the nonverbal behaviors that accompany the skill for the "Looks Like" column (see Figure 3.7). The T-chart is particularly rel-

FIGURE 3.7
Sample T-Chart

Encouraging Others to Participate	
Words and phrases	**Looks like**
What do you think?	eye contact
What's your idea?	leaning forward
Maybe John knows what to do.	hand wave toward body
Would you like to try?	smile at person
Here, you take a look.	turn head toward person
We haven't heard from you yet.	extend hands or materials

evant to students because they generate the examples themselves, in their own vernacular and body language. It is unlikely that students would pay as much attention to a teacher-developed chart.

Practice the Skill

Roy asks the students to focus on encouraging others to participate while they work cooperatively throughout the week. The algebra lessons planned for the week provide many opportunities. For example, on Monday they will construct visual models to illustrate equations. Before constructing the model, the group must solve a difficult equation that will require everyone's input.

Feedback and Reflection

Roy has developed a group form for students to rate their own progress toward attaining the cooperative skill. During the last five minutes of the class period each day, students reflect as a group on how well they have been encouraging others to participate. On Friday, one of the group members will be an observer for the group to count instances of the behavior. The student observers report back to the large group with frequencies of the behavior as well as examples of encouraging participation in the groups (see Figure 3.8). The group reflection on Friday takes about 15 minutes, but Roy believes it is time wisely invested in facilitating the process of active group learning in the classroom as well as enhancing social skills that students will use all their lives.

The "Natural" Approach to Teaching Cooperative Skills

Whereas Johnson and Johnson have developed a specific procedure for directly teaching cooperative skills, Kagan (1987) recommends a more "natural approach." Some cooperative structures, especially those that are

FIGURE 3.8
Sample Group Form

Cooperative Skill Reflection Form

Skill name: Encouraging others to participate

Group name: Cyber whiz kidz

Date: February 12, 1997

Specific examples:

Tara asked Carlos if he would like to play Mario's role.

Jerry said to Joan "I know you can do this, I've seen you before."

Frank suggests that everyone in the group try to play at least one role.

How the skill improved the work of the group:

Everyone participated

No one was ignored

Joan felt encouraged

No one felt rejected

What could be done better or differently in the future:

Tara shouldn't always be the director; she needs to involve others

We need to watch the clock more carefully because we ran out of time.

---

highly prescribed such as Numbered Heads Together, do not require sophisticated social skills. However, less structured activities, such as a long-term group project requiring complex concept development, demand greater cooperative skills. Here are some of the approaches Kagan (1987) recommends for facilitating cooperative skill development:

1.   *Task restructuring.* The task is reorganized so that the acquisition of social skills becomes an integral, or necessary, aspect of completing the task. Example: Students writing a team essay on family holiday traditions are asked to write about the traditions of another student in the group. This enables students to develop listening and interviewing skills.

2.   *Tack-on skill games.* Cooperative skills are reinforced by adding, or "tacking-on," skill-related games to learning tasks. Example: The Talking Chips game can facilitate equal participation in group discussions. Each player is given a chip and when he or she wants to talk, places a chip in the center of the table. This person cannot speak again until all team members have placed their chips in the center of the table. Once everyone has contributed a chip, the chips are redistributed so they can talk again.

3. *Communication training.* Time outside of the lesson is devoted to direct instruction on specific communication skills. Example: Students practice paraphrasing others' ideas in an interview process or validating the feelings or motives of another teammate who is describing a difficult issue or problem they face with another person.

4. *Conflict resolution training.* Students learn conflict resolution skills through direct instruction, then practice them through role plays and simulations. Example: Students learn about and memorize various modes of conflict resolution such as sharing, turn taking, compromise, outside help, postponement, avoidance, and humor. They practice these in a role play requiring decision making, conflict management, and resolution.

5. *Skill development games.* These games use cooperative skills to solve a problem or reach an objective. Some games require specific cooperative skills while others require students to select a cooperative skill for use in the game. Example: In the Broken Squares game students receive several pieces of a broken square. The goal is to put the square together by taking turns and giving each other one piece. A rule of Broken Squares is that teammates cannot speak or ask others for what they need. Students must learn to be sensitive to one another to complete the square.

6. *Group role development.* Students are assigned and taught to perform specific roles in the group. They also spend time analyzing the various productive and nonproductive roles group members play. Example: Students are taught to carry out task roles (e.g., initiating an activity, giving opinions, summarizing) or group maintenance roles (e.g., encouraging, following group decisions) and they are alerted to types of nonfunctional group behaviors (e.g., being aggressive, horsing around, withdrawing). They carry out specific roles in the context of group activities and discuss nonfunctional group behaviors during the group reflection phase of an activity.

7. *Role plays.* Students participate in structured role plays to become more aware of appropriate cooperative and social behaviors. Students may role play desirable and undesirable group behaviors, discussing what they observed and learned from the activity. Example: Students are provided with a scenario that takes place in the school cafeteria, in which one student repeatedly cuts in line in front of a younger student. This conflict forms the basis of a role play in which students try to resolve the situation.

EDUCATIONAL TECHNOLOGY AND COOPERATIVE LEARNING

Cooperative learning is highly compatible with today's educational technology, such as computers, modems, CD-ROMs, and real-time interactivity. This technology can be used for purposes such as the following:

- Written and graphic expression.
- Building data bases.
- Multimedia presentations.
- As an interactive communication device.
- As a device to assist students with disabilities.
- As a means for students to access information from a distance.

Cooperative projects such as sitting together at a computer terminal to complete a joint project work best where there are guidelines. "Putting children together to work at the computer is not enough. They need to feel a commitment and concern for others in their group. When responsible for their own and each other's learning, they learn to understand each other as well as master academic content." (Anderson, 1990, p. 3)

It is essential to be familiar with the software you will be using. Male (1994) urges teachers to move beyond the use of drill-and-practice activities for the computer and to use more "learner-centered" software, which is more consistent with the spirit of cooperation. Learner-centered software focuses on intellectual tasks and problem solving that puts the learner in charge of the goal or the means to reaching the goal, and encourages students to make approximations in the process of solving problems. In addition to preparing a cooperative learning lesson plan suited to computer use, other planning is essential. Planning considerations and decisions that should be made in advance include the following:

- Decide what software you will use. Will it include word processing, graphics, databases? Is it compatible with the networks in your school? Does it lend itself to group learning? Higher-order thinking? Problem solving? More than one answer?

- Adapt the lesson to computer use, using a lesson plan form. You may need to add material not contained in the software.

- Determine the number of computers you will need and how many students will be assigned to each computer. Will you conduct the lesson in the classroom, in several classrooms, or in the computer lab? Which platform will you use? Can some students use one brand of computer in your lab while others use another in the classroom and library? Are the computers equipped with the proper hardware to run the program you have selected?

- Room arrangement is important. Can each student in the group see the screen? Is there enough space between computers to promote concentration and freedom of movement? Are there enough outlets to accommodate the arrangement of computers? Are the screens at eye level? Can students in wheelchairs gain access to the terminal?

- Assess students' keyboarding skills. What level of competence should you expect students to have? Who will help students who are new to the class or who have not obtained these skills?

- Introduce your students to computer etiquette. For example, have a plan for taking turns, proper seating around the computer, and timing the lesson.

- Role assignments can relate to computer use. For example, one student could be responsible for booting up the computer (if necessary) and shutting it down, making certain the work has been saved. This student could also be the courier who retrieves the printed copy from the classroom printer and checks to see if there is paper in the tray.

- Assure individual accountability and positive interdependence. To be certain that everyone has contributed to a group writing project, or to developing some of the slides for a hypercard presentation, for example, students could place their initials or a symbol by their own contributions, such as an "Ω." One student might use *italics*, or each might use a different font, etc. (Adapted from Anderson, 1988)

Global Networking

Students can also participate in cooperative projects with others from schools in distant towns, states, or nations. By logging on to an on-line service, students can interact with other students, families, and experts in real-time. For example, students from the elementary school in Houlton, Maine, collaborate daily on a National Geographic Weather Project with students from Texas and Italy, inputting weather data for future scientific analysis. This type of collaboration tends to be very motivating for students, and increases their global and multicultural awareness.

Multimedia Presentations

Students researching a particular topic can work together to develop presentations that incorporate a variety of media, such as video clips, animation, graphics, sound, and entertaining text formats (e.g., there are many varieties of these entertaining "transitions"—text that flies across the computer screen, fades in and out, or dissolves like rain).

A Cooperative Multimedia Research Presentation

Three students conducted descriptive research on the flora of their island off the southeast coast of Alaska. They sampled the vegetation, graphed their data, and presented their findings using multimedia presentation software that incorporated the following:

> 1. *A video clip of the sampling process (a student laying out the sampling grid and collecting plants).*
>
> 2. *Graphics displaying the histograms of the various plant species.*

3. *Scanned photographs of the most common plant species with brief text descriptions.*

4. *A soundtrack setting the mood for the presentation (they selected jazz).*

5. *A text report describing the entire study, from objective, to methods, to conclusions.*

6. *A landscape of the island using three-dimensional graphics.*

Becky was responsible for the video and the soundtrack. John developed the graphs and took the photographs to be scanned into the computer. Annika developed the landscape of the island using special software and integrated the various media into the final presentation. Each student wrote a section of the report, and all three participated in peer editing, using a spell checker and a grammar check from their word processing program. The technological support and computer hardware was provided through a grant awarded to the school district. More recently, teachers have been trained to use multimedia technology and receive assistance from the school librarian/technology expert.

LESSON PLANNING

A lesson plan form is helpful, if not essential, when planning cooperative learning activities. After years of conducting cooperative activities, a teacher may find that outlining a lesson in advance may not be necessary and can occur mentally (especially for informal cooperative activities). However, my own experience is that if I don't outline my lessons, I tend to forget certain elements or deliver the segments out of sequence. See Figure 3.9 for a cooperative lesson plan form.

In the next section of this chapter you will find the following sample cooperative lessons developed by teachers and university students.

- The Four Stages of the Butterfly (Figure 3.10)
- Said Is Dead (Figure 3.11)
- Cooperative Research (Figure 3.12)
- Groups of Geographers (Figure 3.13)
- The Ins and Outs Game (Figure 3.14)
- The Temperature Conversion Laboratory (Figure 3.15)

As you read these lessons, begin to collect your thoughts about a lesson you will plan using the form provided. Ideally, you should conduct this lesson with students, but if that is not possible, present it to your peers.

FIGURE 3.9
Cooperative Lesson Plan Form

Cooperative Lesson Plan Form

Grade Level: _____ Subject Area: _____

Step 1. Select a lesson _____

Step 2. Make decisions

    a. Group size: _____

    b. Assignment to groups: _____

    _____

    c. Room arrangement: _____

    _____

    d. Materials needed for each group: _____

    _____

    _____

    _____

    e. Assigning roles: _____

    _____

    _____

Step 3. Set the lesson. State, in language your students understand:

    a. Task: _____

    _____

    b. Positive interdependence: _____

    _____

    _____

    c. Individual accountability: _____

    _____

    d. Criteria for success: _____

    _____

    e. Specific behaviors expected: _____

Adapted from Johnson, Johnson, & Holubec (1990)

FIGURE 3.9
continued

Step 4. Monitor and process

    a. Evidence of expected behaviors (appropriate actions): _____

       _____

       _____

    b. Observation form: _____

       Observer(s): _____

    c. Plans for processing (feedback): _____

       _____

Step 5. Evaluate outcomes

    a. Task achievement: _____

       _____

    b. Group functioning: _____

       _____

    c. Notes on individuals: _____

       _____

    d. Suggestions for next time: _____

       _____

       _____

       _____

       _____

Step 6. Determine needed adaptations for students with special needs

       _____

       _____

       _____

       _____

       _____

       _____

       _____

       _____

Figure 3.10
Sample Lesson Plan: The Four Stages of the Butterfly

Subject area: Science

Grade level: Elementary

Lesson summary: By constructing dioramas, students will depict the four stages of butterfly development.

Group size: Four

Assignment to groups: Teacher will assign students by ability level (stratified random method).

Materials: Text book, construction paper, scissors, pencils, and black markers.

Academic task: To start the lesson, each group member draws a slip of paper out of a box. Written on the four slips of paper is either *egg, larva, pupa,* or *adult.* Using the jigsaw method, the students meet in **expert groups.** For example, all group members in the class who chose the slip of paper with *egg* written on it form small groups of three or four to study that phase of butterfly development.

After studying the textbook, the students discuss their assigned stage and generate ideas about illustrating it in the form of a diorama to be constructed by the original group of four, using the information they have gained from studying the textbook.

Upon returning to the original groups, students begin constructing the diorama. At first, each student works on depicting his or her own stage of butterfly development. Then, all the contributions of group members are used to construct the diorama.

To make the diorama, students will use a different color of construction paper for each of the stages. The paper is precut in 9-inch by 9-inch squares. Students fold each corner to the opposite corner and then draw a dotted line for cutting. The lower flaps are overlapped and glued. Next, the name of the stage is written at the bottom along with an arrow to the right of the name (see Steps 1 and 2).

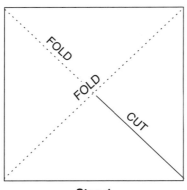

Step 1

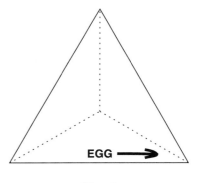

Step 2

Next, students make three-dimensional scenery for the diorama (see Step 3). Upon completion of the scenery, all four stages are arranged to form the diorama. The stages must be placed in correct sequence. Finally, all four stages are glued together (see Step 4).

From Annette Dufner, Glendive, Montana

FIGURE 3.10
continued

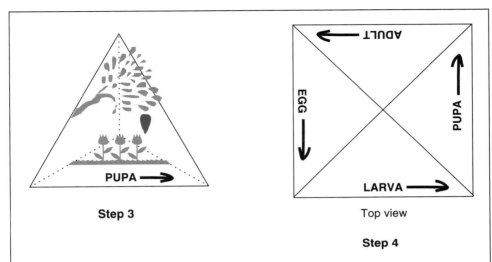

Step 3

Top view

Step 4

After completing the diorama, each student in the group is responsible for teaching the other members of their group facts about their stage. This may require another class session.

The dioramas are displayed in the classroom at eye level. It is best to hang them from the ceiling so that each hangs in the center of the group who created it.

Criteria for success: Dioramas are rated according to three criteria: creativity, accuracy, and neatness. Students receive 0 to 5 marbles for each category (0 = poor, 5 = excellent). At the end of the lesson, students are tested individually on the material with a written quiz. Individuals contribute marbles to the group according to the following scale: 90% to 100%—5 marbles, 80% to 89%—4 marbles, 70% to 79%—3 marbles, less than 70%—no marbles.

When a group has earned 50 marbles, the students can have a popcorn party at the end of the school day or week.

Positive interdependence: Students are assigned specific tasks in the group (task interdependence) and they produce a single product (goal interdependence).

Individual accountability: Each group member will be responsible for learning facts about all four stages of butterfly development. Students will be individually assessed with a 20-item test.

Cooperative skills: Students will practice the skill of encouraging others' participation. This skill will be introduced at the beginning of the lesson and practiced throughout.

Teacher monitoring and student reflection: The teacher observes the groups and records instances of this behavior, providing feedback at the end of the lesson. Students rate their own performance of the social skill and the group task using a self-rating form. Self-ratings are discussed with the group and suggestions for improving performance of the skill are solicited from group members.

FIGURE 3.11
Sample Lesson Plan: Said Is Dead

Subject area: Language arts

Grade level: Middle school

Lesson summary: Working in groups of four, students generate a list of varied words to substitute for *said* in their writings. A goal of the lesson is to encourage students to eliminate overused words in their writing vocabularies.

Group size: Four

Assignment to groups: Teacher assigns students with mixed-ability levels.

Materials: Each group receives one marking pen, a set of colored index cards (a different color for each group), and a roll of masking tape. The teacher prepares a banner with the label "Said is Dead" and a circle with the word *said* and a diagonal line through it.

Group roles: Group members will choose from among the following roles: *time-keeper, organizer* (obtains materials for the group and returns them when done), *facilitator* (assures that the students follow directions, take turns, and stay seated in a circle formation), *reporter* (reads the group cards at appropriate times during the lesson).

Time required: One 45-minute period for the generation of the initial list of words, and a second period for the verification of the conventions, such as spelling and usage.

Academic task: After a discussion by the teacher on the importance of using a variety of words to generate more interesting writing, the students are asked to come up with many unusual words to replace *said.* Using the roundtable structure, each student offers his or her word, writing it on a card. The marker is passed to the next student, who says a new word, writes it, and passes the marker. Students must listen, not repeat a word that has been used, and take turns in a circular order that includes each member.

The teacher emphasizes that groups should strive to produce as many words as they can in a 12-minute period. The timekeeper's job is to remind the group

From Raenelle Lees, Missoula, Montana

FIGURE 3.11
continued

when the allotted 12 minutes is nearly over. When the time is up, students discuss their cards, spreading them out and indicating the ones they like best, or the ones that they believe are the most unusual. They will be sharing the words with the large group in five minutes.

A reporter from each group tapes the group's words to a chart at the front of the room. Members from other groups must listen carefully and eliminate duplicates from their card piles. This process can continue for as long as the teacher desires, or until all the nonduplicative words are on the chart.

Positive interdependence: Group members will share one set of cards and a marker (materials interdependence). Each group will be responsible for having an unusual set of words to share with the entire class (goal interdependence). The color of the paper cards will be a means for demonstrating group effort and productivity (identity interdependence).

Individual accountability: Each member must supply a word before passing the marker to the next student. Each student performs a role in the group.

Cooperative skills: Two skills are practiced in this activity: taking turns and active listening. Because the roundtable format is used, students must honor each person's turn or the activity will not be successful. Active listening is important so that students or groups do not repeat a word that has been contributed.

Teacher monitoring and student reflection: Critical questions to be discussed by the small groups are (1) Of what value was this exercise? (2) What did your group do well? (3) How could you have improved on what your group did? (4) How can you use the information we generated in the future?

Springboards: Several possibilities exist for building on this activity. Students can categorize words in various ways, such as long-short, loud-soft, or negative-positive. Categorization would not only encourage higher order thinking, but would require group interdependence. Students could alphabetize the cards and copy the lists for a minidictionary of their own. The lists could be used when editing and revising their written work.

FIGURE 3.12
Sample Lesson Plan: Cooperative Research

Subject area: English

Grade level: Secondary, Junior Year

Lesson summary: Students research one of five assigned topics, share their knowledge, develop outlines and bibliographies, edit, and present their knowledge to classmates. They also produce individually written research papers and group visual aids for presentation during panel discussions of topics.

Students gain knowledge about a chosen topic, about note taking, summarizing, analyzing, and synthesizing new information, writing outlines and bibliographies, writing in research paper format, editing techniques and presenting information in a panel discussion with group members.

Group size: Three

Assignment to groups: Students select topics they are interested in, then the teacher randomly assigns students to groups.

Materials: Sets of articles (provided by the teacher) on five topics (e.g., Bosnia-Herzegovina civil war, the use of steroids, family issues, nuclear proliferation, the spread of AIDS), handouts on bibliography format, outline forms, evaluation forms for papers and group presentations. Students will also need materials for creating a poster, handouts, or overhead transparencies for use in the panel discussion.

Roles: Each group member is responsible for accomplishing the group goals, so no specific roles are assigned.

Time required: Four weeks

Academic task:

Part 1: Preparing to write.   The first task is for students to individually read all of the articles provided by the teacher. During this reading period (two to three days) students take notes with group members. While they read, they should be formulating ideas for writing a research paper on the topic. After reading the articles, students meet in a group with the goal of developing a list of six to seven main ideas worth including in a paper. Each student must bring two to three ideas with specific examples from the articles. These will be shared with the group members.

Part 2: Writing the papers.   Students continue reading articles, taking notes, and discussing the information with one another. Each student begins writing his or her

From Liz Lousen, Missoula, Montana

FIGURE 3.12
continued

section of the research paper, which will be edited by group members. They also will develop their bibliographies together, consulting handouts and workbooks.

Part 3: Presentation and panel discussion.   The papers are finalized and group members plan a class presentation in which they will equally divide the material to be presented and prepare visual aids (poster, overhead, handout, etc.). The final activity in this project is the panel discussion by group members. The panel is composed to two to three groups, all of whom have researched the same topic.

Criteria for success: All group products, main ideas, outlines, bibliography, and paper are checked by the group members themselves and the teacher. The teacher approves the products or requires additional work by the group. Students receive individual grades on their sections of the paper as well as a group grade for the paper. The panels (and visuals) will be evaluated by the class as a whole, using an evaluation grid.

Positive interdependence: Students must agree on six to seven main ideas to be included in their individually written papers; they must develop an outline, bibliography, and a group presentation (goal interdependence). Students construct one visual aid to be used in the presentation (material and product interdependence).

Individual accountability: Each group member must contribute two to three main ideas they gleaned from reading the articles. Students are responsible for writing their own sections of the paper and for delivering their part of the class presentation.

Cooperative skills: Encouraging other group members to contribute equally.

Teacher monitoring and student reflection: In their groups students discuss the following questions relating to their work:

1.   Was everyone well prepared when we discussed our topics?

2.   Did everyone contribute equally to the discussions?

3.   Did we help each other with the outlines, bibiography, and rough draft editing?

4.   What kind of help did we need from each other that we didn't get? What can we do to improve in this area?

FIGURE 3.13
Sample Lesson Plan: Groups of Geographers

Subject area: Groups must design a city on a landscape using various symbols to denote the apartments, factories, etc. They must justify the placements on a sheet of paper. The groups will then make a class demonstration of the landscape, with the other groups critically analyzing the placements.

Grade level: Middle school

Lesson summary: Students manipulate symbols to learn the importance of location, accessibility, and other variables in the planning of a large city. Students critically evaluate both their placements and the locations chosen by other groups.

Group size: Four

Assignment to groups: Heterogeneous random with high, middle, and low achievers in each group. Two boys, two girls per group.

Materials:
*   Assignment summary
*   Key for symbols on a sheet
*   Laminated, reusable landscape showing coastline, river, mountains, lake, forest, and island
*   Overhead projection pens
*   One sheet of paper for justifications
*   Pen

Group roles:
1. Reader/Questioner—To read all materials and check for understanding within the group.
2. Drawer—To draw symbols on landscape.
3. Encourager/Praiser—To praise contributions and encourage good work from all group members.
4. Recorder—To write down justification for placement of city facilities.

Time required: About two hours.

Academic task (Part 1)
Students are placed in groups before lesson begins. Each group receives materials. Teacher should explain purpose and objective of lesson. Students choose their own roles in groups for this lesson. In my classroom, they will have usually worked in this group for other assignments and I make sure that they rotate roles for every lesson. Stress here that reaching consensus is important to all placements. Also, the teacher should make sure that all students understand that they will be held accountable for understanding their justifications for placing the buildings, roads, etc., where they do. Explain that the teacher will randomly select two students out of the group to make the class presentation explaining placements and their justifications, so all must understand why and be able to explain the decisions of the group.

From John Marks, Missoula, Montana

FIGURE 3.13
continued

Positive interdependence: Students must all agree (reach consensus) on all placements of buildings and facilities. Each student is assigned a group role. Groups receive only one each: landscape, key, explanation of assignment, or limited colored markers, and produce only one sheet of justifications for placements.

Individual accountability: Each member must be able to explain and justify all placements on their landscape to the class. They sign the justification sheet to signify their understanding of and agreement with all placements.

Teacher monitoring and student reflection: Monitor group to check for role assignment and progress of landscape. Monitor also to note the use of group skills.

Intervention: Accept questions from a group only when all the group has the same question. Intervene in each group to ask for a verbal justification for a placement. Listen and praise proper social skill use. When an opportunity to use a skill is passed by, re-explain the proper way of praising or encouraging.

Processing: Have students fill out processing/observation sheet for group assignment. Allow a few minutes to share this in the groups.

Closing: Students all sign evaluation sheet and facility placement sheets.

Academic Task (Part 2)

The task is to present to the class the landscape and justification for placements. Select two students randomly from any group. Allow four minutes to present the material to the class. Then allow two minutes for other groups to discuss and analyze the placements pros and cons. Each group must come up with three questions for the presenters. Call on a number (one for reader, two for drawer, etc.) and have them stand. Randomly select a group (being sure to call on all groups during the course of the presentations) to ask the presenters a question. For example, a group might ask why the dump was placed at the foot of the mountains far out of town when that would increase fuel costs and pollution from diesel exhaust. The presenting group is allowed 30 seconds to discuss and the teacher randomly calls a number from the presenting group to explain and justify placement. This procedure has been labeled "Numbered Heads." Continue this procedure until all groups have presented.

Evaluation: Evaluate on the basis of group cooperative skills with the use of the student checklist. Use checkmarks on a chart for evaluating the presentations. Each time a group asks a *significant* question of the presenting group, give that group a plus. Any *insignificant* questions, give a minus. Tally up to arrive at group grade. Also, groups can be evaluated on the basis of their presentation, public speaking skills, etc.

FIGURE 3.14
Sample Lesson Plan: The Ins and Outs Game

Objective: The students review the concepts of functions, tables of values, algebraic equations, slope, and y-intercept by playing the game.

Grade level: Ninth grade

Grouping: Groups of four (either random or teacher-selected assignment)

Rules and goals: Players try to determine what is "in" and what is "out" of a category (concept) for items revealed one at a time by the teacher. The object of the game is for every team to identify the concept being described by constructing the list of "ins" and "outs." Each team member is assigned a number from 1–4. When the teacher calls his/her number, that student will give an appropriate response from the team's list by holding up a green "in card" or a red "out card."

Procedure:
- To model the procedure, teacher enters one item under each column of the Ins and Outs Game Board. Start with simple patterns or concepts when this game is new to students.
- Teacher displays another item and calls out a number from 1–4, waiting for the students with that number to display their red or green card before entering the item in the appropriate column.
- Students may confer with teammates to discuss before answering.
- The round is finished when every team has identified the pattern and is ready to put in writing the rule or concept that is represented by the ins and outs.
- Call time and have individual team members write their explanations down on paper.
- Teacher calls a number, and the explanation from the student with that number will be collected from each group. Award one point to the group for each correct response.
- Teacher chooses another concept and another round is played.

Sample concepts and items:
- Concept: perfect squares
  Ins: 1, 4, 9, 16, 25, 36, 49
  Outs: 2, 5, 6, 7, 8, −2, −3, −4
- Concept: lines with a slope of 3
  Ins: $2y = 6x - 10$, $3x - y = 9$, $6x - 2y = -2$, $y = 3x + 33$, $y = (6/2)x - 7$
  Outs: $x + y = 10$, $x - 3y = 9$, $6x + 2y = 2$, $y = -3x + 33$, $y = 5x - 7$

The Ins and Outs Game Board	
Where does it go? _____	

IN	OUT

From Mary Jo Messenger (1993), *Cooperative Learning* 14 (1), 53. Reprinted by permission of IASCE.

FIGURE 3.15
Sample Lesson Plan: The Temperature Conversion Laboratory

Objective:
Students will review many concepts they have studied in the course and practice working cooperatively with a partner.

Materials (for each pair):
- one beaker of ice water
- one beaker very hot water
- Celsius/Fahrenheit thermometer
- 25 ml graduated cylinder

Procedure:
1. Gather materials.
2. Carefully place the thermometer in the beaker of cold water.
3. When the reading has stabilized, record both the Celsius and Fahrenheit temperatures in your data table.
4. Now place the thermometer in the beaker of hot water and, after the temperature reading has stabilized, record this temperature in your data table.
5. Measure 25 ml of the hot water using a graduated cylinder and add this to the cold water. Record the temperature of the water.
6. Repeat step 5 six more times. You should have a total of ten pairs of data.

Processing the Data:
1. Assign variables and write the data as ordered pairs using Celsius as the first element and Fahrenheit as the second.
2. On graph paper, label the axes and mark off an appropriate scale.
3. Plot the data points.
4. Draw a best fit line through the data points.

Interpreting the Data:
5. What is the slope of your line?
6. What is the y-intercept of your line?
7. Determine a mathematical model that describes the relationship between Celsius and Fahrenheit temperatures by giving the equation of the line.
8. What is special about the y-intercept?

Questions:
9. Based on this experiment how would you describe the relationship between Celsius and Fahrenheit temperatures?
10. Explain the difference between an algebraic expression, formula, and equation.
11. Explain what a variable is.
12. Explain why this relationship is a function.
13. Explain why scales are important to scientists and mathematicians.
14. Explain the difference between a Celsius degree and a Fahrenheit degree.

From Mary Jo Messenger (1993), *Cooperative Learning* 14 (1), 52. Reprinted by permission of IASCE.

CONCLUSION

Planning cooperative learning activities involves a good deal of front-end work before students are placed into groups. After deciding which cooperative lesson structure you will use (such as a jigsaw, or a round table, as described in Chapter 5), decisions must be made concerning how many students to place in a group, how to best assign students to groups to assure heterogeneity, how to assure positive interdependence and individual accountability, and how to introduce and instruct students about cooperative skills. Lesson plans can be tremendously helpful in organizing the various elements of cooperative learning and in providing a record of the activity when the lesson is completed. Teachers find their most successful lessons evolve as they are carried out and repeated, revised and refined, and shared with other teachers.

In the next chapter, you will be introduced to various cooperative learning activities, or structures, that have been developed by educators and researchers over the years. The recommendations for lesson planning provided in this chapter are generic, and can be used with the array of cooperative learning activities or structures.

◆   ◆   ◆

QUESTIONS AND ACTIVITIES

1. **Lesson plan and round-robin discussion.** Plan a brief cooperative lesson using the lesson plan form in Figure 3.9. If possible, carry out the lesson with a group or classroom of students. Then, present the lesson and your evaluation of it to your peers using a round-robin format. Organize the groups with four or five members, sitting in a circle. A round-robin involves each group member presenting the lesson he or she developed. The presentations moves clockwise around the table.

After providing a brief overview of your lesson and sharing the written lesson plan, answer the following questions: What went well? What would you have done differently? After the presentation of the lesson plan and evaluation, take a few minutes for a group discussion of the lesson. For a round-robin structure to be successful, group members must refrain from interjecting their remarks until the presenter has finished his or her presentation.

2. **Cooperative skill instruction.** Identify a cooperative skill that you would like to teach. Then develop a brief written plan for teaching the skill according to the six-step process presented in this chapter. In class, working in a group of four, hand your cooperative skill instruction plan to one of your group members, who will be teaching from your plan. Form pairs

within the group to discuss the written plans and practice teaching the skills to one another. Reconvene in your groups of four to teach your partner's skill to the other pair. Each group member should teach from his or her partner's written plan. After the four cooperative skills have been taught, take time to reflect on the instructional plans as a group.

3.   Using the types of positive interdependence discussed in this chapter, identify ways in which positive interdependence is fostered in your own community or school. For example, how do individuals work together toward mutual goals? How is interdependence reinforced through role responsibilities, reward interdependence, or sharing of resources? List the ways or design a web to illustrate the various forms interdependence can take.

4.   Discuss violations of the principle of individual accountability in your experiences with groupwork. In retrospect, if you had been able to influence that situation, how would you have assured individual accountability?

SUGGESTED READINGS

Books

Abrami, P. C., Chambers, B., Poulsen, C., De Simone, C. D'Apollonia, S., Howden, J. (1995). *Classroom connections: Understanding and using cooperative learning.* Toronto: Harcourt Brace & Company.

Anderson, M. A. (1990). *Partnerships: Developing teamwork at the computer.* Arlington, VA: MAJO Press.

Bennet, B., Rolheiser-Bennet, C., and Stevahn, L. (1991). *Cooperative learning: Where heart meets mind.* Edina, MN: Interaction Books.

Johnson, D. W., & Johnson, R. T. (1987) *Structuring cooperative learning: Lesson plans for teachers.* Edina, MN: Interaction Books.

Johnson, D. W., Johnson, R. T., & Holubec, E. J. (1993). *Cooperation in the classroom* (6th ed.). Edina, MN: Interaction Books.

Kagan, S. (1992). *Cooperative learning.* San Juan Capistrano, CA: Kagan Cooperative Learning.

REFERENCES

Anderson, M. A. (1990). *Partnerships: Developing teamwork at the computer.* Arlington, VA: MAJO Press.

Bloom, B. (Ed.). (1956). *Taxonomy of educational objectives, handbook I: Cognitive domain.* New York: David McKay.

Gardner, H. (1983). *Frames of mind.* New York: Basic Books.

Hunter, M. C. (1982). *Mastery teaching*. El Segundo, CA: TIP Publications.

Johnson, D. W., & Johnson, R. T. (1989). *Cooperation and competition: Theory and research*. Edina, MN: Interaction Books.

Johnson, D. W., & Johnson, R. T. (1994). Learning together. In S. Sharan (Ed.), *Handbook of cooperative learning methods* (pp. 51–65). Westport, CT: Greenwood Press.

Johnson, D. W., Johnson, R. T., & Holubec, E. J. (1993). *Cooperation in the classroom* (6th ed.). Edina, MN: Interaction Books.

Kagan, S. (1987). *Cooperative learning: Resources for teachers*. Riverside, CA: University of California Riverside.

Kagan, S. (1991). *Cooperative learning lessons for little ones: Literature-based language arts and social skills*. San Juan Capistrano, CA: Resources for Teachers.

Kagan, S., & Kagan, M. (1994). The structural approach: Six keys to cooperative learning. In S. Sharan (Ed.), *Handbook of cooperative learning methods* (pp. 115–136). Westport, CT: Greenwood Press.

Kohn, A. (1987, October). It's hard to get left out of a pair. *Psychology Today*, pp. 53–57.

Male, M. (1994). Cooperative learning and computers. In S. Sharan (Ed.), *Handbook of cooperative learning methods* (pp. 267–282). Westport, CT: Greenwood Press.

Messenger, M. J. (1993) Two cooperative learning activities. *Cooperative Learning, 14*(1), 52–53.

CHAPTER 4

COOPERATIVE CLASSROOM MANAGEMENT

Raymond M. Glass, Ph.D.

◆

This chapter is designed to help you do the following:

- ◆ Explain the concept of cooperative classroom management.
- ◆ Outline specific techniques to prevent or minimize student misbehavior.
- ◆ Describe techniques to help all students behave in ways that promote a safe, cooperative classroom.
- ◆ Identify specific steps to help students learn how to solve conflicts thoughtfully and cooperatively.
- ◆ Outline specific techniques to help individual students improve their behavior during cooperative and other classroom activities.

Raymond Glass is a professor of special education at the University of Maine at Farmington.

Cooperative Classroom Management

It is the first day of school in Jane Fielding's classroom and the students are already working to identify behaviors that will help make this a "good class to be in." In the past, Jane had simply posted and reviewed the rules for good behavior, but this year she wanted her students to play a more active role in the process. After conducting some of the typical activities associated with the beginning of school, Jane asked the students to consider ways students and adults in the class could treat each other to make this a safe, caring, and enjoyable class. To help her students understand the task, she wrote the following example on the board as a model:

Behavior

Listen when someone is talking

Reason

We feel respected and important when people listen to us

She then asked the students to work in pairs to identify other helpful behaviors and the reasons these were important. The students worked diligently in their pairs and then shared their ideas. Jane added each contribution under the appropriate column until all students had a chance to express their ideas. Later, the class worked together to winnow the list down to five or six behaviors and their reasons. This list served as the initial set of class rules, which were posted in full view.

Several days later, Jane intervened in a shouting match and tug of war between two students over who could use a particular reference book. In a calm, firm voice, she told them to stop arguing and come to a table at the back of the room for a conference. Jane asked them to calmly state their needs and concerns, one at a time. She then asked them to work together to think of two or three fair solutions to their conflict that would allow their needs to be met, and to let her know as soon as they arrived at a decision. Judging that it was safe to leave them alone, Jane went back to the front of the room as the students began to discuss possible solutions.

COOPERATIVE CLASSROOM MANAGEMENT: AN OVERVIEW

The examples in the preceding vignette demonstrate the beginning stages of an approach we will refer to as **cooperative classroom management**. Succinctly, the teacher who uses cooperative classroom management seeks ways to involve students in the process of managing the classroom, from helping to determine the class rules to solving actual problems. In employing cooperative classroom management, the teacher does not give up the role of responsible authority in the classroom or even the final say. Rather, students are given a say in some of the key decisions including coming up with ways to solve their own classroom behavior problems.

By providing students with a voice in the development and implementation of classroom management procedures, we begin to meet some important needs described by William Glasser, an advocate for students who demonstrate problematic behavior in school. Glasser (1985, 1990) describes several basic needs that all students, especially those with behavior problems, must have met to improve their behavior and make a commitment to learning. These include the following:

1. The need to feel they **belong** or have a key place in the classroom and school.
2. The need to experience a sense of importance or **power** by being listened to and regarded by adults.

3. The need to experience **freedom** by being able to make choices in some aspects of the daily school curriculum.

4. The need to have **fun**.

Glasser goes on to suggest, "For workers, including students, to do quality work, they must be managed in a way that convinces them that the work they are asked to do satisfies their needs. The more it does, the harder they will work" (1990, p. 22).

Notice that cooperative classroom management differs markedly from highly teacher-directed disciplinary programs such as one put forth by Canter and Canter (1976). Their program, **Assertive Discipline**, emphasizes the authority of the teacher, who establishes the rules, lists the punishments for violating rules, and rewards the class for appropriate behavior. While there may be merit to aspects of this system such as establishing clear classroom rules and guidelines, such systems tend to limit student involvement in the process of solving classroom problems and therefore deny students opportunities to learn interpersonal and problem solving skills and assume responsibility for their own behavior (Curwin & Mendler, 1988).

This chapter focuses on several specific aspects of cooperative classroom management. In the first section we will explore ways to work with students to prevent conflicts from occurring. In the second section we will consider ways to help students develop skills for resolving conflicts. Finally, in the third section, we will examine specific techniques for helping students with persistent behavior problems.

WORKING WITH STUDENTS TO PREVENT CONFLICTS

Most successful classroom teachers would agree with the adage "An ounce of prevention is worth a pound of cure." Because disruptive student behavior takes important time away from learning and can negatively influence the climate of the classroom, we must take steps early in the school year to prevent or minimize such behavior. Fortunately, there is a large body of research that clearly identifies specific steps teachers can take early in the year to help ensure a smoothly running classroom and positive teacher-student interaction (Evertson & Harris, 1992; Evertson, Emmer, Clements, & Worsham, 1994). Some of these steps are described in this section.

Develop Clear Rules and Procedures

Developing clear and reasonable class rules and procedures is a fundamental aspect of cooperative classroom management. In fact, it is difficult to help students learn skills of cooperation and caring without this foundation. Many teachers have observed that a lack of clear rules or guidelines for behavior often results in bickering, arguing, and other negative

Cooperative Classroom Management

responses. Teachers in these classrooms often resort to unconstructive tactics such as threats, shouting, or an excessive focus on negative student behavior in an attempt to control the classroom. It is interesting to note that Kounin (1970) observed that students with behavior problems nearly always behaved more appropriately in classrooms with clear rules and expectations that were consistently reinforced by the teacher.

Rules can be established for the whole class as well as for smaller cooperative learning groups. Rules are most effective when stated clearly and in a positive manner, as demonstrated in the following two examples from the same classroom teacher.

Help Make This a Cooperative Classroom

1. Listen carefully while others are speaking.
2. Use a positive tone when speaking: Avoid put-downs.
3. Share and take turns when appropriate.
4. Respect others' space: Keep hands and feet to yourself.
5. Try to solve conflicts by constructive techniques such as talking and compromising.

Guidelines for Successful Cooperative Groups

1. Form groups quickly and quietly.
2. Listen carefully to each other.
3. Give everyone a chance to participate.
4. Be respectful: Make positive comments and avoid put-downs.
5. Get everyone's opinion before making decisions.

These rules are directly related to broader values such as *caring, respect,* and *cooperation.* These rules are not at all arbitrary; instead, they are designed to bring about a climate of respect and thoughtfulness and should be presented to students and parents with that in mind. Moreover, these rules are stated in a positive manner and therefore provide students with guidance as to what to do instead of what not to do.

These classroom rules typically relate to ways that people in the class should behave with each other to develop a safe, caring classroom. Classroom procedures, on the other hand, focus more on how to move through the day and from activity to activity in a reasonably orderly fashion (Evertson, Emmer, Clements, & Worsham, 1994). Imagine how chaotic classroom life would be if we were constantly barraged by students asking questions such as, "I'm finished, what do I do now?" "Where should I put my math paper?" "Can I go to the bathroom now?" Or if we had to spend 20 minutes after class cleaning the room, rearranging the desks, and sorting math, social studies, and English papers into their own piles because students put them just any place on our desk? When we feel overwhelmed by these problems it is likely that we have not clarified and taught students some procedures necessary for developing and maintaining a smoothly running classroom. These procedures typically focus on **routines** such as the following:

- Where to put coats and other materials upon entering the classroom.
- How to get ready for lunch, music, or recess.
- Where to put completed papers.
- What to do when your work is done.
- How to get help when the teacher is busy.
- How to sign up for and use the computer.
- How to sign up to leave the room to use the bathroom.
- Where to find makeup assignments if you were absent.
- How desks, chairs, bookshelves, and related items need to be arranged before dismissal for the day.
- What activity to engage in upon returning from recess.

Once developed, some procedures can be posted in full view of the students, serving as a constant reminder. Moreover, posting key procedures along with the classroom rules allows us to cue students before an upcoming activity. For example, just as we are about to begin an activity in which students are to work individually, we might ask the class what procedure to follow when their work is completed. In Figure 4.1, four examples of classroom procedures that a teacher posted throughout the classroom are presented.

Involve Students in the Process of Developing Rules and Procedures

In a teacher-directed classroom it would make sense to develop most or all of the rules and procedures and simply announce them on the first day of class. On the other hand, engaging students in the process of identifying helpful rules and procedures represents an important opportunity for establishing a norm of student participation and cooperation. One way to engage students in this process is to place them into groups of two or three and ask each group to identify several rules that would help make this classroom a safe place where everyone feels important and respected. They also should identify their reasons for each rule.

To avoid having groups make long lists of the usual don'ts that occur in schools (don't run, don't fight, don't eat candy, etc.), challenge students to state their rules in terms of what they should do and then provide one example (e.g., listen when someone is talking) as a model. After students have developed several rules, have each group state their rules and the rea-

FIGURE 4.1
Four Examples of Classroom Procedures

Work finished?

- Read a book
- Work on a project
- Pick up an activity from the Free Time Box

Absent yesterday?

- Check class assignment notebook for make-up work
- Put your written excuse in the folder
- Ask the homework/assignment monitor to explain the assignment if you need help

Starting math class

- Move quietly to your desk or your cooperative group
- Find the bonus problem on the board
- Start working on the bonus problem alone, then check your answer with your group members
- Put your assignment on your desk

Ready for lunch?

- Clear off your desk
- Pick things up off the floor
- Line up quietly when your table is called

sons for them much as they did in the opening scenario at the beginning of this chapter. Write the rules on the board, eliminating overlaps until a rough draft of four to six rules is developed. At this time it is important to analyze the list and add any rules that you think are critical, being sure to explain your reasons. Later, a more formal list can be written, posted prominently in the room, with copies sent home to parents.

There are several other activities to further help students understand and become committed to the rules they helped develop. These include the following:

- Have students again meet in small groups to pick one rule to focus on. They then discuss and list several specific examples of the rule as it would apply in the classroom, hallways, and playground and share their results with the class. Students might also be asked to select one of their examples to demonstrate through a brief role play.

- Ask students to independently reflect on one rule they especially value and why. Students then might share their responses using a structure such as "Think–Pair–Share" or write their responses in their journals.

- Ask students to sign a large poster or "Classroom Bill of Rights and Responsibilities" containing a list of the rules or guidelines.

Students can also be involved in developing procedures to help the class run smoothly, although it is to be expected that they won't anticipate all the procedures necessary for a smoothly running classroom. Nevertheless, students often can make useful suggestions about what to do when work is done, how to get help if one is stuck on a problem and the teacher is busy, how to leave the room to use the bathroom, and how to leave the room at the end of the day. Again, small groups of students can make suggestions regarding these procedures with the teacher incorporating some or all of the recommendations. Some students could be enlisted to make posters of the procedures, such as "What to do when you are finished with your work."

Systematically Focus on Positive Behavior

Having clear rules and procedures posted is an important step toward preventing misbehavior, but it is rarely enough by itself. As teachers or prospective teachers, we all know that a concept or skill introduced once is far from learned. Instead, for meaningful learning to take place, concepts and skills must be practiced and reinforced consistently. The same logic needs to be applied to learning rules and procedures. In this section we will examine a strategy, called PARC, that I have developed for reinforcing rules and procedures. PARC stands for praise, anticipatory guidance, reflection, and correction, four powerful steps to take that will help almost every child learn to follow rules and procedures.

Praise.   Praise should be used often during the first few weeks to let students know that we appreciate their efforts at following rules and procedures. As suggested by the following examples, praise can be directed at individuals, or the whole class:

- "OK, I want to thank everyone for remembering to raise their hands. This allowed everyone to get a turn and helped us listen to each other."
- "Great, almost everyone is in their seats and reading."
- "The room looks neat. Chairs are pushed in and I don't see any books on the floor. We're ready to go."
- "I noticed that many people are using their free time quietly. That allows others to work without interruptions and I can help those who need it."
- "Tom and George, I noticed you were sharing the supplies and materials. We didn't have enough materials to go around, so your decision to share allowed everyone to participate."

For praise to be most effective, we should provide reasons for the praise as well as a description of the behavior we are praising. Such praise is informationally rich in that it not only points out the specific behavior (using free time quietly) but also describes a consequence of the behavior or a reason that it is important (allows others to finish their work, etc). Such praise conveys the message that the rules and procedures are not arbitrary but instead, help create a classroom where respect, caring, and responsibility are valued (Deci & Ryan, 1985). Of course, as the school year progresses, the frequency of praise for following specific rules and procedures can decrease, although it should never be eliminated entirely.

Anticipatory Guidance.   In anticipatory guidance we remind students of an upcoming activity in which it is particularly important to follow a specific rule or procedure and thus avoid misbehavior or disorganization (Redl & Wineman, 1951). For example, it is much easier to remind students how they are to line up than it is to call a halt to children who have bolted for the door. Thus, just a minute or two before an important activity or transition we might focus attention on specific rules or procedures through questions or statements such as:

- "We are going to move into our cooperative groups in a moment. Who can remind us of the procedure we should follow as we get into our groups?"

- "In a minute we are going to get ready for lunch. What do we have to do to show that we are ready to line up? Why is this important?"
- "In today's activity, some people might finish early. What are the choices if you finish early and why is it important to stick to the choices?"
- "We are going to have another class join us for a video so the room will be pretty crowded. Look over our rules and see which ones you think will help us the most during this activity."

As with praise, we can reduce the use of anticipatory guidance as students become more familiar with rules and procedures. However, this may remain a much needed technique for children who are impulsive or who have short attention spans. For them we can issue private reminders as needed.

Reflection.   Reflection is the reverse side of anticipatory guidance and occurs after a particular activity. Here, we want students to reflect on or evaluate the degree to which they followed certain rules and procedures. Typical questions for reflection include the following:

- "What went well in today's discussion?"
- "What was a rule or procedure you followed especially well during the morning?"
- "I'd like you to think about our rule about using a positive tone when talking. How do you think you and the class have been doing? Why is this an important rule?"
- "Today we had many people finishing at different times. Let's examine the procedure for what to do when you finish early. What are some examples of helpful things people did today? What suggestions do you have for helping the class to follow this procedure even better?"
- "Let's take some time to reflect on all our rules and procedures. I'd like you to think of a rule or procedure that you think the class is doing a good job with and I'd also like you to think of one that needs some improvement."

Reflection can take place with students working individually, as a small group, or in a "Think–Pair–Share" (Kagan, 1993) activity with the whole class sharing afterwards, or as a large class discussion. As these examples indicate, reflection can take place after an event such as lining up, mid-way through or at the end of an activity such as a discussion, or at the end of the day or week. Taking time to reflect is a way of encouraging students to think about their behavior and its consequences and it conveys the message that you value their observations and opinions.

Correction. Correction is the final component of the PARC strategy. The judicious use of a correction strategy conveys to students that we have clear rules and procedures and that we intend to uphold them. A correction strategy points out a minor misbehavior and asks the student or class to correct the behavior right away (Englemann & Brunner, 1973) as indicated by the following two examples.

- *Example No. 1:* During a discussion Tom speaks without raising his hand. The teacher pauses and says, "Tom, your answer is correct but what is the rule about a discussion?" Tom states the rule (if he cannot recall the rule another student or the teacher restates the rule) and the teacher quickly moves on being sure to praise (through smiles, a thumbs-up gesture, or a "Thanks for raising your hand") other students for remembering to raise their hands. Later, the teacher praises Tom in like fashion when he remembers to raise his hand.

- *Example No. 2:* The desks are clear, the floor is picked up and the teacher asks the class to line up. Many students move too quickly, a chair is knocked over accidentally, and there is more than the usual amount of noise. The teacher firmly stops the class and tells everyone to return to their seats quietly and to read the poster that indicates the procedure for lining up. A student is asked to restate the procedure and the class is invited to try again and then gently praised ("OK, that's better.") when they line up correctly.

Correction strategies are especially useful during the first two months when we are most interested in helping students learn to follow the rules and procedures. However, care needs to be taken to avoid using correction too often, as this focuses attention on inappropriate student behavior.

There are other relatively simple yet powerful suggestions for promoting positive behavior that can be used in addition to PARC that are consistent with the theme of cooperative classroom management. These are briefly described here:

Write the Names of Well-Behaving Students on the Board. Establish a section on the chalkboard in full view of the class with a heading such as "Thanks for Helping." When students follow a rule or procedure, help another student, use self-control, settle down to work right away, or engage in any behavior that appears helpful, the teacher should recognize them by writing their names on the board. At the same time, you quietly thank each student (e.g., "Janet, thanks for getting started on your work right away."). Elementary teachers who successfully use this technique often try to write at least 10 student names on the board each day and then note which students were recognized at the end of the day or a class period to make sure they are not identifying the same students every day or overlooking specific students. This technique represents a dramatic shift away from writing names of misbehaving students on the board and helps teachers stay focused on positive student behavior.

Issue "Caught Being Good Cards." These cards are another way to recognize cooperative student behavior and can be used as an alternative to writing names on the board, which some middle- and secondary-level students find embarrassing. The teacher prints a number of these cards and then issues two or three per class period to different students, filling in the blank spaces with brief messages as indicated in Figure 4.2.

Encourage students to also issue "Caught Being Good" cards. Once students have become familiar with receiving them, they may be ready to take on some of this responsibility themselves. A different student each day might be enlisted to look for examples of helpful behavior and write two or three cards to students other than their good friends. The teacher would co-sign each card to add a measure of approval and to monitor what students are writing. This technique encourages students to focus on and recognize the positive behavior of their classmates. If needed, the entire class can participate in a discussion of what positive behaviors they should be on the lookout for and how to fill out a card with several sample cards placed on a bulletin board.

Enlist Students as Observers. Students can play a key role in observing their classmates during specific activities such as individual seatwork or cooperative learning. A relatively simple way to engage middle- and secondary-level students in this process is to provide a student observer with a clipboard and class list arranged by seating order. The student observer then checks each student on the list, watching each student for a count of three. If the student who is being observed is on task (working quietly if it is a seatwork task; looking at the teacher if the teacher is giving directions, or sitting with the group and interacting appropriately if the task is cooperative) through the count of three, the student observer places a "+" by the student's name as indicated by the example in Figure 4.3.

FIGURE 4.2
"Caught Being Good"
Card

Caught Being Good

TO: Kirby Smith

Thanks for: Speaking to others respectfully

From: Mr. Jones

Caught Being Caring

Notice that more than one student took a turn as the observer. Indeed, the teacher may adopt a convention that each student goes through the list two or three times and then turns the clipboard over to the next observer. Students may observe for an entire class period or a segment of the period such as seatwork or groupwork. When the activity is completed or the time period is up, the teacher or a student could compute the percentage of on-task behavior for the period. A goal of 80 percent might be established for the entire class, or the students might try to match or increase the percentage from the previous day. Although it takes time to explain and demonstrate the process of observation, students' on-task behavior often increases significantly when they know their behavior is being monitored (Broome & White, 1995).

Award Good Behavior Points to the Class.   Good behavior points can be especially helpful for classes that are hard to manage because of the high concentration of students who have difficulty following rules and procedures. This procedure is similar to writing student names on the board with the teacher being on the lookout for small examples of positive behavior. However, instead of writing a name on the board, a tally mark is made signifying a point. Individual students can earn points for the class ("John, thanks for getting to work so quickly. You earned a point for the class.") or the behavior of the entire class can earn a point ("We did a great job of

FIGURE 4.3
*Format for Student
Observation of On-Task
Behavior*

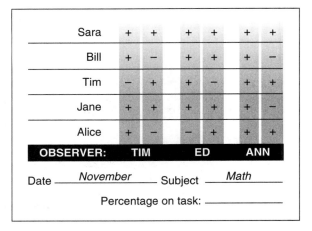

walking quietly through the halls. That's a point for the class." Or, "Everyone is doing a great job of working together in their groups. That's a point for the class."). When the class reaches a predetermined number of points, such as 10, by the end of the day or 50 for the week, the class can earn special privileges.

This technique is applicable to a variety of students and age groups. For example, a second-grade teacher might agree to read her students an extra chapter in a read-aloud book at the end of the day if the class earns 10 good behavior points. A fifth-grade teacher might allow his students to earn an extra recess or art period on Friday afternoon if the class earns 50 points for the whole week. A ninth-grade English teacher might allow her students to skip one homework assignment during the upcoming week if the class earns 50 points during the current week.

The PARC strategy and the additional techniques will help provide a solid foundation for cooperative student behavior. Another important opportunity for developing cooperative classroom management involves how we respond to conflicts between students, the second section of this chapter.

WORKING WITH STUDENTS TO DEVELOP CONFLICT RESOLUTION SKILLS

Conflict among students is almost inevitable, whether it is a dispute over who can use a book or game at the moment or what course of action will be selected for a group project. Many students respond to conflict by arguing, shouting, or grabbing, while others seek adults to mediate for them or simply become passive and withdraw. An important part of cooperative classroom management is to help students learn more constructive skills for resolving conflicts.

Conflict Resolution Required

Conducting Classroom Meetings

Nearly 30 years ago, Glasser (1969) suggested that students should participate in classroom meetings during which they would have an opportunity to discuss a range of problems and concerns in an atmosphere of respect. By having a voice in discussing actual classroom problems and concerns, Glasser believed that students would feel more significant and would also learn critical problem solving skills. This emphasis on student participation continues to be a cornerstone of Glasser's approach (1990) as well as other approaches to developing caring students (Charney, 1992).

One type of classroom meeting is a daily gathering usually conducted at the beginning of each day. The purpose of this meeting is to build a sense of community by establishing a daily ritual of sharing. Here, students generally sit in a circle with some or all of the following typically occurring:

- An opening discussion about the date and the day's events.
- An opportunity for students to share special events happening in their lives or concerns they have about what is happening at school, on the playground, etc.
- Singing a song or reading and discussing a poem, slogan, or saying.
- Asking students to reflect on something specific they can do today to make others in the class or school feel safe, respected, or valued.

Because many students do not come to school with good group discussion skills, it is important to take time to develop and promote such skills. Thus, from the very first class meeting, rules that promote listening, taking turns, and responding to each other with respect and kindness should be stressed and reinforced using the PARC strategy discussed in the previous section.

A second type of meeting is a problem-solving meeting used to identify problems and discuss possible solutions. The range of topics is diverse and includes problems in cooperative groups such as too much talking, not including others, dominating the discussion, as well as typical classroom and playground issues such as name-calling, teasing, tattling, leaving the room too messy, and monopolizing games and class materials. These are all behaviors that, as teachers, we too often try to resolve by making threats or using related tactics to try to suppress the misbehavior. Instead, Glasser (1969, 1990) suggests we pose the problem to the students in a nonjudgmental manner using a format that involves the following steps described by Charney (1992).

1. *Introduce the Problem.* Call the meeting to order, review the rules for discussion, and then make an "I notice" statement such as, "I have noticed that there has been a lot of name-calling and teasing in the hallways and just before class begins. I see that this makes some people feel bad. It is hard to have a classroom where people feel good if there is name-calling and teasing going on. I would like us to work on this problem during this week's meeting." The purpose of such an introduction is to establish a positive tone for problem solving and to spell out the problem or issue as clearly as possible in terms of its effect on people in the class.

2. *Gather Information.* Ask students to share their personal knowledge or experience with the problem under discussion, being sure to establish the ground rule that students focus on their own behavior and experience and avoid blaming others. For example, a teacher might start the discussion by saying, "Let's think about how each of us has been involved in name-calling or teasing this past week or two. Who will start by telling us whether you have been called a name and if you have done this to someone?" Keep in mind that the purpose here is not to blame or moralize but simply to determine the nature and scope of the problem.

Once everyone who wishes to volunteer has had a turn, the teacher may conclude with a brief summary of the concerns that were raised and the apparent reasons why the behavior seems to be occurring (e.g., "It seems as if there has been a lot of name-calling in the hallways and even in this class. People do this sometimes because they are upset and sometimes because they think they are just teasing, and sometimes because they don't know what else to say or do when they are called a name.").

3. *Seek Further Understanding.* Seek further insight about the behavior, focusing on questions such as, "Why does the behavior occur?" "What needs does it meet?"

4. Launch Brainstorming Session.   Ask students to propose or brainstorm possible solutions to the problem by asking a question such as, "What are other ways to meet needs that are less hurtful?" and then listing each solution. During this brainstorming step we need to avoid offering our own solutions. As Charney (1992) wisely points out, "For children to learn to solve problems, we must provide the structure and the focus, but keep our good advice to ourselves. If there is only one solution, and it is ours, the problem is not a subject for a class meeting. It is simply a mandate, and must be presented as such" (p. 84).

5. Evaluate and Choose Solutions.   In this step each solution's advantages and disadvantages may be discussed in terms of whether it is useful and realistic. Students may work in pairs or small groups to review the solutions and then come up with the ones they think will be most helpful. The entire class may then vote on one or two solutions to focus on as a class. Charney (1992) also suggests teachers ask students to spell out ways everyone in the class would be able to tell if the solution(s) were working (e.g., "Fewer people will be name-calling or teasing on the playground." "There won't be as many arguments." "People will be more friendly.").

6. Close the Meeting.   Wrap up by complimenting the students on observing the rules for class meetings, including being respectful and working hard to solve problems.

7. Revisit the Solution in Several Days.   Evaluate the effects of the solution several days later by asking students to describe any improvements they have noticed since the last class meeting or by evaluating their own behavior by answering questions such as, "How often have I engaged in name-calling this past week?" Praise students for the progress they have made and seek additional solutions if they are needed. If the problem behavior persists, students may be asked to discuss possible consequences of continued problematic behavior. The teacher may decide to meet individually with students whose behavior continues to be of concern. Possible approaches for these students are discussed in the final section of this chapter.

Glasser (1969) suggests that problem-solving meetings be convened as often as once a week for 20 to 45 minutes, depending on the age level of the students. More than one topic can be covered in a meeting, and students may request that certain items or problems be discussed at the weekly problem solving meeting. The same process works well in secondary-level classrooms but meetings may take place less frequently than once a week.

Conducting Conflict Resolution Conferences

Not all problems can wait to be addressed in weekly meetings. Sometimes disputes or arguments among two or more students break out and the situation must be addressed right away. However, rather than trying to resolve the conflict for the students and thus denying them an opportunity to practice problem-solving skills, teachers can encourage students to work out their own solutions to some problems by following a fairly simple procedure described by Jones and Jones (1995). In this procedure the teacher acts as a facilitator, guiding each student through a three-step process such as the following example of mediation between two girls:

1. Describe the Problem.   Each student is asked to describe her view of the problem and what happened that caused the other person to become upset, making sure that only one student speaks at a time (e.g., "Mara, would you start by telling what happened?"). After the students have described their views of the problem, the teacher asks each girl to repeat what the other one said (e.g. "All right, Dawn, tell us what Mara's view of the problem is."). If needed, the teacher helps each student accurately describe what the other one said.

2. Describe Feelings.   The teacher asks both students to describe their feelings, again with only one person speaking at a time (e.g. "Dawn, this time you start and tell us how you are feeling and why."). After they both have described their feelings, the teacher asks each one to identify how the other student is feeling and why ("Mara, now you tell us how Dawn is feeling and why.").

3. Identify Fair Solutions.   At this point the teacher asks each student to take turns naming a fair or helpful way to solve the conflict (e.g., "OK, now let's each think of one fair way to solve this that will meet everyone's needs. We'll make a list and then you can decide on the best solution for you."). The teacher lists each solution as it is identified and, if necessary, also offers a suggestion. After several solutions have been listed, the girls are asked to agree on which solution they will try. To further solidify the agreement, they may be asked to shake hands and/or sign an agreement to put their chosen solution into action.

This three-step process won't work if the students are so upset that their ability to think and discuss with reason is restricted. Therefore, a cooling-off period is sometimes needed before students are asked to engage in this process.

Training Students in Conflict Resolution Skills

Once a procedure for resolving conflicts such as the one mentioned in the previous section has been identified, it can be introduced to students through a series of lessons focusing on conflict resolution skills. Simple conflicts such as the following can be presented to students as examples:

Marcus and Juan arrive at the computer terminal at the same time. It is the only computer left of the four in the classroom and both students want to use it. An argument ensues, with each student believing it is his turn to use it.

To develop skills in identifying conflicts and possible solutions, students could be placed into groups of two or three to discuss questions such as (1) What is the conflict? (2) What are three different outcomes that might happen if Marcus and Juan don't use cooperative conflict resolution skills? (3) What are three cooperative or helpful ways Marcus and Juan could solve this conflict? Groups could also be asked to pick one of their cooperative solutions to demonstrate to the class through a brief role play.

A variety of relatively simple, age-appropriate conflict situations can be developed quite easily by simply observing typical conflicts that occur between students. A list of cooperative ways to solve conflicts (e.g., flipping a coin, developing a schedule for the week, sharing, taking turns) can be developed and displayed on a poster or bulletin board.

Once students have had several opportunities to discuss and role play different conflict situations, including how to follow the three basic steps listed previously, they can be encouraged to use the techniques to solve actual problems when they arise. To facilitate this process, some teachers develop a conflict corner or center that lists the conflict resolution steps and different techniques for solving conflicts cooperatively. Students may be asked to go to the corner at a designated time to try to resolve a conflict by themselves or with the teacher or another student serving as a facilitator. Again, the role of the facilitator is to help the students go through the actual steps, not to offer solutions. Students may also be requested to complete a "conflict contract" such as the one in Figure 4.4.

Closely related to the development of conflict resolution skills is the training of peer mediators or conflict managers (Calhoon, 1988; Roderick, 1988; Johnson, Johnson, & Bartlett, 1991). Typically, mediators are trained in how to approach students who are engaged in conflict to see if they want to participate in a mediation or conflict resolution activity. If the students agree to participate, then the student mediators employ a process similar to the three steps already described. Mediators are not discipline monitors and do not try to settle disputes unless the students involved are willing to participate in that process.

WORKING WITH STUDENTS TO SOLVE INDIVIDUAL BEHAVIOR PROBLEMS

While it is true that many behavior problems can be averted by using the techniques reviewed in the previous two sections, it is also true that a few students may require more focused efforts on the part of the classroom

FIGURE 4.4
Conflict Contract

Work together to try to solve your conflict. Take turns answering each question.

1. *What we disagree about:*

    Student #1 _____

    Student #2 _____

2. *How we are feeling:*

    Student #1 _____

    Student #2 _____

3. *What each of us would like to have happen:*

    Student #1 _____

    Student #2 _____

4. *Two or three helpful solutions or options we could try:*

    _____

    _____

5. *We both agree to try:*

    _____

    _____

Signed _____ and _____ Date _____

teacher. In this section we will explore several approaches useful for students who misbehave frequently, despite our efforts at prevention. These techniques will be consistent with the theme of cooperative classroom management in that, whenever possible, they attempt to engage students in the process of improving their own behavior and, ultimately, developing increased self-control.

Improving Participation in Cooperative Groups

An important concern of teachers who use cooperative learning is how to respond to students whose behavior may inhibit the effectiveness of a group. Some of these behaviors include dominating or controlling the discussion, excluding some students from participation, diminishing the contributions of others through put-downs, only passively participating in the group, or refusing to be a part of a group activity. Keeping the size of cooperative groups small enough to ensure active participation as well as making sure that potential "problem" students are placed in groups with strong, positively behaving students is a good place to start (Stainback, Stainback, Etscheidt, and Doud, 1986). I recall one dramatic illustration in which a high school English teacher placed a disruptive male student with three assertive, task-oriented females. When the male student began to speak in a loud voice or make inappropriate comments, the other students were quick to firmly and successfully refocus the student on the task.

In addition to the suggestions regarding group size and composition, Kagan (1993) suggests that we look at specific roles that might help students perform more appropriately. Some of these roles are described in Figure 4.5. Although roles are often used during specific cooperative activities to help all students focus on certain key skills such as including everyone, these same roles can be used to help specific students whose behavior is problematic. For example, the student who dominates or controls might be given the role of encourager, gatekeeper, or checker in an effort to help that student bring others into the discussion. The student who attends the group willingly but participates only minimally might be given the role of recorder or checker in an attempt to increase that student's active participation. Students who are frequently loud or noisy could be given the role of noise monitor.

Students who refuse to participate in group activities can present a much greater challenge. Sometimes they can be offered a role that might seem attractive to them or they can be asked to observe several different groups to provide you, the teacher, with useful information about how each group is progressing. Ultimately, students cannot and should not be forced to participate although they should certainly be held accountable for their share of the work the groups are doing. Some students who initially refuse to participate recognize that it takes more effort to do the work alone and eventually participate more willingly.

In addition to the judicious application of roles to help certain students, Kagan (1993) describes other helpful techniques. One of these is the use of **talking chips.** With this technique, each student in the group may be given four or five chips or cards. Each time the student talks, he or she has to turn in one chip or card. When all four cards or chips are used, the student cannot talk for the remainder of the time period. A different way to use talking chips is to establish a rule that at least two other people in the group have to talk and thus lay down a chip or card, before the same person can talk again. This technique has the effect of regulating communication and ensuring a basic level of participation within each group.

Other chips such as **praise chips, paraphrase chips,** and **encouragement chips** can be used in a similar fashion. For example, if the teacher wants students to work on the skill of paraphrasing the contributions of others before speaking, each student can be given one or two paraphrase chips to use during the activity. At the end of the activity the class totals up the number of paraphrase chips that were used. Students are encouraged

FIGURE 4.5

Sample Roles for Students in Cooperative Groups

Gatekeeper: The job of the gatekeeper is to make sure that each person in the group has a turn and that no one person does all the talking. The gate keeper notices who is not participating and asks for their opinions or ideas.

"What do you think, Sally?"

"Jim, do you agree with that answer?"

Taskmaster: The role of the taskmaster is to keep the group on task and focusing on the assignment. The taskmaster makes sure each step is followed or each question is answered.

"Let's all take a look at the first problem."

"I think we need to get back to our task."

Cheerleader: The role of the cheerleader is to make sure people in the group are encouraged and feel appreciated.

"That's a helpful idea, Tom."

"Let's all tell Tammy how much we appreciate her hard work."

Checker: The job of the checker is to make sure everyone agrees with an answer or everyone understands how to solve a problem.

"Jane, can you show us how to do problem 3?"

"Okay, give a thumbs up if you agree with the decision."

Observer: The job of the observer is to count or write down specific things that people in the group do that the whole class is working on.

If the class is working on making positive statements about each other's contributions during group acitivities, then the observer might make a tally mark each time a group member makes a positive statement such as, "I like that idea," "That's helpful," or "Thanks," in response to another student in the group.

Noise monitor: The task of the noise monitor is to make sure that the group is not getting too loud or disturbing other groups.

"Let's keep our voices down so others can work."

"We need to remember our inside voices."

Adapted from Kagan, 1993

to practice the skill of paraphrasing by striving for a class goal or by trying to exceed their previous total. Artificial devices such as these chips might make students feel self-conscious and possibly inhibit discussion. However, used occasionally, they can be an effective way to focus attention on specific cooperative learning skills.

Another promising technique to help students learn specific social and cooperative skills is the use of **video feedback**. Salend (1995) suggests that students practice specific behaviors such as listening, taking turns, or solving conflicts constructively by participating in videotaped role plays. The teacher replays the role play and encourages students to analyze their appropriate and inappropriate behavior.

Recognizing Goals of Student Misbehavior

Some students misbehave often and in predictable ways. Having some understanding of why students misbehave can help us cope with difficult students and plan long-term strategies for working with them. One framework for understanding patterns and motives for misbehavior is provided by Dreikurs and his colleagues (Dreikurs, Grunwald, & Pepper, 1982). Dreikurs suggests that a small percentage of students find it difficult to fulfill their needs for recognition, power, and approval through typical school activities. Instead, they may engage in misbehavior to gain attention, control, revenge, or withdrawal.

According to Dreikurs, we can determine a student's goal of misbehavior by carefully observing the student's behavior as well as our own reactions to the student. For example, **attention-oriented** students often misbehave to gain recognition from adults, even if the recognition is less than positive or outright critical. These students may talk out of turn, continually ask for help, or make inappropriate comments. Frequently we respond to their misbehavior by giving them attention in the form of reprimands because we feel annoyed or frustrated with their continual demands on our attention. This inadvertent attention can easily reinforce the student's misbehavior, thus creating a vicious cycle.

Control-oriented students often refuse our requests and defy our authority. They may view defiance as a way of asserting their own power and frequently engage us in what Dreikurs refers to as a "battle of the wills." Students who behave this way often make us feel threatened and angry and a typical response may be to try to force a student to comply with our requests through threats or other forms of pressure. While such efforts may occasionally succeed in getting the student to comply, they often escalate the battle of the wills thus creating another vicious cycle of student refusal or resistance followed by increased teacher demands which occasionally end in angry confrontations.

Revenge-oriented students seem less concerned with attention or control. Instead, their goal is to inflict emotional or physical pain on others through put-downs, name-calling, defacing of property, or other more subtle behaviors. The fundamental perspective of revenge-oriented students is that they feel pain and anger in themselves which they in turn create in others through their behavior. Not surprisingly, revenge-oriented students often make teachers feel hurt, and they, in turn, may respond to these students in hurtful ways through threats, sarcasm, or anger. Such responses often confirm the revenge-oriented student's belief that hurtful behavior is both acceptable and commonplace.

Withdrawal or assumed disability is the final goal of misbehavior. Students with this goal have given up on school or on specific subjects, believing they are incapable of learning. They are rarely disruptive or defiant. Instead, they may sit quietly drawing pictures or flipping through magazines, avoiding engagement in classroom activities. We often try to win the involvement of assumed disability students by creating individualized learning activities or by responding to them with large doses of enthusiasm and praise. However, these initial attempts to reach out are often rejected and many teachers soon feel discouraged and reduce their expectations.

Although not every student's misbehavior can be explained by Dreikurs' framework, it does help us understand that student misbehavior may be goal-directed and have a self-protective intention (Foster-Johnson, & Dunlap, 1993). Thus, repetitive misbehavior may be a signal that the student is trying to meet his or her needs for attention, recognition, or self-determination, but has not learned appropriate, socially acceptable ways of doing so. Approaching students with this understanding in mind may prevent us from falling into unconstructive patterns of responses or vicious cycles which tend to worsen the misbehavior.

Typical vicious cycles include the following:

- Reacting continually to the inappropriate behavior of attention-oriented students.
- Engaging in frequent confrontations with control-oriented students.
- Responding to revenge-oriented students with sarcasm punishments, or avoidance.
- Giving up on assumed disability students.

Developing Constructive Responses to Students Who Misbehave

While students who exhibit one or more of the four goals of misbehavior present a clear challenge to our cooperative management skills, there are specific techniques that can help. The following list represents a compilation of suggestions presented by a number of writers in the area of classroom management (Dreikurs, Grunwald, & Pepper, 1982; Glass, 1992; Jones & Jones, 1995; Wolfgang, 1995). Although some techniques are listed under a particular problem area, the same techniques are often useful for many other students.

Attention-oriented students need help learning more acceptable ways to gain recognition and attention. The following techniques can help accomplish this goal:

- Avoid responding to attention-oriented students as much as possible when they are engaging in mild forms of misbehavior.
- "Catch them being good." Quietly notice and praise their appropriate behavior.
- Find ways to give students recognition through legitimate classroom jobs and responsibilities.
- Seek out a moment or two each day to talk with the students. This will help them understand that you are interested in them as individuals and may reduce their need to misbehave to gain attention.

- When students talk too much, ask too many questions, or engage in other easily identifiable minor misbehaviors, consider techniques similar to talking chips (Kagan, 1993). Ask them privately to identify how many times they will need to talk out of turn or request help during a given lesson or period. Then, ask them to keep track by making a tally mark on a piece of paper each time they demonstrate the behavior. Younger students might be required to hand you a chip instead of keeping a tally. Praise students for keeping within their established quotas and encourage them to gradually decrease the quota.

Control-oriented students need to be able to experience legitimate forms of power without having to resort to inappropriate behavior such as defiance. The following techniques often prove helpful for these students:

- Give students reasonable choices. Allow some choice in what assignments need to be done (e.g., select any 10 practice problems on the page), how they are to be done, where the student may work, and whether the student can work alone or with a partner.
- Give students jobs where they regularly experience legitimate control and responsibility. Jobs many students enjoy include working as a library assistant, tutoring younger children regularly, or helping other adults such as the art teacher or school custodian.
- Avoid arguments and confrontations with students by walking away from them if they begin to argue, or by using the "broken record" technique (Silberman & Wheelan, 1980) of continually restating the rules, procedures, or consequences in a calm monotone if a student continues to challenge you, or by putting off discussion to a more convenient time and place such as the end of the period.
- Develop a behavior contract. Meet with a student privately to discuss specific behaviors you would like the student to demonstrate each day (e.g, starting math without complaining, completing math work on time, answering the teacher's questions in a positive tone). Develop a contract or agreement in which the student may earn a certain privilege each day or week for meeting the contract. For example, if the student demonstrates those three behaviors during math period, then he or she may take the last 15 minutes of the day and help the school librarian. Encourage the student to discuss with you the behaviors to improve as well as the possible rewards to promote a sense of cooperation and student ownership.
- Establish and maintain clear limits and consequences. For example, incomplete work must be made up after school or during recess. Impose consequences or limits in a calm, matter-of-fact manner.

Revenge-oriented students need to learn more appropriate ways to express their frustration and anger. The following techniques may prove helpful:

- Attempt to build self-esteem by recognizing and promoting students' positive skills, qualities, and abilities.

- Provide encouragement when students demonstrate appropriate academic or social behavior by privately telling them that you noticed their behavior and appreciate their effort.

- Realize that revenge-oriented students may be wary of relationships because of their lack of trust. Respect their need for some emotional distance and be cautious about overpraising them as they may be unfamiliar and uncomfortable with this type of recognition.

- Teach all students, including revenge-oriented students, constructive ways to deal with conflicts and anger as described in a previous section.

- Model appropriate ways to respond to misbehavior. Respond to hurtful or revenge-oriented behavior calmly. Avoid making threats or giving out punishments on the spur of the moment. Instead, develop a clear set of consequences for certain misbehaviors such as hitting others or name-calling before they occur and review them privately with the student, indicating that hurting others cannot be tolerated. Avoid carrying a grudge, and try to begin the next class period or day with a clean slate.

Students who practice withdrawal assume they are incapable of learning and feel deeply discouraged about their abilities. Teachers need to help such students experience success and regain a sense of competence and confidence. These students need teachers who:

- Encourage and reward small bits of improvement.

- Maintain enthusiasm and a belief that students can learn.

- Employ games, contracts, progress charts, and other motivational devices to keep learning exciting.

- Encourage students to demonstrate their knowledge through reports, projects, and other approaches that are based on their strengths and interests rather than their weaknesses.

Developing Systematic Feedback Programs

In addition to the many techniques just presented, students whose behavior is problematic often profit from systematic behavior change programs that provide frequent feedback on their classroom performance. Feedback, or knowledge of how well we perform can be a powerful motivator (Smith, Young, West, Morgan & Rhode, 1988; West et al., 1995). Two techniques for providing systematic feedback, self-monitoring, and daily progress cards, will be discussed in this section. Each of these techniques can be used in a manner consistent with cooperative classroom management if the teacher uses a problem-solving process that includes student participation. A typical process described by Glasser (1969) and others (Kaplan, 1991) involves (1) meeting privately and asking the student to describe his or her behavior and then adding your own observations, perhaps by using an "I noticed" statement; (2) discussing the effect of the student's behavior on the student's performance and/or others in the class; (3) identifying more appropriate ways of behaving; (4) developing and practicing a plan or strategy for improvement; and (5) evaluating, and if necessary, modifying the plan.

Self-Monitoring. Self-monitoring involves counting how often we exhibit a behavior we are trying to change. For example, if we are trying to increase the number of laps we swim each day, we might keep a daily chart of laps and the amount of time those laps took to swim. Similarly, if we are trying to recognize or praise appropriate student behavior more frequently, we might make a simple tally mark on a piece of paper or clipboard each time we say something such as, "Thanks for raising your hand," or "You have really been working hard on this project." Most of us, including students, want to see ourselves as improving in areas that matter to us. Self-monitoring procedures can provide the structure that is sometimes needed to bring about such improvement (McLaughlin, 1983; Smith, Young, West, Morgan, & Rhode, 1988).

We can teach students to monitor their own behavior by first helping them become aware of the behavior they need to improve. This can be done by initiating a problem-solving discussion and identifying the specific problematic behaviors. For example, there are steps teachers can take with students who engage in identifiable misbehaviors such as talking out of turn, speaking in an angry voice instead of using polite words such as "Please" or "May I," taking things without permission, or not completing assigned tasks such as a math worksheet. First the teacher can help students learn to accurately describe the desirable and undesirable behavior by asking them to demonstrate both the appropriate and inappropriate behavior and discussing possible role playing several examples of each. Once the students clearly understand the difference between the appropriate and inappropriate behavior, teachers can ask them to keep a tally of their own behavior by crossing out a number under the appropriate heading each time they demonstrate either the positive or the negative behavior. They can use a tally chart such as the one presented in Figure 4.6, adapted from Jones and Jones (1995).

Many students improve their behavior almost immediately through this procedure while a few others may need additional steps. One procedure is to select one or two specific time periods or activity periods each day and have the teacher and student independently keep a tally of the positive and inappropriate behaviors during that time. Students could be encouraged and thanked for accurately observing their behavior and for demonstrating a minimum number of behaviors under each heading such as "at least two positive statements during an activity period and no more than one negative

FIGURE 4.6
Sample Self-Monitoring Form

Speaking Politely

Count Your Behaviors

I spoke in a polite voice	**I spoke in an angry voice**
"Please," "Thank-you,"	*"No," "I don't want to!"*
"Yes, I will."	*"This work is terrible."*
1 2 3 4 5 6 7 8 9 10	1 2 3 4 5 6 7 8 9 10
11 12 13 14 15 16 17 18 19 20	11 12 13 14 15 16 17 18 19 20

---

statement during the period". Another possibility is to have the student work with a well behaved student who can serve as a "buddy" or partner. The buddy might remind the student of the behaviors he or she needs to tally and might also assist with the tallying procedure.

Daily Progress Cards.   List the specific classroom behaviors or tasks the student is expected to complete each class period along with a rating system that indicates the degree to which the student meets each objective. For example, a teacher might notice that a student consistently has difficulty with behaviors such as (1) completing math or reading seatwork regardless of whether the student works alone or in a cooperative group; (2) lining up without pushing, running, or hitting; (3) talking in turn; and (4) remaining calm when frustrated. With such a clear description of these behaviors, the teacher can convert them into a daily progress card such as the one in Figure 4.7.

To initiate a daily progress card program with a student, the teacher first reviews the behaviors privately with the student making sure the student understands how to demonstrate some of the appropriate behaviors. If needed, the student and teacher can practice or role play lining up quietly, raising one's hand to gain attention or waiting until an appropriate time to interrupt, and trying to stay calm when upset by taking a deep breath or counting to 10.

Once the student clearly understands the behaviors to work on, the teacher can discuss a procedure for filling out the progress card. Typically, progress cards are completed at logical points such as the end of a class period or the end of the morning. The progress card is often placed on the student's desk each morning, although some students prefer to have the teacher keep it. At the designated time such as the end of the morning, the teacher and student meet for one or two minutes to review progress. Together, the student and teacher evaluate the degree to which the student completed his or her jobs using a rating system such as the one in Figure 4.6. Students can take increasing responsibility for completing the charts

FIGURE 4.7
Sample Daily Progress Card

| Student | Tim Smith | Date | January 15 |

My Job   **How I Did**

1. I need to complete my reading seatwork by 10:15 without
   being reminded by the teacher.   _____

2. I need to complete my math seatwork by 11:00 without
   being reminded by the teacher.   _____

3. I need to line up for recess quietly without running, pushing,
   or hitting.   _____

4. I need to raise my hand and wait to be called on before I talk.   _____

5. I need to use self-control if I get upset. Instead of yelling or
   arguing, I will try to stay calm.   _____

   Key: 3 = Great! I did my job without any reminders.
          2 = Good. I did my job but I needed one or two reminders.
          1 = Needs Improvement. I need to try harder!

as their skill and motivation improve, until they finally engage in self-rating. When self-rating is used, the teacher signs each student's rating to indicate his or her agreement. In the case of a disagreement, the teacher can write in his or her own rating. Usually students no longer need the structure provided by daily progress cards when their behavior becomes consistently appropriate.

Rewarding Positive Behavior

While feedback alone can be a strong motivator for students, additional incentives sometimes need to be applied with students whose misbehavior is deeply entrenched. Certainly, a logical place to start is providing praise and encouragement to the student as you are completing a daily progress chart or reviewing a self-monitoring form. In addition, a student can earn a mutually agreed upon reward when the student reaches a goal agreed upon by both of you, such as "at least two positive statements during a morning and no more than one negative statement," or earns a specified number of daily points on a daily progress card such as 11 out of 15. Typical rewards include a sticker; a brief time to play a game, color, or work on the computer; or running an errand for the teacher. Privileges for slightly older students such as a free homework pass or working as a library or PE assistant for a class period may require meeting a specified goal for a longer period of time, such as five days in a row or five out of six days.

Parents are often pleased to receive daily communication from teachers and sending a completed self-monitoring form or daily progress card home at the end of each day can bring about significant improvement in student behavior (Imber, Imber, & Rothstein, 1979). To initiate such a program, a phone call or conference should be conducted to determine whether the parent is interested in receiving daily feedback. Assuming there is interest, discussion might then focus on details such as setting up a time each afternoon or evening to review the card, what the parent should do if the student does not bring a card home, and what rewards might be used if praise and encouragement need to be supplemented. Typical rewards might include nightly television privileges for reaching a daily goal, an allowance program whereby the student earns a portion of his or her weekly allowance for each day a goal is reached, or a special privilege at the end of the week for reaching the goal on at least four out of five days.

School-home feedback programs are not always successful because they rely on consistency and a positive outlook on the part of both the teacher and the parent. These programs will have little if any effect if the parent is not interested nor available to review the student's progress each day or if the teacher is inconsistent in completing and sending the form home or sends frequent complaints home. Finally, caution is indicated if there is suspicion that the student comes from an abusive home, because the parent may use less-than-perfect school behavior as an excuse to punish. In some of these cases the guidance counselor or building principal can assume the role of the parent and the daily checklist can be sent to that person who might meet briefly with the student at the end of the day to review progress and offer encouragement.

CONCLUSION

Cooperative classroom management is based on the premise that important student needs for belonging, power, recognition, and freedom can best be met in a classroom in which the teacher makes a genuine and skillful effort to include students from the very first day in the process of establishing rules and helping to solve everyday conflicts and problems. Three broad topics were reviewed:

1.   Working with students to prevent conflicts by establishing clear classroom rules and procedures, and systematically promoting positive behavior. This area provides a foundation for increased cooperation among students and between teachers and students.

2.   Working with students to develop conflict resolution skills so that they will become better able to resolve conflicts in a cooperative manner.

Daily classroom meetings, weekly problem solving meetings, and specific instruction on how to solve conflicts are some tools for conflict resolution.

3.   Working with students to solve individual behavior problems. Individual students can be helped to work more productively in cooperative groups and other settings by understanding their motivation for misbehaving, giving them certain roles in cooperative groups, and using self-monitoring procedures and daily checklists.

◆   ◆   ◆

QUESTIONS AND ACTIVITIES

1.   Define cooperative classroom management in your own words. What are the main ingredients of this approach and how does it differ from more traditional approaches?

2.   In groups of three, make a poster of positively stated classroom rules you think would help make your classroom (college or public school) a safe, cooperative place. Display your poster and discuss with the class how you might implement PARC and other techniques to promote rules during the first few weeks of school.

3.   Assume you have a class of active students who do not seem to be following your classroom rules and procedures as well as you think they should. Design a class reward system based on "good-behavior points." Discuss the specific behaviors for which the class will receive points and identify specific rewards toward which the class might work.

4.   Outline a sequence of brief activities designed to teach students conflict resolution skills. Develop additional skits for discussion and role playing and identify several children's stories you might read aloud to help students focus on skills such as sharing, taking turns, and compromising.

5.   Discuss specific ways you might use a video camera to help students learn more effective cooperative skills. What are some potential problems with this approach and how might they be overcome?

6.   Discuss Rudolph Dreikurs' goals of misbehavior. What are the differences between attention- and control-oriented students? Make a list of specific strategies and techniques that would be helpful for these students.

7.   Participate in a discussion using talking chips and paraphrase chips. Discuss your reactions as well as the reactions of others in your group. Discuss how these and related techniques might be used to help students improve their group participation skills.

8. Design a self-monitoring form for a student with a particular type of misbehavior. Assume you have had a discussion with the student and that she is willing to try to improve. List the positive behavior with one or two examples and the negative behavior with one or two examples and then describe how you will teach the student to use this procedure.

SUGGESTED READINGS

Books

Charney, R. (1992). *Teaching children to care*. Greenfield, MA: Northeast Foundation for Children.

Glasser, W. (1985). *Control theory in the classroom*. New York: Harper and Row.

Mendler, A. (1988). *Discipline with dignity*. Alexandria, VA: Association for Supervision and Curriculum Development.

REFERENCES

Broome, S., & White, R. (1995). The many uses of videotape in classrooms serving youth with behavioral disorders. *Teaching Exceptional Children, 27*(3), 10–13.

Calhoon, P. (1988). Mediator magic. *Educational Leadership, 45*, 93–94.

Canter, L., & Canter, M. (1976). *Assertive discipline*. Santa Monica, CA: Canter and Associates, Inc.

Charney, R. (1992). *Teaching children to care*. Greenfield, MA: Northeast Foundation for Children.

Curwin, R., & Mendler, A. (1988). Packaged discipline programs: Let the buyer beware. *Educational Leadership, 46*(2), 68–71.

Deci, E., & Ryan, R. (1985). *Intrinsic motivation and self-determination in human behavior*. New York: Plenum.

Dreikurs, R., Grunwald, B., & Pepper, F. (1982). Maintaining sanity in the classroom. *Classroom management techniques* (2nd ed.). New York: Harper and Row.

Englemann, S., & Brunner, J. (1973). *Distar reading 1*. Chicago: Science Research Associates.

Evertson, C., & Harris, A. (1992). What we know about managing classrooms. *Educational Leadership, 47*(7), 74–78.

Evertson, C., Emmer, E., Clements, B., & Worsham, M. (1994). *Classroom management for elementary teachers* (3rd ed.). Boston: Allyn and Bacon.

Foster-Johnson, L., & Dunlap, G. (1993). Using functional assessment to develop effective, individualized interventions for challenging behaviors. *Teaching Exceptional Children, 25*(3), 44–50.

Glass, R. (1992). Classroom management strategies for students with behavior disorders. In L. Cohen (Ed.), *Children with exceptional needs in regular classrooms.* Washington, DC: National Education Association.

Glasser, W. (1969). *Schools without failure.* New York: Harper and Row.

Glasser, W. (1985). *Control theory in the classroom.* New York: Harper and Row.

Glasser, W. (1990). *The quality school: Managing students without coercion.* New York: Harper and Row.

Imber, S., Imber, R., & Rothstein, C. (1979). Modifying independent work habits: An effective teacher-parent communication program. *Exceptional Children, 46,* 218–221.

Johnson, R., Johnson D., & Bartlett, J. (1991). *Our mediation notebook.* Edina, MN: Interaction Books.

Jones, V., & Jones, L. (1995). *Comprehensive classroom management: Creating positive learning environments for all students* (4th ed.). Boston: Allyn and Bacon.

Kagan, S. (1993). *Cooperative learning.* San Juan Capistrano, CA: Resources for Teachers, Inc.

Kaplan, J. (1991). *Beyond behavior modification: A cognitive-behavioral approach to behavior management in the school* (2nd ed.). Austin, TX: Pro-Ed.

Kounin, J. (1970). *Discipline and group management in classrooms.* New York: Holt, Rinehart, and Winston.

McLaughlin, T. (1983). Effects of self-recording for on-task and academic responding: A long-term analysis. *Journal of Special Education Technology, 6,* 5–11.

Redl, F., & Wineman, D. (1951). *Controls from within: Techniques for the treatment of the aggressive child.* New York: Free Press.

Roderick, T. (1988). Johnny can learn to negotiate. *Educational Leadership, 45,* 86–90.

Salend, S., (1995). Using videocassette recorder technology in special education classrooms. *Teaching Exceptional Children, 27*(3), 4–9.

Silberman, M., & Wheelan, S. (1980). *How to discipline without feeling guilty.* Champaign, IL: Research Press.

Stainback, W., Stainback, S., Etscheidt, S., & Doud, J. (1986). A nonintrusive intervention for acting out behavior. *Teaching Exceptional Children, 19*(4), 12–16.

Smith, D., Young, R., West, R., Morgan, D., & Rhode, G. (1988). Reducing the disruptive behavior of junior high students: A classroom self-management procedure. *Behavior Disorders, 13,* 213–239.

West, R., Young, R., Callahan, K., Fister, S., Kemp, K., Freston, J., & Lovitt, T. (1995). The musical clocklight. Encouraging positive behavior. *Teaching Exceptional Children, 27*(2), 46–51.

Wolfgang, C. (1995). *Solving discipline problems: Methods and models for today's teachers.* Boston: Allyn and Bacon.

SECTION 3

EXTENDING AND EVALUATING COOPERATIVE LEARNING

CHAPTER 5   *Multiple Methods and Modifications for Diversity*

CHAPTER 6   *Assessment and Problem Solving in Cooperative Learning*

CHAPTER 5

MULTIPLE METHODS AND MODIFICATIONS FOR DIVERSITY

This chapter is designed to:

◆ Acquaint you with five important cooperative learning methods that will contribute to your theoretical understanding and your practical application of the techniques.

◆ Introduce you to a variety of cooperative learning formats, including fairly unstructured and informal activities as well as more complex, formally organized activities.

◆ Help you build your repertoire of cooperative learning techniques that are consistent with your personal educational philosophy and approach to teaching.

◆ Introduce you to strategies for modifying cooperative learning to a diversity of learners, including students with disabilities.

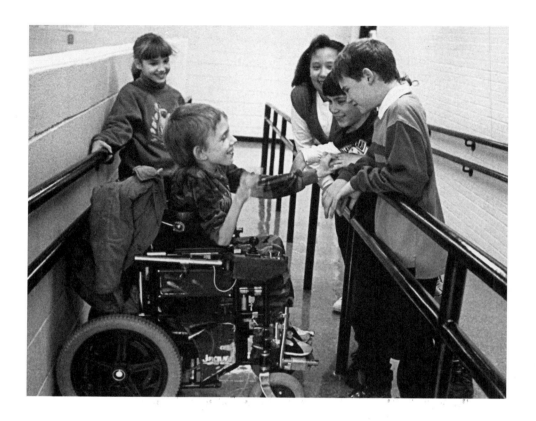

METHODS OF COOPERATIVE LEARNING

Chapters 3 and 4 covered the practical aspects of implementing cooperative learning to improve students' achievement, interpersonal skills, and behavior. After the basics of cooperative learning have been mastered, a wide range of opportunities exists for extending cooperative learning in an array of subject areas. This chapter elaborates on five methods of cooperative learning that teachers have found useful. As with most instructional interventions or behavior management systems, no one method or model of cooperative learning is perfect for all situations. Rather, different approaches are suited to different conditions. As Neil Davidson, professor of curriculum and instruction at the University of Maryland and president of the International Association for the Study of Cooperation in Education, stated:

> In contrast to some other innovations, there is no single guru on cooperative learning who is accepted on all points. The field has a number of diverse viewpoints, which can result in arguments over which approach is better or more "right." However, diversity can be viewed as a source of strength in terms of flexibility and mutually enriching perspectives, with all approaches having more similarities than differences. (Davidson, 1994, p. 13)

Researchers have suggested that it takes three to five years to become skilled at implementing cooperative learning in the classroom, so it is wise to first master the fundamentals of cooperative learning and then assimilate various methods over time. As your repertoire of approaches gradually increases, so will your confidence. While considering the methods and modifications introduced in this chapter, try to determine the unique aspects of each one, the conditions that each approach is best suited for, and the characteristics that are common among all of the approaches.

THE LEARNING TOGETHER MODEL: DAVID JOHNSON AND ROGER JOHNSON

David W. Johnson is professor of educational psychology and Roger T. Johnson is professor of curriculum and instruction, both at the University of Minnesota in Minneapolis. The Johnsons know a great deal about competition and cooperation because they grew up in the same family.

> We are brothers, a year-and-a-half apart in age, and we competed intensely with each other for about 18 years. At the same time, for much of our childhood we lived on a farm in Indiana, working together in the fields, sharing the chores, and generally cooperating with each other to "get the job done." We would compete to see who sat by the window in the car, who got the most ice cream, and who would determine whether our bedroom light was on or off.

David and Roger Johnson

Having experienced what competition among brothers can do, the two have cooperated while at the University of Minnesota by combining David's work in social psychology and Roger's work in curriculum and instruction, science education, and inquiry learning. Since the 1960s they have been reviewing the research, conducting studies, and training teachers on the use of classroom cooperation. The Johnsons are co-directors of the Cooperative Learning Center at the University of Minnesota. With more than 300 research articles and 30 books published, the Johnsons are the most prolific writers on cooperative learning as well as an array of related topics such as conflict resolution, and relationships among diverse team members (Johnson & Johnson, 1989).

Features of Learning Together

The approach to cooperative learning presented in this textbook is based on the Learning Together model, so at this point in your reading, you should be familiar with it. During the past 25 years, the bulk of David and Roger Johnson's research has involved looking at how students learn and interact in individualistic, competitive, and cooperative situations in classrooms. Their conceptualization of cooperative learning incorporates five key features: (1) positive interdependence, (2) individual accountability, (3) face-to-face interaction, (4) direct teaching of cooperative skills, and (5) monitoring and processing of groupwork. The Johnsons stress the importance of **directly teaching students the cooperative skills** that are essential to group functioning. Major categories of cooperative skills addressed in their work include communication skills, building and maintaining trust, controversy and conflict management skills, leadership skills, and peer mediation skills. The emphasis on teaching students cooperative skills is a unique and important feature of the Johnsons' work.

Another aspect of the Learning Together model that sets it apart from other approaches is the elaboration of a variety of **techniques for accomplishing positive interdependence** among group members. You will recall that six of these techniques were discussed in Chapter 3 (e.g., group rewards, identity interdependence, role interdependence). The Johnsons place particular importance on student reflection and goal setting, which takes place in the latter phase of a cooperative lesson or activity. They refer to these activities as **processing,** with the teacher providing input to students based on informal or formal observations made during the cooperative activity.

The Learning Together model has been referred to as the "conceptual" approach to cooperative learning because it is based on the assumption that teachers can learn the key principles of structuring effective cooperative learning activities and then apply them to suit the needs of their own students. The teacher's role is that of an academic expert and classroom manager, and in this capacity, he or she is able to experiment with the procedures in ways that are compatible with his or her predominant teaching philosophy and style.

Learning Together offers an array of group structures, ranging from formal structures, such as laboratory groups or cooperative peer editing groups, to informal activities such as cooperative note-taking pairs or closure-focussed discussion pairs. The generic cooperative learning lesson structures are content-free and may be used with any curriculum and any subject area. Johnson and Johnson (1991) present more than 20 formal and informal structures in their book *Cooperative Learning Lesson Structures*. Samples of lesson structures appear in Figure 5.1 and Figure 5.2.

FIGURE 5.1
Learning Together Model: Peer Editing

Whenever you assign a paper or composition to be written by students, cooperative learning groups should be used. Whenever we give an assignment that requires students to write a paper, for example, we ask them to hand in a paper revised on the basis of two reviews by a member of their cooperative learning group. In other words, we use a process writing procedure requiring a cooperative group.

Task: Write a composition.

Cooperative: All group members must verify that each member's composition is perfect according to the criteria set by the teacher. One of their scores for the composition will be the total number of errors made by the pair (the number of errors in their composition plus the number of errors in their partner's composition). An individual score on the quality of the composition may also be given.

Procedure:
1. The teacher assigns students to pairs with at least one good reader in each pair. The task of writing individual compositions is given.
2. Student A describes to Student B what he or she is planning to write. Student B listens carefully, probes with a set of questions, and outlines Student A's composition. The written outline is given to Student A.
3. This procedure is reversed with Student B describing what he or she is going to write and Student A listening and completing an outline of Student B's composition, which is then given to Student B.
4. The students research individually the material they need to write their compositions, keeping an eye out for material useful to their partner.
5. The two students work together to write the first paragraph of each composition to ensure that they both have a clear start on their compositions.
6. The students write their compositions individually.
7. When completed, the students proofread each other's compositions, making corrections in capitalization, punctuation, spelling, language usage, topic sentence usage, and other aspects of writing specified by the teacher. Suggestions for revisions are also encouraged.
8. The students revise their compositions, making all of the suggested revisions.
9. The two students then reread each other's compositions and sign their names (indicating that they guarantee that no errors exist in the composition).

Johnson & Johnson, 1991

FIGURE 5.1, continued

> While the students work, the teacher monitors the pairs, intervening where appropriate to help students master the needed writing and cooperative skills. When the composition is completed, the students discuss how effectively they worked together (listing the specific actions they engaged in to help each other), plan what behaviors they are going to emphasize in the next writing pair, and thank each other for the help and assistance received.
>
> **Criteria for success:**   A well-written composition by each student. Depending on the instructional objectives, the compositions may be evaluated for grammar, punctuation, organization, content, or other criteria set by the teacher.
>
> **Individual accountability:**   Each student writes his or her own composition.
>
> **Expected behaviors:**   Explaining and listening.
>
> **Intergroup cooperation:**   Whenever it is helpful to do so, check procedures with another group.

FIGURE 5.2
Learning Together Model: Laboratory Groups

> One of the most common ways to involve students actively in the learning situation is the use of laboratory or experimental groups where students use the scientific method to conduct an inquiry. Instructors direct and supervise students working in pairs, triads, or fours to investigate, prove, and formulate hypotheses. In the old paradigm, labs were demonstrations of a theory or concept that followed lectures. The rule was, "Teach them the basic science, teach them the applied science, then give a practicum." Students were often told what to do and what their findings should be.
>
> In the **new paradigm,** labs are introductory activities that build direct experiences in which to understand the procedures, concepts, and theories being studied. The rule is "Give them a problem, coach their problem solving, have them present their solutions, and give the relevant theory."
>
> **Task:**   To conduct an inquiry using the scientific method.
>
> **Cooperation:**   The cooperative goal is for each group to complete the project. Members sign the project to indicate that they have contributed their share of the work, agree with its content, and can present/explain it. When a variety of materials are used (such as microscopes, slides, samples), each group member may be given the responsibility for one of the materials. If appropriate, assign each student a specific role.
>
> **Procedure:**
> 1. Students are assigned an initial problem to solve and are placed in cooperative learning groups to do so. The required materials such as microscopes are given to each group.

Johnson & Johnson, 1991

FIGURE 5.2, *continued*

2. The group solves the problem and prepares a preliminary written report.
3. The instructor presents the relevant algorithm, procedure, concept, or theory required to solve the problem.
4. Students are given a more complex problem that requires them to apply the algorithm, procedure, theory, or concept they have just learned. The instructor systematically observes the groups and provides coaching where it is needed.
5. Students are given an even more complex problem in which they have to go beyond the algorithm, procedure, concept, or theory in order to solve it. The instructor systematically observes the groups and provides coaching where it is needed.
6. Each group writes a report on its solution and hands the report in to the instructor.
7. The instructor pairs each group member with a member of another group. Each presents their group's solution to the other.
8. The groups process how well they worked together.

Individual accountability:
1. Have each group member present his or her group's report to a member of another group.
2. Observe the groups to verify that all members are actively participating.
3. Give an individual test on the content covered by the problems.

Criteria for success: Defensible solution to each problem that all members can explain.

Expected behaviors: All students participate actively in solving the problems and explain their group's solutions to a member of another group.

Intergroup cooperation: If there are any questions about the assignment or procedures ask other groups for help.

THE STRUCTURAL APPROACH: SPENCER KAGAN

Spencer Kagan is director of Resources for Teachers in San Juan Capistrano, California, where he conducts training on cooperative learning and writes about his Structural Approach to team learning. Kagan has researched cooperative learning since the late 1960s, when he was a graduate student at UCLA, and then a professor of psychology in the School of Education at the University of California–Riverside. His research was based on a tradition of scholarly work which indicates that our behaviors are largely determined by the situations we are in.

> We look at someone who's behaving cooperatively or competitively and say, "She's a cooperative person" or "He's very competitive" without realizing that the person's behavior is greatly influenced by the situation. (Brandt, 1989, p. 9)

Spencer Kagan

Kagan's work has been aimed at developing ways to increase the cooperativeness of students and improve race relations. His research led him to cooperative learning as a promising method, which he now shares with educators throughout the world.

Features of the Structural Approach

Kagan has identified the most basic units of student classroom behavior, such as listening, writing, and thinking, and organized them into cooperative structures. A **structure** is defined as a series of steps and prescribed behaviors that are not tied to specific academic content. Depending on the learning objective, teachers may engage students in a single action, such as discussing a problem, or the actions may be combined into structures, such as interviewing a classmate and then sharing the information with teammates. A structure can be applied across curricular areas and levels, from kindergarten through the university, and can be used repeatedly.

Kagan makes a clear distinction between a **cooperative activity** and a **cooperative structure**. To illustrate, teachers can design many excellent cooperative activities, such as making a team mural or a quilt. Such activities almost always have a specific content-bound objective and thus, cannot be used to deliver a range of academic content. In contrast, structures may be used repeatedly with almost any subject matter, at a wide range of grade levels, and at various points in a lesson plan (Kagan, 1990, 1994).

According to Kagan, cooperative structures are most effective when the following features are incorporated into the groupwork:

- Simultaneous interaction
- Equal participation
- Positive interdependence
- Individual accountability

By this point in your reading you should be familiar with the principles of positive interdependence and individual accountability, and equal participation of all students in a group is self-explanatory. The idea of **simultaneity**, however, is perhaps less familiar and deserves more discussion.

Educational research indicates that students learn best when they are actively engaged in learning experiences (Johnson & Johnson, 1989). Cooperative structures, therefore, should be designed to maximize the active participation of all students at the same time. More traditional group activities may require students to participate in sequential order, or by taking turns, with one student responding and then another, and another. It is interesting to observe a reading group of four or five students, in which one student reads at a time. Typically, you will notice that the nonreaders are not really paying attention to the reader, unless, of course, their turn is next. Children often find that waiting for their own turn can be boring, if not frustrating. Many of Kagan's structures are built around groups of four students. Students sometimes work in pairs and sometime with the whole group. The goal is that during some phase of the activity *all* students are actively carrying out some aspect of the task.

One of Kagan's structures is the Three-Step Interview. Four students are assigned to a group, with students forming pairs for the first part of the activity. One member of a pair assumes the role of interviewer and the other is the interviewee. After the members of a pair have interviewed one another, they move to the third step of the interview, which involves sharing what they have learned from interviewing their partner. This reporting takes place in a round-robin fashion, going clockwise around the group, with each person reporting to the group.

As you can see from Figure 5.3, the Three-Step Interview contains all four characteristics of an ideal cooperative structure. The potential topics for an interview are endless. For example, one question might be "What are one or two outstanding qualities of the person you most admire?"

The Numbered Heads Together structure (Figure 5.4) is useful when students are reviewing material at the knowledge or comprehension level. It is highly suited to Kagan's four elements of successful groups.

According to Kagan, the selection of a cooperative structure should be based on its "domain of usefulness" in helping students reach a learning objective. For example, a different structure will be selected based on whether

FIGURE 5.3
Characteristics of Kagan's Three-Step Interview

Step	Characteristics
Pairs are formed within groups of four students.	
Step 1. Individuals interview their partners	Equal participation
Step 2. Reverse roles within the pair, individuals interview their partners	Simultaneous participation Individual accountability
Step 3. Individuals share with the group what they learned in the interview	Everyone gets to share

Adapted from Kagan, 1992

a learning objective requires factual recall or critical thinking. As indicated in Table 5.1, Kagan has classified the structures into the following categories, depending on the particular academic and social functions to be served: class building, team building, communication building, information sharing, mastery, and higher-level thinking (Kagan, 1992). Structures may be combined into "multistructural" lessons, in which each structure is a building block for subsequent structures.

FIGURE 5.4
Characteristics of the Numbered Heads Together Structure

Step	Characteristics
Step 1. Students form teams and count off so each student has a number	Equal participation
Step 2. A question is posed to students by the teacher	
Step 3. Students are asked to literally "put their heads together" to assure that everyone knows the answer	Positive interdependence Simultaneous participation
Step 4. The teacher calls out a number at random, and the students with that number raise their hands or stand up to respond	Individual accountability

Adapted from Kagan, 1992

TABLE 5.1
Cooperative Structures

Structure	Brief Description	Functions Academic & Social
Roundrobin	**Teambuilding** Each student in turn shares something with his or her teammates.	Expressing ideas & opinions. Creation of stories. *Equal participation. Getting acquainted with teammates.*
Three-Step Interview	Students interview each other in pairs, first one way, then the other. Students each share with the group information they learned in the interview.	Sharing personal information such as hypotheses, reactions to a poem, conclusions from a unit. *Participation. Listening.*
Corners	**Classbuilding** Each student moves to a corner of the room representing a teacher-determined alternative. Students discuss within corners, then listen to and paraphrase ideas from other corners.	Seeing alternative hypotheses, values, problem solving approaches. *Knowing and respecting different points of view. Meeting classmates.*
Match Mine	**Communication Building** Students attempt to match the arrangement of objects on a grid of another student using oral communication only.	Vocabulary development. *Communication skills. Role-taking ability.*
Numbered Heads Together	**Mastery: Practice & Review** The teacher asks a question, students consult to make sure everyone knows the answer, then one student is called upon to answer.	Review. Checking for comprehension. Knowledge. Comprehension. *Tutoring.*
Inside-Outside Circle	Students stand in pairs in two concentric circles. The inside circle faces out, the outside circle faces in. Students use flash cards or respond to teacher questions as they rotate to each new partner.	Checking for understanding. Review. Processing. Helping. *Tutoring. Sharing. Meeting classmates.*
Pairs Check	Students work in pairs within groups of four. Within pairs, students alternate—one solves a problem while the other coaches. After every two problems, the pair checks to see if they have the same answers as the other pair.	Practicing skills. *Helping. Praising.*
Think-Pair-Share	**Concept Development** Students think to themselves on a topic provided by the teacher; they pair up with another student to discuss it. They then share with the class their thoughts.	Generating and revising hypotheses; inductive reasoning, deductive reasoning, application. *Participation. Involvement.*
Team Word-Webbing	Students write simultaneously on a piece of chart paper drawing main concepts, supporting elements and bridges representing the relation of ideas on a concept.	Analysis of concepts into components; understanding multiple relations among ideas; differentiating concepts. *Role-taking.*
Roundtable	**Info Exchange: Within Teams** Each student in turn writes one answer as a paper and pencil are passed around the group. With Simultaneous Roundtable, more than one paper is used at once.	Assessing prior knowledge, practicing skills, recalling information, creating cooperative art. *Teambuilding. Participation of all.*
Blackboard Share	**Info Exchange: Between Teams** A student from each team goes to the board and writes an opinion, solves a problem, or shares other information. Usually there is a predetermined place at the board for each team to record its answers.	Sharing information, contrasting divergent opinions or problem solving strategies. *Classbuilding. Participation of eight times as many as the traditional class.*

From Spencer Kagan

Numbered Heads Together

STUDENT TEAM LEARNING: ROBERT SLAVIN

Robert Slavin is co-director of the Center for Research on the Education of Students Placed at Risk at Johns Hopkins University. He received his Ph.D. in social relations in 1975 from Johns Hopkins. For more than two decades he has conducted research on cooperative learning and student achievement. Slavin has authored and co-authored more than 140 articles and 14 books, and is recognized as one of the United States' leading educational researchers.

When asked how he came to be interested in cooperative learning and education, Slavin replied:

> As an undergraduate in the late 1960s, I became interested in simulation gaming. Working with Nancy Madden (now my wife), we designed a complex simulation, World Lab, in which middle school science students worked in small groups to plan the technological development of a newly colonized planet. Nancy and I both wrote our undergraduate theses on the development and implementation of this curriculum in four schools. In the process, however, we found that the dynamics of cooperative learning were more interesting than the simulations, and after a brief teaching career, I went to graduate school (at Johns Hopkins University) specifically to study

Robert Slavin

ways of building on this experience. Incidentally, we shelved the World Lab for almost two decades, but have now brought it back as a project-based learning program for elementary social studies and science! (Slavin, 1995b)

Features of Student Team Learning (STL)

A central focus of Slavin's work has been on enhancing student achievement through cooperative learning. Since the late 1960s, researchers at Johns Hopkins University have been studying cooperative learning and have developed methods, such as Student Teams Achievement Divisions (STAD), Jigsaw II, and Teams–Games–Tournaments (TGT), that can be used with most subject areas and grade levels. They have also developed two programs that are tied to subject matter and materials: Team Assisted Individualization and Cooperative Integrated Reading and Composition (CIRC). These latter two curriculum-based programs are especially suited to assisting low-achieving students as well as typical students in the areas of math and reading.

Team is the operative word in the Student Team Learning approaches. It is used to bring the interdependence and motivation that occurs in team sports into the classroom. All five major Student Team Learning methods involve students in mixed-ability teams that stay together for about six weeks. Each team of four students selects a group name and works together to learn material presented by the teacher. While learning the material, students engage in teaching, explaining, elaborating, arguing, and evaluating one another's understanding.

An essential aspect of Student Team Learning is **assessing student learning individually,** that is, knowing how students perform on their own, without the help of teammates. Assessment can be accomplished through quizzes, essays, compositions, or other means. Rewards, such as certificates or other symbols of achievement, are given on the basis of the progress made by all team members. Students are encouraged to help their teammates succeed and to care about one another's learning. Slavin (1995a) gives thorough explanations of the various team-learning methods. Following are brief summaries of several of the Student Team Learning approaches:

Student Teams–Achievement Divisions (STAD).   STAD is considered the simplest of the Student Team Learning methods. It involves students in a cycle of:

1. *Class presentation.* Lesson material is presented to the class, typically through direct instruction, or a lecture/discussion format by the teacher; the presentation may include audiovisual materials.

2. *Teamwork.* Heterogeneous groups of students form teams of four or five with the goal of preparing for quizzes by completing assignments such as worksheets; students also are responsible for making sure their team members do well on their quizzes, because team scores are determined by individual scores.

3. *Individual assessment.* Students take individual quizzes to assess the degree to which they learned the material.

4. *Team recognition.* Students can earn certificates and recognition based on the extent to which team members improve over their past performance. **Individual improvement scores** are given when students achieve better than their past performance.

Slavin (1995a) notes:

> Any student can contribute maximum points to his or her team in this scoring system, but no student can do so without doing his or her best work. Each student is given a "base" score, derived from the student's average past performance on similar quizzes. Students then earn points for their teams based on the degree to which their quiz scores exceed their base scores. (p. 73)

Teams–Games–Tournaments (TGT).   The format of TGT is similar to STAD, with one exception: instead of individual assessment of students, the assessment is based on team competition. Students compete in academic tournaments, with members contributing to their group scores. Academic games add a bit of competitive excitement to the STAD approach. Both STAD and TGT are appropriate for grades 2 through 12. The process for TGT is as follows:

1. *Class presentation.* (same as in STAD)
2. *Teams.* (same as in STAD)
3. *Games.* The content of the games consists of content-relevant questions designed to test comprehension of the material from class presentations and team practice. Three students from different teams sit at tables to answer questions. Numbers are randomly drawn and students respond to or answer the question that corresponds with their number. Players may challenge one another's answers.
4. *Tournament.* After students have had a chance to practice the material to be learned (usually at the end of the week or a unit), students are assigned to tournament tables in threes. An attempt is made to create equal competition by assigning highest achieving students to one table, the next highest to another table, and so on. After the tournament, students move to different tables based on their performance in the most recent tournament. The winner from a table moves up to the next higher tables and the low scorer moves down to the next lower table. If two top scorers receive the same score, a coin is flipped to decide who will be the winner. Eventually, students will be moved up or down until they reach their true level of performance.
5. *Recognition.* (same as in STAD)

Jigsaw II.   This structure is appropriate for working with written or narrative material. Each team member is assigned a specific topic of study, such as reading one section from a chapter. The students study their particular material and then meet with those students from other groups who have been assigned the same topic. These groups are referred to as **expert groups.** Once the expert groups have discussed what they have learned, students return to their original groups to discuss their findings. Assessment of individual achievement takes place and teams are rewarded according to the progress of all team members, as in STAD. Jigsaw is appropriate for students in grades 3 through 12.

Two additional Student Team Learning methods are curriculum-based approaches that are excellent alternatives to ability grouping, or remedial and special education pull-out programs. These approaches are tied to particular reading or math content and materials. One method, **Cooperative Integrated Reading and Composition (CIRC)**, has been developed for reading and writing instruction with students in grades 1 through 8 (Stevens, Slavin, & Madden, 1991; Slavin, 1995a). Students follow a sequence of teacher instruction, team practice, team pre-assessments, and quizzes. Novels or basal reading books and reading groups are used and materials are adapted to the levels and needs of individual learners. Teachers meet with students to introduce and discuss stories for about 20 minutes each day. Following the introduction of the story, students are given a story packet that contains a series of activities involving partner reading, story grammar and story-related writing, reading words aloud, finding word meanings, retelling the story, spelling words, partner-checking, and tests.

The Team Learning features of team rewards, equal opportunity for success, and individual accountability also are incorporated. Team rewards consist of certificates issued to teams based on the average performance of all team members on all reading and writing activities. Students have equal opportunities for success because they work on materials at their own reading levels. Individual accountability is assured when students take quizzes and write compositions that contribute to team scores. This program is highly appropriate for students with special needs.

> CIRC gives teachers strategies to accommodate the students' needs without detracting from the education of the rest of the students. The student interaction in cooperative groups also furthers the goals of inclusive education by increasing the social acceptance of special education students. (Stevens, Slavin, & Madden, 1991)

Team Assisted Individualization (TAI).   TAI focuses on mathematics for grades 2 through 8. Students are placed in heterogeneous groups to help one another learn as they work on a series of cooperative activities. Both approaches also offer some homogeneous group or individualized instruction that addresses the specific learning needs of students. Students use self-instructional materials designed for their particular learning and skill levels. Teachers work with homogeneous teams of students who are at the same point in the curriculum. While the teacher works with one team, the other teams work on their own modules. Students take quizzes, which are graded by team members. When they reach the criterion for success (typically 80 percent mastery), they can move on to another unit. If they fail to reach criterion on their test, they receive individualized attention from the teacher.

GROUP INVESTIGATION: SHLOMO SHARAN AND YAEL SHARAN

Shlomo Sharan and Yael Sharan live in Tel Aviv, Israel. Shlomo was born in Milwaukee, Wisconsin, and moved to Israel in 1966 after receiving his Ph.D. in clinical psychology at Yeshiva University in New York. He is professor of educational psychology at the School of Education, Tel Aviv University, and is the author of many books, articles, and research studies—in both Hebrew and English—on cooperative learning and school organization. A recent publication is the *Handbook of Cooperative Learning Methods* (1994), an excellent resource for educators on cooperative learning methods, their application to a wide range of academic disciplines, and the

Shlomo Sharan   *Yael Sharan*

methods needed to introduce and sustain cooperative learning in elementary and secondary schools.

Yael and Shlomo are co-authors of the book *Expanding Cooperative Learning Through Group Investigation* (1992). Shlomo was a founder of the International Association for the Study of Cooperation in Education, and served as secretary from 1979–1982 and president from 1982–1988.

Yael worked as a classroom teacher, specialized in remedial reading, and little by little focused on training teachers in cooperative learning. She trained the teachers for many of Shlomo's research studies. Since 1979 she has combined cooperative learning with the use of television in the classroom, as part of her work as coordinator of teacher training at the Israel Educational Television Center. She also has written numerous articles and chapters in books on group investigation.

Features of Group Investigation

Group investigation actively engages students in the instructional process by requiring that they carry out investigations, integrate their findings, and make presentations to the class. This method encourages students to determine what they will study and how they will conduct their investigation. Empowering students to make decisions about the *what* and the *how* of their own learning is a unique and essential feature of Group Investigation (Sharan & Sharan, 1992). The Sharans have identified four basic features of the group investigation model: investigation, interaction, interpretation, and intrinsic motivation: **the 4 I's**.

1. *Investigation.* The investigation is stimulated by a **challenging, multifaceted problem** posed by the teacher. Students seek an answer to the problem by searching out information from various sources. They rely on their own initiative as well as on mutual assistance they uncover information and construct their own knowledge.

2. *Interaction.* Each student investigator interacts with his or her peers to address the group's problem, thus creating an "inquiring community." A number of opportunities for interaction occur, such as when students initially plan their approach to the investigation, when they discuss the sources they will use, when they exchange their ideas and information, when they determine the approach they will use in synthesizing their findings, and when they plan their class presentation. As they cooperate, their thinking is influenced and enriched by the ideas and experiences that their peers bring to the task (Sharan & Sharan, 1994).

3. *Interpretation.* During the process of conducting their individual inquiries, students convene regularly with group members to exchange information and ideas to analyze what they have learned about different aspects of the topic. "The cooperative interpretation of information gathered by group members promotes their ability to organize, confirm, and consolidate their findings and thus to make sense of them" (Sharan & Sharan, 1994, p. 100).

4. *Intrinsic motivation.* When students are able to make decisions about *what* problem they will investigate and *how* they will investigate it, their personal interests are served and motivation is increased. Motivation is also enhanced by the positive interaction with one another.

Group investigation consists of six stages, into which the previous four features—investigation, interaction, interpretation, and intrinsic motivation—are embedded. The activity begins with the teacher posing to the class a broad, multifaceted problem that has no single correct answer. Of course, the problem should be interesting, and be relevant to their lives both inside and outside school.

Six Stages of Group Investigation

Stage 1: Class Determines Subtopics and Organizes Into Research Groups.   Based on the question posed by the teacher, the students formulate questions they would like to investigate to understand the topic more fully. Next, they categorize the questions to develop subtopics for investigation. Students then select the subtopic they are most interested in and groups are formed to investigate the subtopic.

Stage 2: Groups Plan Their Investigations.   Group members discuss and decide what sources they will use in their investigation, how they will

FIGURE 5.5
Group Investigation Lesson Worksheet

Are Birds of Prey the Same as Raptors?

Our research topic: How do birds of prey differ from raptors?

Group members: Mark, Lara, Aaron, Miguel, Linda

Roles: Mark: manager; Lara and Aaron—resource persons; Miguel—recorder; Linda—steering committee

What do we want to find out?

Mark and Lara—What behaviors does a bird of prey exhibit? Identify various birds of prey.

Miguel and Linda—What behaviors does a raptor exhibit? Identify various raptors.

Aaron—Why do raptors have such a bad reputation in the public eye?

What are our resources?   Books, articles, and videos are listed in this section. The group will contact a biologist who is a raptor specialist. Group members will visit the raptor house of the state zoological garden.

From Sharan & Sharan, 1989–1990

conduct their investigation, and how the work will be divided among the group members.

Stage 3: Groups Carry Out Their Investigations.   Working individually or in pairs, group members find information from a variety of sources; gather that information; present it to group members; and discuss, interpret, and integrate the findings. They also determine whether they should seek out more information.

Stage 4: Groups Plan Their Presentations.   The group presentations are planned for the purpose of teaching classmates their main findings. Students select a presentation mode, such as a role play, a video drama, or a written report, and they develop handouts containing the main ideas and their resources. A lesson planning worksheet can be filled out for the group at this stage, to be posted in the classroom (see Figure 5.5). It helps remind group members of what they need to accomplish as well as communicate their plans to the class.

Groups are encouraged to adhere to the following guidelines:

• Emphasize the main ideas and conclusions of the inquiry.

• Make sure everyone in the group takes an active part in the presentation.

• Set and observe time limits for the duration of the presentation.

- Plan to involve classmates from the "audience" as much as possible by giving them roles to perform or otherwise having them be active during the presentation.
- Allow time for questions.
- Make sure all the necessary equipment and materials are available. (Sharan & Sharan, 1994, pp. 107–108)

The teacher's role in all stages of group investigation is to meet with each group and review what the group plans to do that day. During the fourth stage, the steering committee—composed of members from the groups—meets to hear each group's plan for its report, making sure the plans make sense and can be accomplished. The teacher's role is that of adviser, intervening only when necessary.

Stage 5: Groups Make Their Presentations.   Each group presents its findings in one of many engaging ways, including exhibitions, models, dramatizations, written reports, etc., avoiding lecture as much as possible. The other students in the class participate in evaluating the presentations.

Stage 6: Teacher and Students Evaluate Their Projects.   A variety of methods are used to assess students' understanding of the main ideas, new knowledge acquired, and conclusions drawn about the different problems. For example, groups may be asked to submit several questions concerning the topic of their presentation for a class test. Students are also asked to reflect on their performance as investigators and as group members, and to set goals for the improvement of their group behavior.

COMPLEX INSTRUCTION: ELIZABETH COHEN

Elizabeth G. Cohen received her Ph.D. in sociology in 1958 from Harvard's Department of Social Relations. For many years she has researched problems of unequal status within small mixed-status groups. Using Expectations States Theory, she has developed and evaluated interventions suitable for classroom teachers. She has published many articles on status problems in classrooms and their treatment.

Since 1982, Cohen has been director of the Program for Complex Instruction at Stanford University. Complex Instruction is a strategy designed to produce equity in heterogeneous classrooms while permitting the teacher to teach to a high cognitive level. Complex Instruction is now implemented widely in the United States, Israel, the Netherlands, and Sweden. Cohen has written a book for teachers, *Designing Groupwork: Strategies for the Heterogeneous Classroom* (1994).

Complex Instruction is targeted for heterogeneous (e.g., academically, linguistically, and ethnically diverse) classrooms of students from grades 2

Elizabeth G. Cohen

through 5. The methods are designed to foster higher-order thinking and conceptual development through challenging, intrinsically motivating, multi-dimensional tasks. The tasks require multiple abilities of students in the group, including traditional academic skills (language arts, mathematics, social studies) as well as artistic abilities, reasoning abilities, visual/spatial abilities, observation skills, communication skills, interpersonal skills, kinesthetic abilities, and others.

It is important for students to understand that multiple abilities are essential for successful completion of the activity. Cohen (1994) explains that a good multiple-ability task:

- Has more than one answer or more than one way to solve the problem.
- Is intrinsically interesting and rewarding.
- Allows different students to make different contributions.
- Uses multimedia.
- Involves sight, sound, and touch.
- Requires a variety of skills and behaviors.
- Also requires reading and writing.
- Is challenging. (p. 64)

In Complex Instruction, problem-solving activities are open ended and built around a central concept or idea. The teacher is responsible for organizing students into groups of up to five students, at learning stations throughout the classroom. Each group has a different task that relates to the central concept. Groups rotate among tasks so that students have the chance to understand the central concept through different media and modes. The teacher fosters interaction between the students by delegating authority to students and groups.

Cohen also places great importance on student roles in Complex Instruction. Students perform procedural roles such as facilitator or materials manager in their groups. Every person has a role to play and roles rotate over time.

A unique aspect of Complex Instruction is the focus on addressing the problems associated with social status differences of students in the groups. The two most important sources of social status in the classroom are perceived academic ability and peer popularity. Cohen (1994) states the following:

> High status students are generally expected to do well on new intellectual tasks and low status students are generally expected to do poorly on these same tasks. When the teacher assigns a groupwork task, general expectations come into play and produce a self-fulfilling prophecy in which the high status students talk more and become more influential than the low status students. The net result of the interaction is that the low status students are once again seen as incompetent. (p. 117)

Teachers use several techniques to raise classmates' expectations for low-status students. One is called the multiple-ability treatment. Students must understand that no one is good at all the abilities the tasks require, but that everyone is good on at least one of these important intellectual abilities. Teachers explicitly give the students this message and may ask students to think of the different abilities that the tasks require.

At the elementary level, the bilingual curriculum *Finding Out/Descubrimiento* (De Avila, Duncan, & Navarrete, 1987), designed to develop thinking skills and using concepts from math and science, has been developed for Complex Instruction. An example of a multiple-ability unit for the middle school is a set of group activities on the Crusades. Different groups of students study castle floor plans and pictures of ruins, listen to recordings of Crusader songs, analyze the text of a speech by Pope Urban, and examine pictures of half-human infidels in the *Crusader's Handbook*. Students spend several days on this project, experiencing each of the media: text, music, and art/architecture. The group works with an activity card and creates a group product for presentation to the class. Individuals write reports of their answers to the questions the group has discussed.

Group products include a student-created version of a Crusader castle with a plan for its defense, a song about current events that echoes the purpose of the music of the Crusades, and a skit illustrating how the *Crusader's Handbook* was used to recruit naive villagers. As students present these products, the teacher stimulates a discussion on the different sources used by historians (Cohen, 1994).

Another method developed by Cohen is "expectation training," in which the teacher has a low-status student become the teacher of a novel, challenging, and valued task. Culturally specific or stereotyped tasks are avoided, such as asking a French student to sing *Frere Jacques*. Teachers also publicly point out the competence of low-status students to the class by mentioning what they are doing well and how important their contributions are to the group and successful completion of the task (Cohen, 1994).

The needs of bilingual students are varied and pose challenging problems to educators. Students for whom English is a second language have complex needs: linguistic, academic, and cultural. To complicate matters further, many limited-English speaking students come from poor economic conditions and have little preparation for school. They face the difficulty of gaining proficiency in English and basic academic skills at the same time. A mistaken assumption, according to Cohen, is that students must learn English before they can profit from instruction in basic skills. Too great an emphasis on teaching English at the expense of instruction in basic skills results in students falling further behind in academics. Cooperative learning can be a powerful tool for helping students simultaneously attain both English and basic skills, in addition to higher-order thinking skills (Cohen, 1994).

Curriculum materials have been developed for Complex Instruction that are highly appropriate for bilingual classrooms, such as *Finding Out/Descubrimiento* (De Avila, Duncan, & Navarrete, 1987). As mentioned above, this math and science curriculum provides learning materials in Spanish, English, and pictographs. Themes such as crystals and powders, balance and structures, clocks and pendulums, reflection/refraction, and optical illusion form the basis of the curriculum, which is designed to develop thinking skills.

Finding Out/Descubrimiento learning stations are set up with two activity cards that describe the activity and pose key questions. One activity card is written in English and the other in Spanish. The questions usually involve students in describing what happened and why they think it happened. Students engage in activities that require measuring, constructing, hypothesizing, and analyzing using concrete materials. They complete worksheets requiring basic skills such as reading, writing, and computation as well as inference skills such as estimation. Students are encouraged to ask one another for task assistance, so if one child cannot read well, another can serve that function. Children with limited-English proficiency are exposed to a rich language experience and English-speaking students are exposed to input from Spanish speakers. Cohen's research has found that students participating in the *Finding Out/Descubrimiento* curriculum made highly significant gains in language arts, reading, and on standardized mathematics subtests. Cooperative groupwork is an ideal context for learning language because students are able to practice their language skills as they work to accomplishing meaningful tasks.

SIMILARITIES AND DIFFERENCES AMONG THE VARIOUS COOPERATIVE METHODS

Similar Attributes

All cooperative approaches, as well as the cooperative methods discussed in this chapter, have five attributes in common (Davidson, 1994):

1. Common task or learning activity suitable for groupwork
2. Small-group learning
3. Cooperative behavior
4. Interdependence (often referred to as positive interdependence)
5. Individual accountability (p. 14)

Cooperative methods and approaches also vary in a number of ways, as you have noted in reading about the five methods presented in this chapter. For example, Slavin's Team Learning and Johnson's Learning Together methods differ with respect to collaborative skill instruction: In Team Learning, collaborative skills are not explicitly taught as they are in Learning Together. Complex Instruction addresses status differences more directly than the other methods, through techniques such as expectation training. Group structure is highly explicit in Kagan's Structural Approach through use of specific structures with specific steps, whereas student groups determine the structure at different stages of Group Investigation.

Different Attributes

Davidson (1994) has identified nine major ways in which cooperative approaches *differ* from one another:

1. Various grouping procedures (e.g., heterogeneous, random, student selected, common interest).
2. Different types of positive interdependence (e.g., goals, tasks, resources, roles, division of labor, rewards).
3. The explicit teaching of varied skills (e.g., interpersonal, relationship, cooperative, or collaborative skills).
4. Reflection (or processing) in different areas (e.g. social skills, academic skills, or group dynamics).
5. Climate setting through either class building, team building, trust building, or cooperative norms.
6. Explicit or nonexplicit group structure.
7. Varied attention to student status by the teacher (e.g., identifying competencies of low-status students and focusing peers' attention on them).

8. Group leadership roles may or may not be designated to a student.

9. Varied roles, functions, and involvement for the teacher.

Because cooperative learning has become a fundamental aspect of instruction in many of today's classrooms, the methods used by teachers are often creative and innovative variations of cooperative fundamentals discussed in this book. The teacher's application of cooperative strategies is based on the goals of instruction, his or her personal philosophy, the needs of the students, and the classroom settings. What is exciting about cooperative learning is the flexibility within a unified approach based on the six commonalities listed earlier (Davidson, 1994).

MODIFICATIONS FOR DIVERSE LEARNERS

Today's classroom has a more diverse population than ever. Experiencing diversity in the classroom and school is important for all students, because for them to succeed in the 21st century they will need to know how to live and work with people who have different abilities, ethnicities, and cultures (Nevin, 1994). Because of this diversity of learning styles and student behaviors, teachers must deal with a wide range of learners, often with very

Cooperative Activities for Diverse Learners

different educational needs. Fortunately, cooperative learning is ideally suited to the needs of heterogeneous groups of learners (see discussion in Chapter 2 on academic and social outcomes and students with disabilities).

Team Assisted Individualization (discussed earlier in this chapter), is designed for students of different performance levels working as a team to earn points through completion of modules, tests, and assignments. Students use their own curricular materials and work at their own level of mastery. Complex Instruction takes into account the differences in students' intelligence by designing multiple-ability tasks to incorporate all levels of performance, such as cognitive, interpersonal, spatial, etc. The teacher also identifies low-status students, seeks out their areas of competence, and brings these to the attention of the others in the class through public recognition.

It is essential that teachers attempt to meet individualized educational or social needs of students while they participate in their cooperative groups. As you can imagine, this is not always an easy task! In the next section, five strategies for modifying cooperative activities for students with exceptional learning needs are presented. Suggestions for modifying the evaluation system for students with exceptional needs will be discussed in Chapter 6.

Modifying Learning Objectives

1. *Same Objective–Modified Manner of Student Response.* Although the lesson objective does not have to be modified, a different type of student response will be needed for assignment completion. For example, in a writing assignment the students may need to answer in a language other than English, draw pictures rather than write words, or type on a computer due to a fine motor or written expression disability. Assistive technology, such as a microphone or amplifier may be needed by a student with a voice disorder.

2. *Same Objective–Modified Presentation of Material.* The lesson objective is not changed, but to receive the input, the student may need (a) another student to read the material, (b) an interpreter due to a hearing impairment or limited-English proficiency, (c) to listen to an audiotape of the material due to slow auditory processing capabilities.

3. *Same Objective–Reduced Workload.* The objective is not changed, but students are required to contribute less. They are asked to offer fewer ideas, complete fewer problems, or write fewer words than others in the group. For example, Brenda, who is still recuperating from a serious bicycle accident involving a pickup, has little stamina and requires frequent rest periods. She is able to accomplish only a portion of the work, nevertheless, she is capable of mastering the learning objectives with less practice than most students require.

4. *Same Objective–Lower Level Expectations.* Expectations may be set at a lower performance level, such as a lower grade level or developmen-

tal level. In writing, for example, while other group members concern themselves with the mechanics of writing and punctuation, the student with a cognitive disability due to fetal alcohol syndrome will copy vocabulary words and define them.

5. *Personalized Objective.* Unique functional or interpersonal skills can be learned in the context of a cooperative activity. Four students with exceptional needs can focus on their own objectives in the same classroom, placed in different cooperative groups. For example, a student could work on mobility skills by obtaining materials and handing in the finished product to the teacher; a student with a behavioral disorder could practice a social skill in a group context; a student with a communication disorder might work or on communication skills by summarizing the story using sign language; and a gifted student could practice leadership skills by leading the group in a conflict resolution activity (Putnam, 1991).

Modifying Materials and the Environment

Students participating in a cooperative activity may benefit from specialized materials to complete the learning objective. For instance, a special felt-tip marker to produce enlarged and darker print, a keyboard, or a communication board may be necessary. Talking books and manipulatives, such as a plastic model of the DNA helix, can be helpful to students who are visually impaired. A legally blind student may benefit from a Kurzweil Reading machine, that can read books and printed matter aloud via synthesized speech and computer technology. Teachers can make slight variations of the same materials used by others in the class to be more "manipulable, concrete, tangible, simplified, and matched to the student's learning style or comprehension level" (Udvari-Solner, 1994).

Environmental adaptations for students with physical disabilities or sensory impairments should be made. The lighting, seating arrangements, the height or width of desktops can be adjusted to help students. In one case, a student with a severe hearing impairment who was able to read lips was having difficulty participating in cooperative groups because he could not identify who the speaker was in a rapidly moving conversation or interaction. The teacher gave the group a red bean bag, and whoever was speaking held the bean bag. This visual cue was all the student needed to identify the speaker and orient to the speaker's lips to understand his or her speech.

It should not be assumed that the classroom is the best environment for a cooperative activity. Students may need to use another location in the school, such as the library, or the computer room to access the Internet through a computer modem. They may also need to work away from the school campus—in the community. Consideration should be given to the mobility needs of physically impaired students who may require wheelchairs and accessible buildings.

FIGURE 5.6
The Wind Project

Wind Project Gives Students of All Abilities a Sense of Discovery

Academic goals: The students were to work in cooperative groups to design and make a sail for a pre-made boat furnished with a mast. Then each group was to create wind to power the boat, without using their breath or electricity of any kind.

Social goals: The students were to work cooperatively, respectfully and with care and consideration for each other. They were to listen without judgment and remember all ideas were a possibility. The outcome or finished project was to be built with the agreement of all.

Teaching students with exceptionalities in the regular classroom

Leslie Fesq-Lavallee's second-grade classroom at Readfield Elementary School, Readfield, Maine, is a mixture of students, including some with learning exceptionalities. We asked her to describe in detail how she structured and implemented a Wind Project for her Weather Unit, using the techniques of Cooperative Learning.

Question: Let's begin this account at square one. Given your mix of student abilities and personality types, how did you form the learning groups?

Fesq-Lavallee: I secretly number each of my students each time I set up cooperative groups, in order to mix strengths and needs as much as possible. First, I decide on the number of groups. For this particular project I chose to divide the kids into five groups of four each. The next step was to separate the students with challenging behaviors and number them *one's.* Students who are strong academically and also kind to others (I have a few who are not) are my number *two's.* Students who are low or nonreaders but good orally and/or verbally are my *three's.* The other kids are my *four's.* I just divide them as evenly as possible, always keeping in mind those children who cannot be together.

Question: In this project, how is interdependence fostered?

Fesq-Lavallee: Each group member has a specific job. The leader is to keep everyone sharing and on track. The materials person is the runner who gets material or asks for something not readily available. The secretary writes down ideas, needs, plans and comments. The messenger runs errands, such as taking questions or comments from the whole group to adults or other teams.

Question: Do you assign specific tasks to each child?

Fesq-Lavallee: No. Students decide on jobs. Often my lower ability or L.D. kids are chosen as leaders, because they are known to be good listeners or fair. Then they brainstorm ideas. For this project the groups brainstormed ideas for their sails—design and materials. When they completed a design and had the boat ready their next step was to come up with a way to provide wind. They again brainstormed ideas and tried their boats and wind in the wading pool we had set up in our room for several weeks.

The kids were able to head back to their drawing boards and try new designs as many times as their group wanted as long as all were ready to present their work at the end of the second week. They were allowed about an hour three or four times a week for two weeks. A lot of discussion went on during choice time and recesses as well.

"Wind Project," 1994

Question: With so much going on, how did you ensure accountability?

Fesq-Lavallee: I ensured individual accountability in two ways. First, I used Numbered Heads Together. The child whose number is rolled on the dice was expected to demonstrate the boat and wind power. The child was expected to explain the process by which the team arrived at its final design. The description was to include the trial and errors, and the contributions of the team (without naming names).

Each team member evaluated the team as a whole. We then reviewed the evaluations together. Based on their evaluations of their team, the members decided what their team would try to improve upon next time.

Question: How actively did you coach during the design phase?

Fesq-Lavallee: The students were on their own unless all requested help by sending their messenger to an adult in the room. Children who brought material from home were required to bring enough for our materials box so others had access to the same materials. I stood back, but moved about listening for too many "I's" and "me's."

Through questioning, the kids caught on quickly and moved back to "we" and "our."

One table with a particularly bright but difficult little girl had problems. Her team was very patient with her although I had to remove her several times for short periods so the projects could continue. I felt the academic and social goals were accomplished with extreme interest and enthusiasm. All were able to contribute and feel successful.

Question: What are your major reflections? Would you do it again?

Fesq-Lavallee: I was somewhat skeptical about undertaking this project. It was all too easy to imagine having a wading pool in my room for a few weeks: there were two daredevil boys sure to be soaked every day! My hamsters would be set afloat on someone's sailboat, fall off, and drown. I was wonderfully surprised. We set some very specific rules and expectations around the pool. At no time was it a true problem. However, the pool sprang a leak on the third day. Several kids volunteered their tubes to catch the water and we were OK for a little while. A couple of the kids and I found the leak and plugged it with clay. We were able to keep the pool full for the duration of the project. They had a wonderful time building and testing their sailboats. It gave them an incentive to keep working.

One student asked to take the boat out at recess time to float it in a puddle. The duty teacher was quick to let me know how well this little guy, who has language difficulties, explained the project to children from other classes. He was able to really shine for a few moments. Since this project, I've seen a big jump in his willingness to take risks in the classroom. I will definitely repeat this project the next time we do our weather unit.

Question: Thank you for giving us such an exciting look at cooperative learning in action, and sharing your strategies with us. What's next for the lucky children in your classroom?

Fesq-Lavallee: Birds! Our next unit is on birds and I hope to have a similar activity ready to fly.

Providing Tutorials, Study Skills, and Individualized Support

To maximize the success of a student with exceptional needs in a cooperative group, teachers can arrange to provide additional support within or outside of the cooperative activity. There may be occasions when a student requires the assistance of an adult or peer tutor to function in the group. The student may need an interpreter due to a hearing impairment or a facilitator due to a communication problem associated with autism. An adult or peer tutor who has been trained to help a student in a particular area may provide assistance with a behavioral or instructional program, for instance, by providing verbal prompts, reinforcers, and physical assistance. Such assistance may be especially helpful when the student first enters the group, as it provides a model to other group members of how to best help this student (Udvari-Solner, 1994).

Ideally, the students in the cooperative group will learn how to perform these support functions for the student, when it is appropriate or possible. A word of caution: Sometimes adults or peer tutors can *inhibit* the natural interaction between a student with exceptional needs and his or her group mates. The more direct the interaction and communication among students in cooperative groups, the better!

Another way teachers, particularly special education teachers, can support students with exceptional needs is to provide tutorial sessions *outside* of class that support *in-class* performance. Tutorials may take the form of pre-teaching or reinforcing/reviewing previously introduced academic skills or social behaviors. Vocabulary words and concepts associated with a history or social studies lesson may be introduced to the student before the class. Review of previously learned skills and content in preparation for a test may involve working with the student to identify the most important material to be learned. Study skills involved in the comprehension and retention of information can also be imparted outside of class (Jakupcak, 1994).

Tutorial sessions can be used to prepare students to perform specific roles in their cooperative groups. If the student will be assuming the role of encourager, the teacher can provide examples of encouraging phrases with a T-Chart (sounds like: good job) and body language (looks like: smiling, nodding). Teachers may also role play the cooperative behavior before class sessions. If the student has been assigned the role of materials manager, the teacher can show the student where to find the materials, what materials will be required, and where to put the materials at the end of the activity.

Cooperative Learning in Inclusive Classrooms

King Kaumuali'i Elementary School is in Lihue, Kauai, one of the Hawaiian islands known as the "garden island." Alicia Pelas, a fourth-grade teacher, and Jennifer Fenner, a special educator, team teach in an inclusive fourth-grade classroom. Eleven students certified to receive special education are an integral part of this innovative classroom.

Students work in heterogeneous cooperative learning groups on interdisciplinary thematic units throughout the day. For an hour in the afternoon, six groups of four students are assigned to learning centers where they participate in Writer's Workshop, Literature Activities (Book Chats, Reports), Mathematics, Record Oral Reading, Class Newspaper, Computer, Music, and Art.

Groups are rotated each day of the week so that students participate in all the learning center activities. Student assignments are modified to address individualized learning objectives. For example, all the students at the Writer's Workshop compose stories appropriate to their own written expression abilities, which vary substantially. At the end of the learning center activities, each group makes a presentation so the students can share what they accomplished and learned in their particular center. All the students in the group take part in the oral presentation. During the presentations, the entire class practices communication and social skills, such as speaking ability, expression, fluency, volume, and content. The audience works on active listening, asking good questions, and giving appropriate feedback to the groups presenting about their improvements. Being a good audience has been directly taught by the teachers and reinforced by the students themselves.

Unit activities are connected with the Hawaiian culture. For example, students' artwork reflects the Pacific region, as illustrated by the volcano drawings in the accompanying photo. Displayed on the class bulletin board are the eight major Hawaiian islands for S.U.R.F.—Silent Uninterrupted Reading for Fun. Each student's name is written on a colorful paper surfboard, which moves across the water from island to island as points are earned for reading in and out of the classroom. Sixty points are required to

King Kaumuali'i Inclusive Classroom, Kauai, Hawaii

move from the first island to the second, 120 points to the next island, and so on, with 500 required to reach the last island of Hawaii.

While cooperative learning is highly compatible with the Hawaiian culture, this program is unique to King Kaumuali'i Elementary School. Cooperation among teachers makes this inclusive classroom community possible—Alicia and Jennifer model cooperation in action as they practice what they preach.

Culturally Sensitive Instructional Practices

Culturally sensitive teachers make every effort to help a diversity of students achieve their full potential, and understand that students from the nondominant social and cultural background may not respond to traditional instructional practices. The following suggestions for fostering culturally sensitive instructional practices are adapted from Franklin, 1992:

1. *Incorporate cultural practices from the learner's nonschool environment.* Try to reduce the discrepancy between a child's home and school environments by infusing cultural variables into the classroom and interactions with students. In Browning, Montana, I learned from members of the Blackfeet tribe that it is customary to sit in a circle, which promotes face-to-face communication, and no one must look at someone else's back. A classroom with rows of desks and the teacher in the front inhibits interaction and is discrepant from the cultural norms. In addition, when a Blackfeet student diverts his or her gaze from the teacher, it is a sign of respect. This same behavior in a nonnative white classroom might be interpreted as disrespect.

2. *Identify and build on a student's strengths and interests.* Determine what the student knows, and then build on it. Avoid always targeting weaknesses or gaps in learning for remediation. It can be argued, for instance, that it is more important for a child to learn basic skills than to gain fluency in the English language. Focusing on learning the English language at the expense of learning mathematics will result in a narrowing of a child's intellectual development. Cohen (1994) notes that "Groupwork is an alternative approach that puts language in a useful perspective; language serves as communication in order to accomplish various learning objectives" (p. 161).

3. *Understand and dignify the language that is used at home, even if it differs from that used at school.* Build on prior language learning and experience. Don't view the responses of linguistically diverse learners as wrong; rather, use the child's prior experience to understand how the child uses language and makes sense of the world.

4. *Build bridges between prior learning and a variety of instructional activities.* Discover the interests, developmental levels, and

prior experiences of a student before developing instructional activities. Activities must take place with the student's current understandings and knowledge base in mind. This may require research into a child's culture and community.

Franklin (1992) makes a number of recommendations to teachers for fostering culturally sensitive teaching approaches for African American learners based on these four recommendations. They include being *people focused, using dialect judiciously, incorporating cooperative learning,* and *presenting real-world tasks* that are related to the child's culture.

People Focused.   African American students are often reared in people-focused families, and respond better to affective-oriented, as opposed to task-oriented teachers. Affective-oriented teachers are described as "kind, optimistic, understanding, adaptable, and warm" (Franklin, 1992, p. 118). They are affirming and provide lots of positive reinforcement. Use of curriculum materials that include a people focus is recommended, particularly emphasizing credible people and heroes with whom African American students can relate (e.g., the late Arthur Ashe—tennis champion and social activist).

Use Different Methods of Presentation.   Variety in presentation is also helpful to students. For example, a teacher might speak rhythmically and with varied intonation; incorporate oral and visual media along with print; and emphasize verbal interaction by planning expressive, creative activities that incorporate rap music, chants, and responsive reading into the instruction. The research shows that effective teachers also try to bridge home and school cultures by using greater verbal interaction with verve and rhythm.

Dialect.   At times it is appropriate to use Black English dialect in the classroom, such as "jive talkin'." However, because Black English dialect is not acceptable in some environments, it should be used judiciously to establish rapport with children. Take care not to appear patronizing or condescending to students by using *their* language when it is obviously not *your* language.

Real World Tasks.   Incorporate into classroom instruction real-world tasks that reflect the student's cultural home, community, and school environment. For example, secondary English students from inner-city Los Angeles could be engaged preparing essays for Black History month, or papers that address current social problems in their urban environment.

Grouping of Students.   Cooperative learning, peer tutoring, and cross-age groupings are recommended grouping patterns for African American students. Such activities encourage social growth and cross-racial friendships and introduce students to a variety of learning strategies that they might not be exposed to otherwise.

Native American Students.   Cooperative learning is highly compatible with the learning and interactional style of many Native American children, according to Swisher (1990), who reviewed the literature on the cooperative nature of Native American/Native Alaskan children. Because these children traditionally avoid individual competition, and shun being singled out in front of an audience, cooperative learning is preferable. Indian children tend to dislike the type of competition that is often used in classrooms, that is, *individual* competition. These students do not wish to stand out in a group, a preference which has cultural roots and is sanctioned today through teasing. Group competition, however, has its place outside the classroom in the form of team sports (Brewer, 1977).

The following vignette describes a cooperative learning unit that involves a real-world task (an archaeology dig) to teach secondary students mathematics and science skills. Cultural heritage is emphasized in the context of cooperative activities and the involvement of elders.

Maliseet Archaeology Project

Integrating Math and Science

Secondary students from the Houlton Band of Maliseet Indians are learning about the prehistory of the native people of northern Maine as they participate in an authentic archaeological investigation. The purpose of this project is to provide Maliseet students with a broad foundation in science and mathematics through a real archaeological dig. Students gain academic skills as they conduct all aspects of the project—from planning, sampling, excavation, field recording, cataloging of artifacts, radiometric dating, and statistical artifact analyses to report preparation and presentation.

Students also learn about their own history and culture in the course of the project. The project archaeologist states the following:

> *Although the Maliseet people played a fundamental role in the early settlement of Aroostook County in northern Maine and influenced its ultimate possession by the United States, the Band is hardly mentioned in local histories. Recognition of this rich heritage can promote cultural awareness and enhance the value placed on cultural diversity within the broader community. Moreover, the contributions of the Maliseet people should be included the local history. Certainly, the more than eleven thousand years of cultural experience that precedes contact with Europeans some four hundred years ago provides a rich backdrop to the contemporary community. (Putnam, 1996)*

Throughout the project, students conduct their work in cooperative teams of three, using the jigsaw model with "expert teams"
each investigating a different topic. All teams engage in project
planning as well as the excavation phases. First, each team
selects a special topic to work on exclusively after the completion
of excavation. Some of the topics include geochronology and
radiometric dating; and quantification and analysis of artifacts
(stone, bone, and antler tools; and other manmade objects) and
ecofacts (animal and plant remains of human subsistence).

Each team has an adult mentor and a list of qualified professional archaeologists in the state that have agreed to assist in the
project for advice and guidance. Tribal elders have been invited to
work with the teams, particularly in the realm of scientific ethics
and determining the religious significance of archaeological
remains. Tribal traditions favor involving elders in the education of
their youth and the "collectivity orientation" of cooperative learning.

Two sites have been identified by the project archeologist. The
first is convenient to the school and on tribal lands. In the fall, students will learn the skills of the archaeology trade as they survey
the nearby lands. Early next summer, they will participate in the
second excavation at a site about 75 miles away. This site is a
deeply stratified and undisturbed riverbank, and is a known occupation site of repeated use through prehistory. The second location is sufficiently rich in artifacts to provide adequate samples
for simple statistics.

The archaeologists will avoid disturbing any features of potential religious significance to Native Americans, and their focus will
be on the refuse of daily life. Should a grave or ceremonial feature
be inadvertently exposed, they will ask a tribal shaman to re-
establish the spiritual balance. Artifacts uncovered will be forwarded to the Maine State Museum for curation. This project is a
collaboration between the Houlton Band of Maliseets in Houlton,
Maine, and the Maine Mathematics and Science Systemic Initiative, a project funded by the National Science Foundation.

Activities and Science and Mathematics Skills

1. **Project planning.** Logistical planning, sampling theory.
2. **Site excavation.** Setup and basic use of a transit, metric
   measurement, basic soil science and stratigraphy, field
   recordkeeping, sample collection and management.
3. **Analyses.** Geochronology and radiometric dating, artifact
   quantification and attribute analyses (computer data-
   base), stratigraphic analysis, special sample identifica-
   tion (flora, fauna, and unknown objects).
4. **Report preparation** Articulation of results in written
   report form and oral presentation of results.

Creating a Climate of Support and Helpfulness

A warm and friendly classroom atmosphere, in which the teacher models supportive and helping behavior toward students with diverse learning needs is most conducive to successful cooperative learning—and student motivation in general. During the past decade, I have observed, both informally and formally, using systematic observational research, cooperative learning in numerous classrooms that included students with disabilities. In classrooms across the country, across age levels and subjects, I have found the behavior of typical students to be positive or neutral—but rarely, if ever, negative. The general attitude of acceptance toward students with disabilities is one reason that cooperative learning is a recommended strategy for inclusive classrooms. And systematic research findings lend support to the practice of cooperative learning with students with exceptional needs to promote peer acceptance and liking, as was pointed out in Chapter 2.

While cooperative learning, when appropriately implemented, should creative a supportive classroom climate, there are some techniques teachers can use to enhance a positive classroom climate; they fall under the categories of **modeling supportive behavior** and **helpfulness to the students**.

One technique for modeling support to diverse learners or learners with exceptional needs is to publicly point out the student's strengths and successes. This must be done thoughtfully so that (a) it is sincere, (b) the remarks are valued by classmates, (c) it does not underscore student differences, and (d) it does not promote competition or jealousy. Teachers are the most powerful models in the classroom—you should always be aware of this and treat all children with respect. Videotapes and movies also provide examples of supportive behavior, such as *Regular Lives* by Biklen at Syracuse University.

Teachers can promote helping behaviors towards diverse learners by remembering two critical classroom values (Sapon-Shevin, Ayres, & Duncan (1994). "1) Everyone is good at something and can help others, and 2) everyone is entitled to and can benefit from help and support from others" (p. 50). They suggest that teachers create a "Classroom Classifieds." This newspaper enables students to identify their own strengths and skills for the "Help Offered" column and to indicate their needs in a "Help Wanted" column. Examples of "Help Offered" are help with the computer, chemistry tutoring, and playing ice hockey; examples of "Help Wanted" are learning how to play chess, surf the internet, identify the planets, and make tacos (see Figure 5.7).

Cooperative Learning and Parent/Family Involvement

Cooperative learning does not stop at the boundaries of the classroom or the school—it involves parents, families, and the community as well. Since the mid-1970s, special education has had a tradition and legal mandate to involve parents in the education of their child with a disability. Parents are

FIGURE 5.7
Sample of "Classroom Classifieds" Ad

Help Wanted	Help Offered
I need to learn how to play chess (A. Brown)	I make World Wide Web pages (P. Lambrecht)
Help needed with surfing the Internet (F. Cote)	Help with editing (D. May)
Artistically impaired student needs help with science project! (N. Rodrigues)	Hockey tips after school (K. Meyers)
Need a team to prepare tacos for the next school dance (L. Wu)	Chemistry tutoring (for a minimal fee, namely food) (J. Mullen)

members of a team that develops the child's individualized educational program and meets periodically to follow the child's progress. Research tells us that family actions influence a child's achievement and success in school (Clark, 1983). For example, the degree to which parents become involved with homework, and the academic aspirations and expectations they have will affect their child's achievement. Research also tells us that attempts by teachers to build collaborative partnerships between parents and school enhances student achievement (Davies, 1991; Walberg, 1994).

To promote partnerships between parents and teachers, Chrispeels (1994) suggests developing the following collaborative roles between the home and school:

- co-communicators
- co-supporters
- co-learners
- co-teachers
- co-advocates
- co-advisors
- co-decision makers (p. 19)

Parents should feel welcome in the cooperative classroom. They may want to engage in tutoring, assist with activities, or simply attend classroom or school events. Some parents may want to participate in training in a particular curriculum area to assist their children.

When parents observe children in cooperative learning activities, they may glean ideas for fostering greater cooperation in their own families through practicing cooperative skills and conflict resolution techniques. When parents attend meeting at schools, they can be encouraged to participate in cooperative pairs or groups to discuss issues and share their ideas.

Parents can be invited to school events such as a Hands-on Math and Science Night or a Family Read Aloud Night. Teachers can also reach out to parents by making "good news" phone calls (as opposed to only bad news phone calls), and they may visit the homes of students, when they are invited and welcome. Home visits are an excellent way to heighten cultural sensitivity and understanding.

Home Visit Increases Student Teacher's Sensitivity to Socioeconomic and Cultural Diversity

Home visit programs can inform a teacher about the parents' culture and the family's situation. In rural Appalachia, I once supervised a student teacher, Amy, who was concerned about the appearance of a teen-age girl in her class. What bothered Amy the most was Jenny's disheveled hair. She bought Jenny a new brush, shampoo, conditioner, and hair spray, which she taught her to use at school.

Amy was overly judgmental about Jenny's appearance, and she lacked tolerance for the family's lifestyle, even though she had never met Jenny's parents. Toward the end of the semester, Amy had an opportunity to make a home visit. She learned that Jenny and her family of eight lived in a log cabin at the top of a mountain, with no running water and no road going up the mountain. What water was available had to be hauled from a spring to the top of the mountain on foot, and heated on a wood stove. Jenny's hair was identical to her father's—long, red, curly, and tangled.

Amy's home visit may have had more effect on her than any other aspect of student teaching. She began to appreciate the fact that Jenny was from a different cultural background and socioeconomic circumstances than herself. The home visit also increased Amy's respect for Jenny's culture, as she enjoyed the family's traditional music, which included fiddles, banjos, a mandolin, and a guitar.

CONCLUSION

In this chapter you have been introduced to five popular methods of cooperative learning: Learning Together, the Structural Approach, Student Team Learning, Group Investigation, and Complex Instruction. Each method has unique aspects and purposes, but all the methods are tied together by five critical attributes: (1) a common task or learning activity suitable for group-work, (2) small-group learning, (3) cooperative behavior, (4) interdependence, and (5) individual accountability and responsibility. It is important to emphasize all five aspects in cooperative learning activities—they are the defining characteristics of the method.

Beyond these generic approaches exists an array of cooperative methods; some are specific to curricular areas, some to age and developmental levels, and many more based on the creative imagination of teachers throughout the world. No one method is adequate for all instructional goals; rather, different cooperative methods are selected for various instructional purposes.

While the generic model of cooperative learning lends itself to educating heterogeneous groups of learners, specific strategies exist to maximize the success of students with exceptional learning and behavioral needs. Major categories of modifications include altering instructional objectives, instructional materials, and the environment. The profound effect of teachers as positive role models for helping create a cooperative classroom climate cannot be overemphasized. Teachers should exhibit cultural sensitivity in the way they organize and conduct learning activities to foster the growth of all children.

◆   ◆   ◆

QUESTIONS AND ACTIVITIES

1.   The letter in Figure 5.8 was written to the State Superintendent of Education in Montana. Given my involvement in cooperative learning and inclusion training in the state, the letter was forwarded to me for a response. The student has given me permission to print her letter (I have deleted the name of her high school). With the understanding that the letter states only one side of the story—the student's perception—form groups of three and discuss your reactions and how you would respond to the letter. Answer these questions:

1. What could done differently in the classroom with respect to cooperative learning?
2. Were the key features of cooperative learning adhered to?
3. What modifications could be made for the students with disabilities?

Put your reply in the form of a letter, signed by all three members of your group.

2.   What five critical attributes are common to all the models of cooperative learning discussed in this chapter (Learning Together, the Structural Approach, Student Team Learning, Group Investigation, and Complex Instruction)? To answer this question, form a group of five stu-

FIGURE 5.8
Student's Letter to Superintendent of Education

Superintendent of Education
Office of Public Instruction
State Capitol Room 106
Helena, MT 59523

Dear Superintendent:

  My name is Darcy Schilling. I'm a freshman at a high school
in Montana. I am writing this letter in concern with kids
with learning disabilities. Before I continue I'd like to
tell you I have grown up with people with disabilities all my
life. Some used to live with us. My mother works with them.
  In my world history class there are some of these
students. I don't mind them being in my class as long as they
don't interfere with my learning as they are interfering
right now. We have to work in groups and our teacher puts me
with two or three of these students. He won't let me go on
without them, so it slows me down. They don't want to work.
All they want to do is copy my paper which is unfair to me. I
am there to learn, not to teach. I am being punished for
being smarter than they are. It's very aggravating for me and
other students. I believe they have a right to a good
education as citizens of the United States and as human
beings, but so do I. Because they are slower than me they
shouldn't be able to make me have to slow down. I understand
that people believe in cooperative learning as I do, but one
person shouldn't get stuck doing all of the work. This seems
to be what is happening in my world history class.
  It is as important for me to learn everything I am capable
of as it is for them to learn everything as they are capable
of. I would appreciate it if the school boards would look
into alternate solutions for this problem.

Sincerely,

Darcy Schilling

dents in your class and select one attribute (or the instructor can assign the attribute), such as interdependence. Each group member works independently to determine how that attribute is featured in a particular method (this should take about five minutes). Then, as a group, discuss all five methods and how the attribute is incorporated. After the groupwork, a whole-class discussion of the attributes can take place.

3.   How could you modify a cooperative learning activity for eighth-grade students on identifying trees? Briefly describe a cooperative lesson and how you would modify the activity for a student with a hearing impairment, a student with a visual impairment, and a student with a cognitive delay. You will need to describe the students and make some assumptions about their characteristics and abilities. Feel free to use another lesson objective if you prefer.

RECOMMENDED READINGS

Books

Cohen, E. G. (1994). *Designing groupwork: Strategies for the heterogeneous classroom.* (2nd ed.). New York: Teachers College Press.

Putnam, J .W. (Ed.). (1993). *Cooperative learning and strategies for inclusion; Celebrating diversity in the classroom.* Baltimore: Paul H. Brookes Publishing Company.

Sharan, S. (1994). *Handbook of Cooperative Learning Methods.* Westport, CT: Greenwood Press.

Sharan, Y., & Sharan, S. (1992). *Expanding cooperative learning through group investigation.* New York: Teachers College Press.

REFERENCES

Brandt, R. (1990). On cooperative learning: A conversation with Spencer Kagan. *Educational Leadership, 47*(4), 8–11.

Brewer, A. (1977). On Indian education. *Integrateducation, 15,* 21–23.

Chrispeels, J. (1994). Home-school collaboration: A review of research. *Cooperative Learning, 14*(4), 18–21.

Clark, R. (1983). *Family life and school achievement: Why poor black children succeed or fail.* Chicago: University of Chicago Press.

Cohen, E. G. (1994). *Designing groupwork: Strategies for the heterogeneous classroom.* (2nd ed.). New York: Teachers College Press.

Davidson, N. (1994). Cooperative and collaborative learning. In J. S. Thousand, R. A. Villa, & A. Nevin (Eds.), *Creativity and collaborative learning* (pp. 13–30). Baltimore: Paul H. Brookes Publishing Company.

Davies, D. (1991). Schools reaching out: Family, school, and community partnerships for student success. *Phi Delta Kappan, 72,* 376–382.

De Avila, E. A., Duncan, S. E., & Navarrete, C. (1987). *Finding out/Descubrimiento.* Northvale, NJ: Santillana.

Franklin, M. E. (1992). Culturally sensitive instructional practices for African-American learners with disabilities. *Exceptional Children, 59*(2) 115–122.

Jakupcak, J. (1994). Innovative classroom programs for full inclusion. In J. W. Putnam (Ed.), *Cooperative learning and strategies for inclusion.* (pp. 163–180). Baltimore: Paul H. Brookes Publishing Company.

Johnson, D. W., & Johnson, R. T. (1989). *Cooperation and competition: Theory and research.* Edina, MN: Interaction Books.

Johnson, D. W., & Johnson, R. T. (1991). *Cooperative learning lesson structures.* Edina, MN: Interaction Books.

Kagan, S. (1992). *Cooperative learning: Resources for teachers.* San Juan Capistrano, CA: Kagan Cooperative Learning.

Kagan, S. (1990). The structural approach to cooperative learning. *Educational Leadership, 47*(4), 10–15.

Kagan, S., & Kagan, M. (1994). The structural approach: Six keys to cooperative learning. In S. Sharan (Ed.), *Handbook of Cooperative Learning Methods* (pp. 115–133). Westport, CN: Greenwood Press.

Putnam, D. (1996). Personal communication.

Putnam, J. W. (1991). Curriculum adaptations for students in cooperative groups. *Cooperative Learning, 12*(1), 10.

Sapon-Shevin, M., Ayres, B. J., & Duncan, J. (1994). Cooperative learning and inclusion. In J. S. Thousand, R. A. Villa, & A. Nevin (Eds.), *Creativity and collaborative learning* (pp. 45–58). Baltimore: Paul H. Brookes Publishing Company.

Sharan, S. (1994). *Handbook of cooperative learning methods.* Westport, CT: Greenwood Press.

Sharan, Y., & Sharan, S. (1994) Group investigation in the cooperative classroom. In S. Sharan (Ed.), *Handbook of cooperative learning methods* (pp. 97–113). Westport, CT: Greenwood Press.

Sharan, Y., & Sharan, S. (1992). *Expanding cooperative learning through group investigation.* New York: Teachers College Press.

Sharan, Y., & Sharan, S. (1989–90). Group investigation expands cooperative learning. *Educational Leadership, 47*(4), 17–21.

Slavin, R. E. (1995a). *Cooperative learning.* (2nd ed.). Boston: Allyn and Bacon.

Slavin, R. E. (1995b). Personal communication.

Slavin, R. E. (1990). *Cooperative learning: Theory, research and practice.* Englewood Cliffs, NJ: Prentice Hall.

Stevens, R., Slavin, R., & Madden, N. (1991). Cooperative integrated reading and composition (CIRC): Effective cooperative learning in reading and language arts. *Cooperative Learning, 11*(4), 16–18.

Swisher, K. (1990). Cooperative learning and the education of American Indian/Alaskan Native Students: A review of the literature and suggestions for implementation. *Journal of American Indian Education, 29*(2), 36–43.

Udvari-Solner, A. (1994) A decision-making model for curricular adaptations in cooperative groups. In J. S. Thousand, R. A. Villa, & A. Nevin (Eds.), *Creativity and collaborative learning* (pp. 59–77). Baltimore: Paul H. Brookes Publishing Company.

Walberg, H. J. (1984). Families as partners in educational productivity. *Phi Delta Kappan, 65*(6), 397–400.

Wind project gives students of all abilities a sense of discovery. (1994, Fall). *Incline,* pp. 3–4.

CHAPTER 6

ASSESSMENT AND PROBLEM SOLVING IN COOPERATIVE LEARNING

◆

This chapter is designed to:

- ◆ Acquaint you with the purposes of assessment relative to cooperative learning.
- ◆ Provide guidelines for assessment based on current recommended practices.
- ◆ Introduce you to a variety of techniques for evaluating academic achievement, ranging from more traditional methods to current approaches.
- ◆ Introduce you to techniques for evaluating students' cooperative behaviors and group process outcomes.
- ◆ Identify some persistent problems that interfere with successful groupwork.
- ◆ Develop your repertoire of practical solutions for some of the most common problems associated with cooperative learning group processes.

How Do We Know What We Know?
Assessment in Cooperative Learning

By Liana Nan Forest, Editor, Cooperative Learning Magazine

How many of you have had a nightmare from which you wake trembling, sure that you have forgotten to study for an important test, or even have forgotten you were taking that class, so you are miles behind? I would bet it's a pretty common occurrence, especially among those of us who have gone as far as a tertiary degree. For me such a nightmare ranks in terror right above dreams where I discover I have absent-mindedly gone to school in my pajamas. Most often the class is one in some advanced form of mathematics, which in my school days was all right or wrong answers, and I'm sure I know nothing and I'll be wrong, wrong, wrong!

How refreshing to banish those dreams to the Dumpster with the realization that not only has the study of mathematics (and other subjects) changed with a focus on thinking skills, problem-solving strategies, discussion of alternatives, and discovery meth-

ods, but also our whole view of how to assess where we are in our learning process is evolving as well. No longer need we feel alone, terrified, and angry that our views of what is relevant and interesting to learn are ignored.

I once read a science fiction story about an alien who was astounded at how few humans knew what they knew. From the alien's perspective, humans were unaware of what vast storehouses of wisdom and strategies for attaining knowledge they actually were. Perhaps this was in part because we have had narrow and primitive ways of knowing what we know. And we also were neglecting two important sources of information to gain that discernment: our own **self-assessment abilities,** *and the* **perspective of our peers.***

Cooperative classrooms and teacher learning communities are where students and teachers can learn to generate, with supportive workmates, the criteria to use in self- and peer evaluations. Cooperative learning is on the forefront of deciding which outcomes are to be sought, what is "authentic" and "relevant," and how to use the power of the group combined with that of the individual to expand how we know and what we know.

ASSESSING COOPERATIVE LEARNING

Consider these two student's comments on testing and cooperative learning. Upon reading and understanding this chapter, you will know why the assessment used by the teachers of these two students was not appropriate or consistent with the principles of cooperative learning.

> *Ian, an eighth-grade student. Last quarter, my eighth-grade health class was working on a unit covering the respiratory system. Our teacher, Mr. Louder, split the class into groups of four or five children so we could study together and take a cooperative test. The test covered a chapter in the textbook, so we needed to learn the material. On the day of the test, Mr. Louder handed out one test per group. Practically the whole period, the classmates in my group were feuding over which answers were the correct ones. As it turned out, of the entire class, not one group received more than 86% on the test. My group only got 80% correct. What was frustrating is that I really did know some of the right answers but the group wouldn't listen to me or accept my input. Personality-wise, I'm laid back, and certainly not as dominating as some of the other kids in the group. My grade was dragged down to a B–. In my opinion, group testing is the point where cooperative learn-*

ing breaks down, and may not be as helpful to all the students in the group. A student should work on his or her own to take a test. A test is too personal, too individual, and too important for several people.

Srijana, a high school student. *Our biology class has been working on solving experiments at learning stations. We work in teams of four, with role assignments changing when we move to the next station. Each group member serves as a recorder at one of the stations. Last week we worked on stations for two days. It was a big rush to get through the work and there was no time to discuss our findings or check on what the recorders were writing at each of the stations. When the teacher returned our grades on the experiments, our group received 78%! I was shocked to see some of the reports—they were awful. One recorder didn't even fill in the names of the plants or record the answers to the questions we had discussed. The experiment I recorded was correct and had no points taken off. What really irritates me is that we never had a chance to go over the write-ups because we were in such a rush. I shouldn't have to live with the work of a lazy recorder. Next year I was hoping to apply to our state's science and mathematics magnet school for gifted and talented students. Grades of B– are simply not acceptable. I can accept working on a group project with one write-up, but not if I don't have an opportunity for input. This grade does not reflect what I know or can do.*

One of the more controversial topics in education today is assessment. Many citizens and educators disagree about how learning should be evaluated and they debate the use of certain terminology, such as **outcomes-based assessment.** Testing is another emotionally charged subject in U.S. education. Educators and noneducators alike question the value of testing, particularly if it is used as a primary tool in determining how much students know.

Historically, however, a test score in our society has assumed importance. It may signify potential success or lack of it; it may tell us whether the test taker is functioning at an appropriate level; and it may provide us with relevant diagnostic information that is germane to a successful program. A test score may also provide us with inappropriate or biased information that can be detrimental to students (Adler, 1993). For students like Ian and Srijana, tests can be highly important because they are used as exit criteria for most high schools and as entrance criteria for most colleges and special programs.

By definition, tests pose a series of questions, problems, or tasks to be completed. However, they constitute only one type of evaluation. Assessment is much more broadly defined than that—it involves the observing, gathering, and / or recording of information for the purpose of making educational decisions. The first goal of this chapter is to examine assessment as it relates to cooperative group learning. A key assumption of the chapter is that *cooperative learning does not create a totally new agenda in assessment*. Rather, teachers simply need to apply to cooperative learning instruction what they already know about sound assessment practices (Bennett, Rolheiser-Bennett, & Stevhan, 1991).

Performance Assessment

What to Assess.   Assessment of student learning in cooperative groups encompasses three major areas: (1) *academic performance*—such as the ability to solve math problems, write an essay, or make a presentation; (2) *social skill performance*—such as the ability to be a good listener, make contributions to the group, or encourage others in the group; and (3) *general group functioning*—such as the ability to achieve positive interdependence, stay on task, or behave respectfully toward one another.

How to Assess.   One of the first questions a teacher may ask regarding assessment in cooperative learning is how to assess performance outcomes (academic and social) and process outcomes (group functioning) in cooperative groupwork. A variety of techniques involved in assessment are introduced in this chapter, ranging from more traditional approaches to more contemporary, or "alternative," approaches.

Who Assesses?   Another question teachers need to answer is *who* conducts the evaluation of cooperative learning outcomes: the students, the teacher, or both?

The final section of this chapter ventures into what I consider the most fascinating aspects of using cooperative learning methods in instruction, which is trying to answer the following questions: "Why do cooperative groups experience problems?" and "What can be done about them?" It is not sufficient to evaluate student and group success. Teachers must then decide why students and/or groups are not faring well, and then *do something about it!*

ASSESSMENT CONSIDERATIONS

Suggestions for assessing cooperative learning outcomes and processes include the following practices:

1.   *Align the assessment method with the instructional objective.* Approaches for examining student and group outcomes in cooperative learning situations are similar to the general classroom assessment approaches.

First, the instructional objective should be clearly stated and the evaluation criteria identified up-front during the lesson planning phase. The evaluation method to be used should be based on the instructional objective and the purpose of the cooperative activity. A variety of strategies and tools (described later in this chapter) can be employed, whether to measure student learning results, or determine whether the groups are functioning well, or improve your own instructional methods and organization.

2.   *Use criterion referenced evaluation.* Criterion referenced evaluation establishes the standard for student success at the *onset* of the cooperative learning activity. The criterion for success is tied to the curricular objectives, such as solving 17 out of 20 chemistry problems, completing a unit math test, writing a technical paper, or reading a score of music. Performance is judged by the degree to which students achieve the preset standard or goal. Norm referenced assessment, which compares students' scores or performance with that of other students, is not consistent with cooperation. Rather, it is more appropriately used in competitive situations, such as standardized testing, or for rating individuals in an ice skating competition.

3.   *Evaluate individually to determine student growth.* Miller (1992) posed the following questions: "If you instruct using groupwork, shouldn't you assess in the same way? But if you use group assessments, how do you measure and evaluate individual growth?" (p. 48). The best answer is to use both group and individual assessments, but for different purposes. Even when students work together to learn, the best way to determine what each student has mastered is to conduct individual evaluations. A group test will tell you what the group knows, or what a particular member of the group knows, but it will not allow you to verify what each student in the group knows.

The students in one of my university courses tried to persuade me to give them group exams rather than individual exams. They argued that a group exam would be most consistent with the spirit of cooperative learning. To their dismay, I argued that my purpose for testing was to find out what *each* of them had learned from the class, the activities, and the readings. This is not to minimize the importance of evaluating group endeavors, such as their group presentations, solutions to problems, or group products—which received group grades or recognition.

Both Ian and Srijana, who wrote about their cooperative testing experiences at the beginning of the chapter, recognized the problems with assessing the group as opposed to individuals. In this author's opinion, the *only* justification for grading students as a group is when the specific purpose of the activity is to promote interdependence, when a project or presentation requires some type of group evaluation (but this can be used in addition to individual evaluations), and when the activity is set up to allow ample time for thoughtful and critical group input and editing.

4.   *Adapt evaluation criteria to suit the capabilities of a student with exceptional needs.* All students do not have to perform at the same level or in

the same manner in cooperative groups. Expectations should correspond to the student's abilities and learning needs—and these may vary slightly or even greatly from the rest of the group. For example, a student who reads at a lower level than peers may not be expected to read the test questions, but may work with a volunteer adult reader or teaching assistant who presents the questions orally during the test. Students with personalized objectives may have very different criteria for success with different evaluation approaches. A social studies lesson developed by teacher Karen Noone of Vermont included an eighth-grade student with limited reading and spelling skills and memory deficits. The curriculum (covering material about African countries) was adapted to address the student's Individualized Education Plan objectives.

The teacher asked each of six groups of four students to develop a memory aid, or mnemonic, to represent each of three sets of African countries being studied. The student with memory deficits was held accountable for one of the sets (a reduced assignment). All the groups were successful in creating mnemonics that enabled them to remember both the names of the nations and their locations, for example, "MATLE"—for the contiguous North African states of Morocco, Algeria, Tunisia, Libya, and Egypt, and "My Mother Never Cooked Soup Every Night During Supper"—for the contiguous middle states of Mauritania, Morai, Niger, Chad, Sudan, Ethiopia, and North Djibouti (Nevin, 1993).

5.   *Use unbiased assessment approaches with language minority and bilingual students.* Cooperative learning lends itself to assessing language minority and bilingual students because it affords observation of how students are able to use their resources and what they already know. Standardized methods of assessment do not reveal what a child knows, nor do they guide us in the delivery of instruction (Calderon & Hertz-Lazarowitz, 1992). Alternative assessment practices yield more relevant information about students' understandings and abilities. When students are engaged in cooperative learning activities, teachers can gather information about their communication capabilities, use of manipulatives, learning strategies, and study skills, as well as the products they generate. Using these techniques, language minority and bilingual students can be evaluated in either language by evaluators who may or may not be fluent in their language (Raborn, 1992).

6.   *Use equal-opportunity-for-success-grading procedures.* Teachers should try to create cooperative situations in which each student is able to demonstrate growth beyond his or her own past performance (Slavin, 1991). Students who are evaluated on their improvement can be successful whatever their level of ability. High performers, students who are gifted, average performers, and students with learning problems alike are challenged to surpass past expectations. An unfortunate misunderstanding about cooperative learning is that everyone in the group must perform in exactly the same manner or at the same level. When strict conformity is the expectation, it is unlikely that the activity will stimulate student motivation or high achievement.

7. *Incorporate authentic performance assessment in your repertoire of cooperative learning evaluation procedures.* Authentic performance assessment involves evaluating students as they perform tasks similar to those they will encounter in the "real world." Recall Figure 1.1 in Chapter 1 that demonstrates the situations in which people learn, ranging from when they learn the least (10%) to the most (95%). The figure indicates that when you *apply* what is learned to real-life situations, you learn more than when you simply read or listen to a presentation. When real-life tasks are used, individuals select and apply information in sometimes unpredictable, but more authentic, situations. When students work in authentic situations, the quality of performance is assessed through rubrics, focus lists, and standards of quality which are described in the next section of this chapter. Multiple-choice or true-false test questions are of limited value in such situations.

Anchorage Public School elementary students (typical students and those with special needs) participated in a summer school program that involved studying basic economics principles. Students worked in teams at various levels in multigrade classrooms to plan and carry out a "market day" at the school. Each team developed a product (e.g., friendship bracelets, plastic jewelry, pizza) to be sold at the market. A variety of strategies were used to assess student performance in mathematics, economics, and language arts, such as teacher observation, work sample analysis, and reading students' "learning logs." Students studying business in high school can work together to develop a marketing strategy or an improved management approach for addressing the real-life problems of a local business. Both of these examples are interdisciplinary activities, with integration of the subjects of mathematics, writing, social studies, and the use of technology.

Evaluating Academic Performance

Student progress in academic areas can be measured in a number of ways. Below are some of the techniques that can be used. We begin with a listing of traditional approaches that should be familiar to you, as well as more current, holistic approaches (Calderon & Hertz-Lazarowitz, 1992).

Student Products

Quizzes	Student notebooks
Tests	Papers
Homework	Learning logs
Reports	Journals

Participation Points.   Students can also be assessed on their participation in the group and their completion of assignments or homework. Points may be awarded on an individual or group basis for the following types of participation (Calderon & Hertz-Lazarowitz, 1992):

A Student Report

1. Attending class
2. Submitting completed homework
3. Contributing to the groupwork
4. Completing a project or unit
5. Behaving appropriately

Portfolios.   A portfolio is a purposeful collection of student work that exhibits the student's efforts, progress, and achievements in one or more areas. The collection must include student participation in selecting contents, the criteria for selection, the criteria for judging merit, and evidence of student self-reflection (Northwest Education Association, 1990).

Portfolios can contain writing samples, drawings, selections from learning logs or journals, tests, tapes, CD-ROMs, or videos. It is important that students select samples of their work to be placed in the portfolios, and that they understand what a sample is! A *cooperative group portfolio* may also be maintained for groups that stay together for longer periods of time.

Digital portfolios containing writing samples, scanned drawings, audio samples, and even video clips can be maintained using computer technology.

Periodically, teachers and students should review the portfolios. Reflecting on the quality of work, the improvement over time, problem areas, and areas of success are all part of the assessment process. Students should be able to identify, with the teacher and eventually on their own, which behaviors and skills will improve their future performance. Portfolios are an excellent communication device about class progress, and can be shared with parents and others.

Grading.   Another way student achievement can be evaluated is through the assignment of grades. Some grading options are:

1. *Individual grades.* Student products and participation can be graded individually for each member of the group.

2. *Shared group grade.* If students take a test as a group, or submit one product, or make one presentation, a single grade can be awarded to all students.

3. *Averaged individual grades.* A group score is arrived at by averaging the individual grades on a test.

4. *Individual and group grade.* A combination of individual and group grades can be awarded. For example, students receive an individual grade on their own section of a paper and a group grade for the paper overall.

A good deal of controversy exists regarding whether students in cooperative learning groups should receive a group grade on a test or product. An argument in favor of group grades is that in the real world of work and in the community, we are often held accountable for the results of a product developed by a team. Students may object to this approach because the group grade can lower the grades of all students in the group for reasons not always in their control, such as one or several students not studying, off-task behaviors, or because they have a student with learning difficulties in their group. A single group grade or averaged group grade may also artificially raise the grades of poor performers.

Insisting on group grading also can incur parents' wrath and opposition to cooperative learning, especially the parents of secondary students who are college bound and risk lowered grades due to groupwork. The best advice is to use group grades sparingly, and for only those projects and products that lend themselves to a single grade. A rule of thumb is *don't lower the grade of a high performer due to the poor performance of another.* A few exceptions to this rule are when you are trying to build positive interdependence, or a greater level of student concern for the performance of others in their group, or when the grade has little effect on a student's overall average. And be sure to have a way to determine how individuals are achieving the learning objectives.

5. *No grade.* There are occasions when no grade should assigned for a cooperative activity, such as when the groups have just been formed; when an ad hoc, or informal group, has been formed to work on a task for a short period of time; when new material is being introduced and students are in the early acquisition phases of learning; or when students are focusing on learning the cooperative skills they will need to perform in their groups (Bennett et al., 1991).

Hot Issue: Extrinsic Versus Intrinsic Rewards in Cooperative Learning

In a thought-provoking article titled Group Grade Grubbing Versus Cooperative learning, Kohn (1991) argues that there are two perils of using rewards to bribe students to work together: decreased motivation and lower levels of performance. Citing research on motivation, Kohn gives three explanations for the possible negative effects of rewards on motivation and performance. The first is that people who think of themselves as working for a reward tend to feel controlled by it, which results in a lack of self-determination that interferes with creativity. Second, when a person strives for extrinsic, or external, rewards—as opposed to intrinsic, or internal, rewards—the focus is more on the self. The self-focus results in ego involvement, as opposed to task involvement, which is more predictive of achievement. The third explanation is that attaching a reward to an activity implies that the activity is not worth doing for its own sake, resulting in the task being devalued and the goal becoming the reward.

Should cooperative learning be used for learning tasks that have little intrinsic appeal? Kohn proposes that cooperative learning models should be created that do not rely on extrinsic rewards, but incorporate the key components of successful cooperative learning: an **appealing curriculum** *emphasizing challenging and interesting tasks,* **student autonomy** *that empowers students to make choices in the classroom, and the promotion of* **caring relationships** *through encouraging social and collaborative skills.*

While an interesting curriculum incorporating student autonomy and positive relationships sounds ideal for cooperative learning, most of us can identify tasks that are made less objectionable through the use of an outside reward. My children would cite numerous examples of housework, such as washing dishes or cleaning rooms. And some tedious, boring, or inconsequential schoolwork may be made more palatable by using extrinsic rewards (such as practicing three-digit multiplication problems). Moreover, we cannot neglect the results of more than 35 studies by Slavin (1991) indicating that cooperative classes using group rewards and individual accountability achieved more than tradi-

tional control groups not using extrinsic group rewards. Slavin explains that cooperative learning creates peer norms that favor achievement. Students must ensure that everyone in the group learns the material to attain the group reward. Answer-sharing will not accomplish this goal; students must sometimes teach their groupmates.

> *With the possible exception of Summerhill, just about every school in the world uses grades, praise, recognition, and other rewards to maintain student motivation. Cooperative learning simply focuses the classroom reward system on helping others learn (as well as on one's own learning). (Slavin, 1991, p. 90)*

Intrinsically rewarding cooperative activities may be the ideal, but it is unrealistic to expect that all learning activities are suited to intrinsic reward structures. Sometimes students have to expend great effort to learn material or master a subject—and extrinsic rewards "sweeten the pot."

Peer Evaluation

Students can contribute to the cooperative learning effort by evaluating the work or contributions of their peers. Editing the written work of classmates is one example of peer evaluation. For example, students can use calculators to check computations as shown in the photo, or be given criteria for evaluating essays written by teammates for mechanical and grammatical errors. A laminated bookmark with editing symbols can be prepared by the teacher and distributed to students, who work in teams of four (Figure 6.1). Students form pairs to read and correct each other's essays, using a colored pencil to indicate their suggestions for editorial changes. Each student then revises his or her draft using the word processor. Students can compare their original drafts and revised drafts to show improvement.

Students can work together with or without the teacher to develop the standards for assessing quality performance in their groups. They brainstorm and discuss the task or project to be accomplished and identify standards for effectiveness and high quality. A continuum of quality can be developed, sometimes referred to as **rubrics**. See Figure 6.2 for a sample evaluation form for debates.

Students also reflect on the group process through peer evaluation. They consider how well their group has functioned and the degree to which they accomplished their goal(s). Periodically, students can complete written evaluation forms to analyze their strengths and weaknesses (Figure 6.3). An important aspect of the group process evaluation is for students to identify the behaviors they need to improve on in the future. If the groups reflect on their functioning on Friday, the next Monday they should review the goals they plan to address.

FIGURE 6.1
Bookmark With Editing
Symbols

EDITOR'S MARKS
≡   capitalize
⊙   make a period
∧   add something
⋏   add a coma
ᵛᵛ   add quotation marks
⸰   take away something
◯   spell out
⌗   indent the paragraph
╱   make lowercase
⇄   transpose
⌒   move something

Occasionally, a student can serve as an outside observer for the group. Observations are recorded on an observation form. Various approaches can be used for documenting observations:

1. An anecdotal running record can be kept of the group actions and verbalizations (Figure 6.4).

2. One or more behaviors can be tallied, such as paraphrasing others' ideas, making summary statements, and asking others for their opinions (Figure 6.5).

3. A student observer can also reflect on what is seen, noting personal perceptions and judgments about the groupwork (Figure 6.6). A student comment might be, "I noticed that every time Mary tried to talk, she was interrupted."

Students are provided with feedback from the observer, who shares the observation forms and reflections. Group members then discuss the

Peer Evaluation

observer's data and conclusions. The discussion should lead the students to goal setting for improving future groupwork.

PROBLEM SOLVING IN COOPERATIVE GROUPS

When people affiliate with one another for the purpose of accomplishing a goal, the potential exists for problems. When cooperative group learning is selected as the instructional method, positive results can be anticipated if the procedures are used correctly. But even with the most careful planning and implementation, difficulties can be expected.

It has always surprised me to hear statements such as, "I tried cooperative learning in my social studies class last Friday for the first time. It was awful. The kids were off-task and we hardly accomplished anything! I'll never try that again." What is even more surprising is when the reaction to an initial attempt at cooperative learning leads to a hasty and negative conclusion about its value: "I'm convinced that cooperative learning doesn't work because some students weren't participating and there was conflict in

FIGURE 6.2
Peer Evaluation Form for Debates
Dippong, 1992, p. 51

Key:

1 = disorganized, unclear

2 = barely interesting, uncreative

3 = quite interesting, satisfactory

4 = organized, very interesting

5 = very well organized, stimulating

Topic: _____

Position: Pro   Con   (circle)

Names: _____

Marks

Understood material	1	2	3	4	5
Quality of voice	1	2	3	4	5
Convincing	1	2	3	4	5
Overall	1	2	3	4	5

Total points: _____ /20

two of the groups." What makes this conclusion even more troublesome is that the teacher who stated it had only experienced a one-day awareness level in-service training session on cooperative learning at her school the week before. Despite her lack of experience and background in conducting groupwork, she felt competent to evaluate it and lightly dismiss it.

We know that human relationships can be troublesome. But we also know they are mostly worth the trouble, and we usually attempt to make them better. The divorce rate illustrates difficulties with the institution of marriage, yet our society is not willing to abandon it just because it is problematic. People read books and magazine articles about improving relationships, sometimes they seek counseling, and they turn to their friends and family for advice. Some people even call psychic hot lines! Our families and friends are important enough for us to make the effort to deal with the problems that inevitably arise. And, learning and working in groups is no different—sometimes groups thrive and sometimes they struggle. If they struggle, we search for solutions to the problems. If a group seems hopeless, we may choose to disband it, but we cannot abandon the goal of working together—it is too critical to our future.

To me, the most interesting aspect of using cooperative learning in instruction is analyzing *why* groups are successful or unsuccessful. So many variables interact when two or more people try to accomplish something together! To consider these variables adequately would take volumes.

FIGURE 6.3
Cooperative Group Reflection and Goal Setting

Group name: _____

Date: _____

We have serious problems   Need some improvement   Well done   Excellent job
       1   2   3   4

How well did we:

1. Complete the task? _____
2. Use our time? _____
3. Listen to others' ideas? _____
4. Help other group members? _____
5. Each contribute to the work? _____

What we did especially well: _____

_____

What we should improve on: _____

_____

Future goal(s): _____

_____

FIGURE 6.4
Peer Observation Options: Anecdotal Running Record

Observer: Jamie _____

Date: April 13 _____

Team investigation topic: Viruses, HIV/AIDS _____

Ramon handed out the assignment.

Carla read the directions.

Mark elaborated on the directions.

Anita asked a question about using the Internet to see if there is a list on the topic.

FIGURE 6.5
Tally Sheet for Behavior Observations

Observer: _Jamie_

Date: _April 13_

Team investigation topic: _Viruses, HIV/AIDS_

Behaviors	Team members				Total
	Ramon	Carla	Mark	Anita	
Contributes ideas					
Invites other's contributions					
On-task talk					
Total:					

FIGURE 6.6
Sample Form for Noting Observer Reflections

Observer: _Jamie_

Date: _April 13_

Team investigation topic: _Viruses, HIV/AIDS_

What I noticed or felt about the groupwork: _____

_____

Suggestions for the group: _____

_____

What follows is a discussion of some of the common problems that arise in cooperative learning. As mentioned in Chapter 2, the literature points out that cooperative learning is most effective when the following conditions exist: positive interdependence, individual accountability, frequent face-to-face interaction, and the direct teaching and frequent use of interpersonal and small-group skills (Johnson & Johnson, 1989). For a comprehensive, research-based discussion of why cooperative learning fails, see *Cooperation and Competition: Theory and Research* (Johnson & Johnson, 1989). Another resource is the book *Small Group Teaching: A Trouble-Shooting Guide* (Tiberius, 1990). A major barrier to effective groupwork is student misbehavior and the lack of cooperative skills. Because these topics were discussed in Chapters 2 and 4, they will not be covered in this section. Additional sources of difficulty in groupwork may relate to problems with the group objectives, lack of experience with cooperative learning and cultural differences, and problems with the task itself.

Problems with Group Learning Objectives

Problems with learning objectives may be attributed to four common causes:

1. Lack of a clear objective
2. An unobtainable objective
3. Objective doesn't align with the activity
4. An objective judged unacceptable by students (Tiberius, 1990).

Unclear Objectives.   Have you ever attended a class or workshop, been asked to start working, and realize that you have no idea what you are supposed to do? And you were even paying attention! The objective must be made clear to students through careful explanation. Displaying the goal statement on an overhead projector or chalkboard may reinforce understanding and is especially helpful to students whose preferred input mode is visual.

Check students' understanding of the learning objective by asking them to **paraphrase** it in their own words. By paraphrasing the objective to the large group or the cooperative group, the teacher or students can detect misunderstandings. Paraphrasing also prevents students from straying off task or allowing their conversations to digress. Carefully **explaining the criteria for success** to students will also reinforce the objective: "Give four explanations for the loss of energy. Write them in your log books, and quiz one another to make sure everyone in the group knows them. Each group member will have to write accurately about all four explanations for the quiz tomorrow."

Especially for long-term cooperative activities, **restate the learning objective** each time groups are convened. If the groups have a notebook or chart, the objective can be written down and students reminded of their purpose. When group members are reflecting on their progress, they can assess how well they are doing relative to attaining the objective.

Allow for modification or alteration of objectives if necessary. Sometimes students may want to alter their objective as the groupwork progresses if they have decided to take a different direction or have taken on too much work. Sometimes teachers will realize they have been too ambitious with their learning objectives and may decide to scale back the work or modify the objective to be more appropriate to student capabilities and interests.

Unobtainable Objectives. Objectives may be unattainable by students because (1) there isn't enough time, (2) students don't have the resources to complete the task, (3) the material is too difficult for students, or (4) the group structure being used doesn't match the assigned task. Teachers have run into difficulties with their earliest attempts at cooperative learning because they were asking students to do too much in too short a time period. One teacher planned a jigsaw activity for one class period that really needed three class periods. Students became frustrated because they weren't able to accomplish the work and had to rush through it.

Sometimes teachers don't provide students with the information they need to accomplish the objective. A friend of mine described an activity she planned in which students were asked to discuss concerns with underground water quality in the local region. Unfortunately, she had not given them enough background information to enable an informed discussion. After making the assignment, the students were silent because they simply were not prepared to respond. She realized she should have provided the class with advanced readings, lectures, or opportunities to search out information in the library or through computer networks.

Individuals in the groups may have learning problems that prohibit them from attaining the objective. The needs of individual students can be addressed by modifying the student response mode (oral response versus written), modifying the presentation method (using manipulatives rather than written materials), reducing the workload (fewer problems), expecting work at a lower grade level (reading at the fourth grade level versus the seventh grade level), or assigning personalized objectives (accomplishing a task suited to an Individualized Education Plan). See Chapter 5 for a discussion of modifications for students with disabilities.

Sometimes in our zeal to capitalize on the many human resources in the classroom, we overuse students as teachers and presenters. For example, if a group of students is asked to research a topic and make a presentation to the class, the teacher may feel "off the hook" in having to cover that topic. Sometimes using students as teachers/presenters backfires and the class becomes frustrated, perhaps because the knowledge and capabilities of the students to adequately cover the material has been overestimated. A student once complained, "I pay my tuition to listen to what you, the professor, have to say—not to my classmates!" If we expect students to teach students, we have to be sure they have the expertise to do so, and, when necessary, we must supplement what is taught and sometimes intervene to assure accuracy and quality (see Chapter 2).

Objectives Don't Align With the Activity.   Selecting the appropriate lesson structure to suit the learning objective of the activity is also essential. Noting that the effects of different structures and elements lead to the selection of appropriate lesson designs, Kagan and Kagan (1994) have identified "domains of usefulness" for cooperative structures. For example, if the objective is to generate creative solutions to a problem, select a structure that fosters divergent thinking, such as a roundtable, a brainstorming activity, or a word-webbing activity. If the objective is to recall factual information, select a structure that fosters convergent thinking, such as Numbered Heads Together or cooperative flash cards. You can expect problems if the structure doesn't match the objective of the activity. For example, if the task is to correctly solve 10 assigned math problems, a brainstorming activity would not focus students on the step-by-step procedures involved in reading the problem and solving it. A Numbered Heads Together activity would not be suited to considering alternative hypotheses, dealing with controversy, or considering different values.

Unacceptable Objectives.   Another obstacle to successful cooperative learning is choosing an objective that students do not consider relevant, interesting, or purposeful (Hunter, 1982; Tiberius, 1980). Students want to know why they should spend their time on a learning activity. Middle school students participating in a library unit I once observed were required to memorize the letters on the spines of books (e.g., F represents fiction). It was no surprise that they were disengaged. Isn't it more productive to target the effective use of databases or electronic networks to develop library skills?

If teachers cannot provide a rationale for an activity for themselves, they should consider doing something else. The usefulness of some tasks, particularly those that are tedious or abstract, may not be evident to students. In this case, it is up to the teacher to help students understand the potential benefits of accomplishing the objective or pursuing a course of study.

In high school and college, I was unaware of how important keyboarding would be to my future work as a researcher and writer. I spent many hours practicing at the typewriter, feeling resentful because the subject was uninteresting and I could not see how it was related to my future goals. Now I use keyboarding skills every day and I can't imagine how I would get along without them. At the same time, there are some objectives that I never understood the value of, such as diagramming sentences in English class. I remain unconvinced of its relevance for me.

Students also may have difficulty accepting an objective if it conflicts with their values or sensibilities. In my high school biology class we were required to dissect frogs and worms. As an animal lover, I found this task extremely objectionable. It is gratifying to know that interactive software technology now exists that enables students to dissect "virtual" animals.

Objectives Don't Match Students' Ability Levels. Learning objectives may not meet student needs when they are not matched to their cognitive/developmental stages. Engaging students in the analysis and debate of a controversial topic, such as gun control and the U.S. Constitution, requires students to consider multiple perspectives and viewpoints.

Considering multiple perspectives may not be easy for students who tend to be "black or white" or "right or wrong" in their thinking. At the lower stages of moral development, the tendency is to arrive at one absolute answer rather than to deal with alternate viewpoints or critically analyze conflicting information. Challenging students to stretch themselves by considering a problem that requires higher-level cognitive or moral reasoning can result in increased levels of cognitive or moral reasoning (Johnson & Johnson, 1989). However, if the disparity between the students' level of reasoning and the cognitive demands of the task are too great, they will experience frustration.

Even in small cooperative learning groups the diversity among student ability levels can be great. You will recall that in Chapter 5, five strategies were provided for modifying objectives to accommodate individual students with lower ability levels. In addition to modifying student objectives, tasks can be developed to accommodate a diversity of cognitive levels. For example, the Complex Instruction (Cohen, 1994) approach poses challenging and multifaceted problems requiring multiple abilities and diverse talents among students. Another way to address a diversity of ability levels is to use peer tutoring, which encourages more able students to help less able students. While peer tutoring should not be overused, benefits can accrue to both tutor and tutee. Tutors "learn twice" when they teach another student. They can also enhance communication and interpersonal skills by providing practice opportunities.

The jigsaw method is an excellent technique for addressing differing ability levels through the cooperative task itself (Figure 6.7). The task is

FIGURE 6.7
Sample Jigsaw Activity

Student 1: Identify the states that Lewis and Clark traveled through. Color the states on a map provided by the teacher.

Student 2: Explore the characters of Lewis and Clark. What were they like? What drew them to exploration?

Student 3: Explore the question of why Lewis and Clark embarked upon their journey. Why did Thomas Jefferson send them?

Integration: The three students, after sharing with one another their findings, produce a written report and presentation in which they share their information and address the questions posed about the Lewis and Clark expedition.

divided into pieces, and each piece requires a different level of ability. For example, a jigsaw activity on Lewis and Clarke's expedition is divided into three parts, each with a different demand.

Lack of Experience, Cultural Differences, and Physical Distance

Another troublesome problem that occurs in cooperative learning situations is the lack of student participation and interaction. Unless the teacher has purposefully built individual work or reflection into the cooperative activity, students should be conferring with one another about the task. It is important to discover why are students are not interacting when the groupwork is slowing down and students are not accomplishing the group task. Some of the reasons for lack of interaction are discussed below.

Inexperience With Cooperative Learning.   One of the most obvious causes for prolonged silences after the group assignment is given is students' lack of experience with cooperative learning. You cannot expect students who have learned one set of rules for classroom behavior, such as "work quietly at your desk, on your own," to suddenly shift to "sit in groups and talk with one another." If students have not encountered cooperative groupwork before, teachers should provide an orientation. Showing a videotape about cooperative learning, visiting another class where cooperative learning is taking place, and providing written guidelines on cooperative learning as well as training in cooperative skills will help to prepare students (Putnam & Spenciner, 1993).

Cultural Differences.   One summer, I taught a course at Beijing Normal University in China. It was a lecture class and I had to rely on an interpreter to translate my speech. Having grown accustomed to lively discussions in my U.S. courses, I was thrown off-balance by the silence during the classes. Even when I specifically asked students to discuss a topic, or to ask questions or react to my ideas, there was no response. Not only were our language differences contributing to the interaction problems, there were also cultural reasons for the lack of responsiveness. The reluctance of Chinese students to interact with a professor or one another is a sign of respect for the professor. I was told that asking a question or making a comment was disrespectful because it questioned the teacher's authority. Nevertheless, I persisted in my effort to receive student feedback. Eventually the students became willing to write down their questions, which they anonymously passed along the long rows and aisles of the lecture hall to the interpreter who translated them for me.

Similarly, Native American students in my courses have told me that it is customary to listen carefully to others and to talk only when one has achieved understanding of a subject. The silences should not be interpreted as a lack of attention; rather they constitute a thoughtful and reflective response to the interaction. Some non-Native people, like myself, have been socialized to be uncomfortable with periods of silence in an interaction and may need to exercise restraint when there is a lull in the conversation. Unfortunately, the urge some students have to chatter and fill in gaps of conversation further prevents meaningful contributions from the more thoughtful group members.

Students Are Unfamiliar With One Another.   If students don't know one another very well, they are less likely to interact comfortably. An array of team-building cooperative activities have been developed to help students get acquainted (Johnson & Johnson, 1985; Kagan, 1992). A common team-building activity is asking newly acquainted students to ask each other questions, such as "What are your life dreams?" or "What adjectives best describe you?" or "Where is your favorite place in the world?" Although these activities are not strictly academic, they are well worth the time spent in developing a classroom climate that is conducive to cooperative learning.

> What appears like time-off-task can be viewed as an important investment in creating the social context necessary for teams to maximize their potential. Again and again, we have observed greater long-run efficiency, learning, and liking of class, school, and subject matter if teachers take time for team building and class building." (Kagan, 1994, p. 129)

Group Size or Physical Proximity.   When groups are too large, students may not be able to maintain the close physical space that enables all members to participate in the discussion or activity. Sometimes it is difficult to hear others in the group, and students will simply tune out. If there are five or six people in a group, the tendency is for students to break off into sub-groups to manage their conversations. Some group members may retreat from the conversation entirely. Kagan (1992) has developed structures that require groups of four, with students occasionally pairing off in twos to accomplish a task or engage in a discussion.

As was pointed out earlier in this text, large tables may inhibit interaction and place a "psychological distance" between group members. Johnson and Johnson (1990) suggest that students be arranged so they are "knee-to-knee, nose-to-nose, and eye-to-eye." Group interaction is supported by arranging students into groups that are close in proximity without physical barriers to inhibit interaction. Also, it is important to teach students to modulate their voice levels to ensure that their group is not disturbing other groups.

Problems With the Task

If students are not motivated to engage in the cooperative activity, it may be due to a lack of interest in or commitment to the task itself. (See Johnson and Johnson, 1989, for a discussion of the cooperative task and its effects on achievement.) In Chapter 3, several factors related to student motivation and cooperative learning were discussed—level of concern, feeling tone, interest, success, and knowledge of results (Hunter, 1982). Two of those factors focus on the task: how interesting the task is to the students and students' level of concern for succeeding at the task. It is crucial that tasks are relevant to the lives of students, and that their attention is captured and maintained.

An Uninteresting Task.   All of us have experienced boring classes and we all find some subjects to be intrinsically more interesting than others. Nonetheless, teachers can draw out student interest by engaging students in an *authentic activity* that is relevant to their experience or interests, focusing on the unusual or the novel, and avoiding overdoing an activity.

The Physics of Logging

A high school teacher from a rural community in Maine was having difficulty engaging one of his students in physics class. The student's absences were piling up and he was on the verge of dropping out of school. He told the teacher that for generations his family had worked in the woods as loggers. How was physics going to be of any help to him? Based on the student's interests, the teacher put aside the traditional text and engaged several students in a cooperative physics activity that involved felling trees and dismantling and reassembling a chainsaw. The student began attending school regularly. He impressed his classmates with a culminating presentation that involved a demonstration of how chainsaws work and the physics of felling trees.

Another way to foster interest in a subject is to *emphasize the unique or unusual*. One of the finest middle school teachers I know captures students' interest in social studies, and in particular, the history of the Renaissance, by sharing stories of bizarre or even morbid events—including the story of Vlad the Impaler (the *real* Dracula). The students were eager to learn about the French Revolution when the teacher built the "anticipatory set" by telling the story of the invention of the guillotine.

Novelty also entices students to engage in an activity. Those of us who, during our entire elementary, secondary, and even college education, experienced mostly lectures, reading, papers, and exams became satiated and bored by the standard format. A former undergraduate sociology professor of mine sent his students out to systematically observe and record social behaviors. One cooperative activity involved observing eye-contact of people in elevators. My team learned that in an elevator, most people look up, or they look down, or they look at the operating panel, or sometimes they stare straight ahead—even if it's at the back of someone's head. It is unusual, however, for eye contact to occur among people who are unacquainted with one another, especially for extended periods of time. Part of our experiment was to look at people's faces, which made them extremely uncomfortable. A lifelong interest in social psychology was kindled as a result of this professor's novel approach, which he dared to use at a time when sitting passively and listening to 50-minute lectures was the standard in higher education.

Satiation With a Task. When students are filled, or glutted, with doing something they become bored. Satiation leads to the progressive loss of interest in the task and to the likelihood that student misbehaviors will increase. Students may try to escape from boredom by looking out the window, asking for a hall pass, sharpening their pencils, passing notes, drawing on the desk, stepping on each other's toes, or poking one another. I have vivid memories of studying the oak tree outside my classroom window during third grade *Weekly Reader* time. Every Friday the same format was used: a student was called on to read an article to the class and the teacher asked questions of the large group. I was satiated with this format by October. And my teacher quickly became satiated with my inattentiveness. Perhaps what I lost in my understanding of current events I gained in the realm of aesthetics and a beginning awareness of the process of photosynthesis. Satiation interferes with learning and good behavior. Remedies for satiation suggested by Kounin (1977, cited in Charles, 1989) are to provide progress, challenge, and variety.

1. *Progress.* Provide students with a feeling that they are progressing in their work, that they are moving on to new and more demanding tasks. Going over and over the same multiplication table that was mastered the previous week will quickly lead to satiation.

2. *Challenge.* Offer students a challenge to build enthusiasm for the lesson. "Last year it took my class three days to solve this math problem. I'll bet, with hard work in your groups, you can do it in one or two days."

3. *Variety.* You can incorporate variety into your lessons in any number of ways. Vary the group format using a variety of the structures that have been introduced in this book, from informal structures to formal structures. Vary the materials and technology to be used. For example, in group writing activities, use colored markers, chalk or marker boards, overhead projectors, and computers. Use manipulatives or musical instruments, or bring in live animals (with permission) to spice up the lessons.

Artificial Cooperative Tasks. According to Glasser (1986):

> We are mistaken if we believe that discipline, dropouts and drugs are what is wrong with today's schools. Serious as these are, they are symptoms of a much larger underlying problem which is that far too many capable students make little or no effort to learn.

One solution to the problems with student motivation is engaging students in cooperative learning activities. Glasser advocates the use of *genuine* as opposed to *artificial* cooperative assignments. An artificial cooperative assignment is one that can actually be accomplished just as well by an individual who is willing to make the effort. If students prefer to be graded individually, then it is likely that such an activity lends itself to individual work. Also, it is hazardous to award team grades for work that was not actually cooperative, as was pointed out in the vignette about Shrijana at the beginning of this chapter. Both students and parents resent it when a team grade is lower than what an individual might have achieved alone.

Assignments that lend themselves naturally to team cooperation are referred to as *genuine* cooperative assignments. These are activities that cannot be completed alone and lend themselves to a team grade. A high school English teacher I know uses a cooperative approach in his journalism class. The students in his class are put in charge of producing the school newspaper from start to finish. They are responsible for writing the articles, doing the layout, editing, typesetting, and printing, as well as marketing and sales. Students assume different roles in the process, and it is essential that all students do their share. Empowering students to work autonomously involves a risk on the teacher's part. And, there have been times when the teacher wanted to intervene (especially with the editing process) but he restrained himself. One year, a class put out their first newspaper that was fraught with typos and misspelled words. When the students read the printed product themselves, they were chagrined. Their awareness of the need to edit more carefully was raised. The next newspaper was almost flawless.

Lack of Task Completion.   If students aren't able to complete a task in the allotted time, the teacher needs to consider the following questions: Was the task too complex or demanding for the given time period? Did the teacher fail to anticipate the need for an extended group discussion, student reflection, or a break? Careful planning of the activity will assist in time management. Also, with experience in conducting group activities comes a better sense of how long particular processes take.

Are students in a group off-task too much of the time? What is interfering with the work completion? Following are suggestions for helping students who have poor time management skills:

1. Provide students with a schedule for the activity. Display the schedule in a prominent place in the room or give each group a copy of the schedule.
2. Remind students of the schedule, pointing out transition times and providing warning of transition times and ending times. "You have 15 minutes to finish your discussion and compile your findings into a written response."
3. Assign a student to the role of time manager. The time manager is responsible for reminding students of timelines and the need to refocus when they are straying from the task at hand.
4. Directly teach students time management skills and encourage them to practice the skills in their groups.

*Classroom Store, Trapper
School, Nuiqsut, Alaska.*

A Need for More Powerful Rewards.   To increase motivation to learn and
perform, it is important to know what is relevant, fascinating, valuable, or
novel to your students (Hunter, 1982). Unfortunately, not all subjects meet
these criteria. In such a case, you may need to explain to students *why* it's
important to learn the material or perform the skill. You may also need to
supply an extrinsic form of reinforcement for completing the task. Just as a
parent sweetens the drudgery of housework or yardwork with the promise
of playing a table game or renting a videotape, a teacher may need to do the
same. (Earlier in this chapter we discussed the controversy surrounding
the merits of extrinsic versus intrinsic rewards.)

Joyce McCarthy, a fourth-grade teacher, is highly creative in planning
motivating lessons, yet she also issues tokens to the students in her cooperative groups throughout the week. The tokens are given as reinforcers, but
may also be taken away for certain prespecified misbehaviors. On Fridays,
students exchange their tokens for items at the classroom store, which they
run themselves. Some students have individualized behavior plans and
receive tokens for behaviors they are trying to change. In this class, it is difficult to distinguish the students with special education needs from the general
education students. The reward system is a motivator for all the students.

CONCLUSION

This chapter has discussed assessment in cooperative learning, particularly
as it relates to the evaluation of student academic performance, social
skills, and group functioning. Methods for assessment include the more tra-

ditional practice of evaluating student products (quizzes, tests, reports, papers, journals), as well as the evaluation of student participation and group or individual portfolios. A distinguishing feature of cooperative learning is that it has traditionally involved both students and teachers in the assessment process. Students engage in observing themselves, their own group, and other groups. Teachers help students through the evaluation process by helping establish evaluation criteria, teaching students how to gather information and conduct observations, and providing students with evaluation instruments and tools. Teachers also serve a critical role in the assessment process by observing student progress and group functioning.

Careful planning and implementation of cooperative lessons does not assure a trouble-free learning environment. Given the variables involved in the cooperative learning process, such as the quality of the learning objectives, student interaction, and the task itself, it is predictable that difficulties will arise. Teachers lament that they haven't achieved perfection with cooperative learning because their students are struggling, or they just don't seem to "get it." Cooperative learning is such a dynamic and complex process that the standard of achieving perfection is unrealistic.

> The road called learning is endless and that's exactly the way it's supposed to be. No one on this journey is expected to get done, be finished, or fully arrive. (Moorman, 1992, p. 53)

Educating students in cooperative groups requires that teachers and students continually address problems as they surface. Each day in today's diverse classroom brings new opportunities for both success and failure. In truth, we often learn more from our failures than from our successes, especially if we are willing to persevere in determining what went wrong and work to make it right.

QUESTIONS AND ACTIVITIES

1.   Define *assessment* in your own words. Do you think that assessing student outcomes in cooperative learning situations requires a unique approach to the evaluation of students?

2.   Assessing academic achievement in cooperative learning involves more than quizzing and testing students. What other techniques can be used?

3.   How can you involve students in reflecting on their own performance in cooperative groups? Design a simple form that students might use

to monitor the frequency of several different types of student verbal contributions during the activity. Discuss how students would use the information obtained from the observation form to improve their group functioning.

4.   In groups of three or four, discuss an unsuccessful cooperative group experience that one of you has experienced. Analyze the difficulty and try to isolate what went wrong. Was the problem related to poor implementation of the key features of cooperative learning (e.g., individual accountability, positive interdependence), an individual's "misbehavior," or problems with the learning objectives or the task itself? Share your analysis with the class.

SUGGESTED READINGS

Books

Bennett, B., Rolheiser-Bennett, C., & Stevahn, L. (1991). *Cooperative learning: Where heart meets mind.* Toronto: Educational Connections.

Tiberius, R. G. (1990). *Small group teaching: A trouble-shooting guide* (Monograph Series/22), Toronto: OISE Press, The Ontario Institute for Studies in Education.

Magazines

Assessment in Cooperative Learning. (1992, Fall). *Cooperative Learning. The Magazine for Cooperation in Education, 13*(1).

REFERENCES

Adler, S. (1993). *Multicultural communication skills in the classroom.* Boston: Allyn and Bacon.

Bennett, B., Rolheiser-Bennett, C., & Stevahn, L. (1991). *Cooperative learning: Where heart meets mind.* Toronto: Educational Connections.

Calderon, M., & Hertz-Lazarowitz, R. (1992). Dynamic assessment of teachers and language minority students through cooperative learning. *Cooperative Learning, 13*(1), 27–29.

Cohen, E. G. (1994). *Designing groupwork: Strategies for the heterogeneous classroom.* (2nd ed.). New York: Teachers College Press.

Dippong, J. (1992). Two large questions in assessing and evaluating cooperative learning. Teacher challenges and appropriate student tasks. *Cooperative Learning, 13*(1), 6–8.

Charles, C. M. (1989). *Building classroom discipline.* New York: Longman.

Glasser, W. (1986). *Control theory in the classroom.* New York: Harper & Row.

Hunter M. C. (1982). *Mastery teaching.* El Segundo, CA: TIP Publications.

Johnson, D. W., & Johnson, R. T. (1985). *Cooperative learning: Warm-ups, grouping strategies, and group activities.* Edina, MN: Interaction Books.

Johnson, D. W., & Johnson, R. T. (1989). *Cooperation and competition: Theory and research.* Edina, MN: Interaction Books.

Johnson, D. W., & Johnson, R. T. (1990). Personal communication.

Kagan, S. (1992). *Cooperative learning.* San Juan Capistrano, CA: Kagan Cooperative Learning.

Kagan, S., & Kagan, M. (1994). The structural approach: Six keys of cooperative learning. In S. Sharan (Ed.). *Handbook of cooperative learning methods* (pp. 115–133). Westport, CT: Greenwood Press.

Kohn, A. (1991). Group grade grubbing versus cooperative learning. *Educational Leadership, 48*(5), 83–88.

Kounin, J. (1977). *Discipline and group management in classrooms.* York: Holt, Rinehart, and Winston.

Miller, E. (1992). Tips on assessment and evaluation in cooperative work. *Cooperative Learning, 13*(1), 48.

Moorman, C. (1992). You never get there. *Cooperative Learning, 13*(1), 53–54.

Nevin, A. (1993). Curricular and instructional adaptations. In J. W. Putnam (Ed.), *Cooperative learning and strategies for inclusion: Celebrating diversity in the classroom* (pp. 41–56). Baltimore: Paul H. Brookes Publishing Company.

Noone, K. (1990). *Locating African countries.* (Report completed in partial fulfillment of requirements for Prof. J. Thousand, EDSP 322). Burlington, VT: University of Vermont.

Northwest Evaluation Association (1990, August). C. Meyer and S. Schuman (Eds.), White Paper presented at the Conference on Aggregating Portfolio Data, Union, WA.

Putnam, J. W., & Spenciner, L. (1993). Supporting young children's development through cooperative activities. In J. Putnam (Ed.). *Cooperative learning and strategies for inclusion: Celebrating diversity in the classroom* (pp. 123–144). Baltimore, MD: Paul H. Brookes Publishing Co.

Raborn, D. T. (1992). Cooperative learning and assessment: A viable alternative for language minority and bilingual students. *Cooperative Learning, 13*(1), 9–11.

Slavin, R. E. (1989). *Cooperative learning: Theory, research, and practice.* Englewood Cliffs, NJ: Prentice Hall.

Slavin, R. E. (1991). Group rewards make groupwork work. *Educational Leadership, 48*(5), 89–92.

Tiberius, R. G. (1990). *Small group teaching: A trouble-shooting guide* (Monograph Series/22), Toronto: OISE Press, The Ontario Institute for Studies in Education.

INDEX

Ability grouping, of gifted students, 43
Ability levels, 197
Academic performance
    assessment of, 181, 184–188
    cooperative learning and, 31–33
Accountability
    individual, 12–13, 32, 68–70
    motivational strategies and, 69–70
Achievement, and cooperative learning, 31–33
Activity
    authentic, 200
    cooperative, 140
Adler, S., 17, 180
African Americans
    culturally sensitive instructional practices
        for, 165–166
    integration and, 30
    interpersonal space of, 17
    as percentage of population, 26
Alcorn, M. D., 8n
Allport, G., 36
American Indians. See Native Americans
Anderson, M. A., 79, 80
Antarctic expedition, 12, 14–16
Anticipatory guidance, 105–106
Artificial cooperative tasks, 201–202

Asian-Pacific Islanders
    culture of, 162–164
    interpersonal space of, 17
    as percentage of population, 26
Assertive Discipline, 100
Assessment, 6, 178–190
    of academic performance, 181, 184–188
    authentic, 184
    considerations in, 181–184
    criterion referenced, 182
    of general group functioning, 181
    grading and, 183, 186–187
    of learning, 146, 181
    outcomes-based, 180
    of participation, 184–185
    by peers, 179, 188–190, 191, 192, 193
    of portfolios, 185–186
    self-assessment, 179
    of social skill performance, 181
    of students with exceptional needs, 182–183
    testing in, 180–181
    unbiased, 183
Assumed disability, 119–120, 122
Attendance, 41
Attention-oriented students, 119, 120–121
Authentic activity, 200

Authentic performance assessment, 184
Autonomy, 187
Ayres, B. J., 168

Bartlett, J., 115
Base groups, 62–63
Behavior. *See also* Positive behavior
  cooperative learning and, 41
  in mixed ability pairs, 38–39
  supportive, 168
Behavior problems, 115–126
  constructive responses to, 120–122
  goals of, 119–120
  improving participation and, 116–118
  violence, 28
Bell, Andrew, 30
Belonging need, 99
Bennett, B., 181, 187
"Best-evidence synthesis" technique, 31
Bias, in assessment, 183
Blackboard Share, 143
Black English dialect, 165
Bloom, B., 57
Bloom's taxonomy, 57
Bracey, G. W., 25
Brainstorming, 196
Brandt, R., 139
Brewer, A., 166
Broken Squares game, 78
Broome, S., 109
Bruininks, R. E., 27
Brunner, J., 107
Byrd, Richard E., 12, 14, 15

Calderon, M., 183, 184–185
Calhoon, P., 115
Canter, L., 100
Canter, M., 100
Cards
  "Caught Being Good," 108
  daily progress, 124–125
Caring, 13
Caring relationships, 187
Carter, G. C., 38, 39
Carter, S. A., 30
Catanzarite, L., 36
"Caught Being Good" cards, 108
Charles, C. M., 201
Charney, R., 111, 112, 113
Checker role, 66, 118

Cheerleader role, 118
Chrispeels, J., 169
CIRC (Cooperative Integrated Reading and
    Composition), 147
Civil Rights Act of 1964, 30
Clark, R., 169
Classroom(s). *See also* Cooperative classroom
  changes in, 4–5
  inclusive, 162–164
  traditional, 4–5, 29–30
Classroom management. *See* Cooperative
    classroom management
Clements, B., 100, 102
Cohen, E., 36, 152–155, 197
Collaborative teaching, 7
Common School Movement, 30
Communication
  parental involvement and, 126
  student skills in, 72
Community members, 7
Competition
  interdependence through, 68
  learning and, 10–11
Complex Instruction, 152–155
Computers, 79–81
Concern, level of, 69
Conflict contract, 115, 116
Conflict prevention, 100–110
Conflict resolution
  conferences for, 113–114
  example of, 99
  skills in, 42, 72, 110–115
  training in, 78, 114–115
Consensus, 65
Contact Theory, 36
Contract, conflict, 115, 116
Control-oriented students, 119, 121
Cooperation
  caring and, 13, 187
  in dangerous situations, 14–16
*Cooperation and Competition: Theory and
    Research* (Johnson and Johnson), 194
Cooperative activity, 140
Cooperative classroom
  educational technology in, 78–81
  environmental considerations in, 61–62
  example of, 5–8
  modifications for diverse learners, 164–167
  parental involvement in, 7, 126, 168–170
  physical proximity in, 17, 199

teacher in, 5–6, 7–8, 56–57
Cooperative classroom management, 98–128
  behavior problems and, 115–126
  conflict prevention, 100–110
  example of, 98–99
  focusing on positive behavior, 104–110
  PARC strategy in, 104–107
  rules and procedures, 100–104
  solving individual behavior problems,
    115–126
  student needs and, 99–100
Cooperative groups. *See* Group(s)
Cooperative Integrated Reading and Composi-
    tion (CIRC), 147
Cooperative learning
  academic outcomes of, 31–33
  benefits of, 20
  components of, 11–17
  controversial issues in, 42–45
  difficulties of, 19
  historical aspects of, 30–31
  inexperience with, 198
  methods of. *See* Methods
  social outcomes of, 33–34, 42
  student response to, 54–55
  traditional group learning vs., 18, 19
Cooperative Learning Lesson Structures
    (Johnson and Johnson), 137
Cooperative skills, 16–17, 60
  defined, 71
  demonstrating, 73, 75
  developing, 70–78, 136
  encouraging participation, 74, 75–76
  examples of, 72
  feedback on, 73–74, 76
  goals for, 74–75
  identifying, 71–72
  natural approach to teaching, 76–78
  need for, 72, 75–76, 136
  observation of, 73–74
  opportunities to practice, 73, 76
  reflection on, 74–75, 76, 77
  steps in teaching, 71–76
Cooperative structures, 140–141, 143
Cooperative Student Support Teams, 7
Coopersmith, S. A., 40
Corners, 143
Correction strategies, 107
Courier role, 66
Criterion referenced evaluation, 182

Crowley, E. P., 44
Crusader's Handbook, 154
Cultural differences, 198–199
Culturally sensitive instructional practices,
    164–167
Curriculum, 187
Curwin, R., 100

Davidson, N., 33, 134, 156–157
Davies, D., 169
De Avila, E. A., 154, 155
Deci, E., 105
*Designing Groupwork: Strategies for the Het-
    erogeneous Classroom* (Cohen), 152
Deutsch, M., 38
Dewey, J., 30
Dialects, 165
Dippong, J., 191n
Disabilities, students with
  assumed disabilities, 119–120, 122
  benefits of cooperative learning for, 44–45
  evaluation criteria for, 182–183
  interpersonal relations of, 36–37
  law on, 27
Disadvantaged children, 27–29
Discipline, Assertive, 100
Diversity, 6, 26–29. *See also* Modifications for
    diverse learners
  cultural differences and, 198–199
  disadvantaged children, 27–29
  ethnic minorities, 26–27, 35–36
  in interpersonal space, 17
  planning for, 18
  students with disabilities, 27
Doud, J., 117
Dreikurs, R., 119, 120
Drug abuse, 28
Dufner, Annette, 84n
Duncan, J., 168
Duncan, S. E., 154, 155
Dunlap, G., 120

Editing, peer, 137–138, 188, 189
Education
  crisis in, 25–30
  expectations in, 24–25
Education, U.S. Department of, 27
Educational technology, 78–81
  global networking, 80
  multimedia presentations, 80–81

Effort, valuing, 38
Emmer, E., 100, 102
Encouragement chips, 117
Encourager role, 66, 74, 75–76
Englemann, S., 107
Environment
    educational technology in, 78–81
    for groups, 61–62
    modifications for diverse learners, 159
Equalizer role, 66
Equal opportunities for success, 18, 32, 70, 183
Equal opportunity scoring, 32
Ethnic minorities, 26–27, 35–36. *See also* Diversity; *specific minorities*
Etscheidt, S., 117
Evaluation. *See* Assessment
Evertson, C., 100, 102
Exceptional learners. *See* Disabilities, students with
Exemplars, negative, 73
Expanding Cooperative Learning Through Group Investigation (Sharan and Sharan), 149
Expectations, for schools, 24–25
Experience, lack of, 198
Expert groups, 84, 147
Extrinsic rewards, 65, 187–188

Face-to-face interaction, 17
Family. *See* Parental involvement
Feedback
    on cooperative skills, 73–74, 76
    daily progress cards, 124–125
    developing systematic programs for, 122–126
    on performance, 70
    school-home, 126
    self-monitoring, 123–124
    video, 118
Feeling tone, 69–70
Fenner, Jennifer, 162
Finding Out/Descubrimiento (De Avila, Duncan, and Navarrete), 154, 155
Forest, Liana Nan, 178–179
Forms
    for cooperative lesson plan, 82–83
    for goal setting, 192
    for observation, 74, 192, 193
    for peer evaluation, 191

    for self-monitoring, 124
Foster-Johnson, L., 120
Franklin, M. E., 164–165
Freedom, need for, 100
Fun, need for, 100

Games, skill-related, 77, 78
Gardner, H., 70
Gatekeeper role, 118
Gerard, H. B., 35
Gifted education teacher, 6
Gifted students, 42–43
Glass, R. M., 41, 97–130
Glasser, W. J., 17, 99–100, 111, 112, 113, 123, 201
Global networking, 80
Goal setting
    for cooperative skills, 74–75
    form for, 192
    in groups, 17, 64, 65
Goldring, E. B., 43
Good behavior points, 109–110
Goodlad, J. I., 29, 30, 43
Grades
    assessment and, 183, 186–187
    equal-opportunity-for-success, 183
    group, 65, 186
    individual, 186
    no grade, 187
Grant, C. A., 24
Group(s), 56–70
    assessment of, 181
    assigning students to, 58–59
    base, 62–63
    caring in, 13
    duration of, 60–61
    expert, 84, 147
    forming, 58–62
    goals of, 17, 64, 65
    grade for, 65, 186
    heterogeneous, 18, 58
    individual accountability in, 12–13, 32, 68–70
    interdependence in, 11–12, 63–68, 136
    introducing lesson to, 62–63
    laboratory, 138–139
    learning in, 10
    logo for, 68
    planning, 57–58
    rewarding, 32, 64–66
    roles in, 66–67, 78, 117, 118

size of, 60, 199
structuring, 56–57
"Group Grade Grubbing Versus Cooperative Learning" (Kohn), 187
Group Investigation, 148–152
Group learning, vs. cooperative learning, 18, 19
Group management skills, 72
Grunwald, B., 119, 120
Guidance, anticipatory, 105–106

Handbook of Cooperative Learning Methods (Sharan), 148
Harris, A., 100
Hawaiian culture, 162–164
Helpfulness, climate of, 168
Helping others, 38
Hertz-Lazarowitz, R., 183, 184–185
Heterogeneous groups, 18, 58
Hispanics
  interpersonal space of, 17
  as percentage of population, 26
History, of cooperative learning, 30–31
Hodgkinson, H., 26, 27
Holubec, E. J., 11, 30, 31, 41n, 56, 60, 64, 68, 71, 82n
Home visit programs, 170
Hunter, M. C., 69, 196, 200, 203

IAEP-2 (Second International Assessment of Educational Progress), 25
Identity interdependence, 67
IEP (Individualized Educational Plan), 6, 183, 195
Imber, R., 126
Imber, S., 126
Inclusive classrooms, cooperative learning in, 162–164
Individual accountability, 12–13, 32, 68–70
Individual improvement scores, 146
Individualistic learning, 9–10
Individualized Educational Plan (IEP), 6, 183, 195
Individuals with Disabilities Education Act, 27
Inside-Outside Circle, 143
Instructional objectives
  assessment method and, 181–182
  determining, 57–58
Instructional practices, modifications for diverse learners, 164–167
Intelligence, interpersonal, 70

Interaction, face-to-face, 17
Interdependence
  through competition, 68
  in cooperative groups, 63–68
  identity, 67
  positive, 11–12, 136
  task, 67
Interest level, 70
Interpersonal intelligence, 70
Interpersonal relations, 35–39
  cross-ethnic, 35–36
  of low-performing students, 37–39
  of mixed ability pairs, 38–39
  of students with disabilities, 36–37
Interpersonal skills, 33–34, 70–71, 72
Interpersonal space, 17, 199
Interrogator role, 66
Intrinsic motivation, 150
Intrinsic rewards, 65, 187–188

Jaeger, R. M., 27
Jakupcak, J., 162
Jigsaw activity, 197
Jigsaw II, 147–148
Johnson, D. W., 5, 11, 17, 18, 30, 31, 32, 33, 34, 36, 37, 38, 40, 41n, 43, 44, 56, 60, 63, 64, 68, 71, 76, 82n, 115, 135, 136, 137, 138n, 194, 197, 199
Johnson, R. T., 5, 11, 17, 18, 30, 31, 32, 33, 34, 36, 37, 38, 40, 41n, 43, 44, 56, 60, 63, 64, 68, 71, 76, 82n, 115, 135, 136, 137, 138n, 194, 197, 199
Jones, L., 114, 120, 123
Jones, M. G., 38, 39
Jones, V., 114, 120, 123

Kagan, M., 70, 196
Kagan, S., 70, 71, 76–78, 106, 117, 118n, 121, 139–142, 143, 196, 199
Kaplan, J., 123
Kennedy, John F., 25
Keyboarding skills, 79
Kinder, J. S., 8n
Kohler, F., 44
Kohn, A., 60, 187
Kounin, J., 101, 201
Kozol, J., 28

Laboratory groups, 138–139
Lancaster, Joseph, 30

Language, 164
Laws
  on civil rights, 30
  on students with disabilities, 27
Leadership skills, 72
Learning. *See also* Cooperative learning
  competition and, 10–11
  in groups, 10
  individualistic, 9–10
  sources of, 8–9
Learning objectives
  modifying, 158–159, 195
  problems with, 194–198
  restating, 194–195
Learning Together model, 135–139
Lees, Raenelle, 86*n*
Lessons
  introducing, 62–63
  planning, 81–93
Letter, student, 172
Level of concern, 69
Lloyd, J. W., 44
Logo, 68
Lotan, R., 36
Lousen, Liz, 88*n*
Low-performing students, interpersonal rela-
    tions of, 37–39

Madden, N., 147, 148
Male, M., 79
Maliseet Indians, 166–167
Manager role, 66
Marks, John, 90*n*
Maruyama, G., 5, 11, 36, 37, 44
Match Mine, 143
Materials
  modifications for diverse learners, 159
  sharing, 67
McCarthy, Joyce, 203
McLaughlin, T., 123
Meetings, 111–113
Mendler, A., 100
Messenger, M. J., 92*n*, 93*n*
Methods, 134–157
  Complex Instruction, 152–155
  differences among, 156–157
  Group Investigation, 148–152
  Learning Together model, 135–139
  similarities among, 156

structural approach, 139–142, 143
  Student Team Learning (STL), 144–148
  traditional, 4–5, 29–30
Mexican-Americans, interpersonal space of, 17
Miller, E., 182
Miller, N., 35
Minorities. *See* Diversity; Ethnic minorities;
    specific minorities
Misbehavior. *See* Behavior problems
Mixed ability pairs, 38–39, 43
Modeling, of supportive behavior, 168
Modifications for diverse learners, 157–170
  climate, 168
  instructional practices, 164–167
  learning objectives, 158–159, 195
  materials and environment, 159
  parent/family involvement, 168–170
  tutorials, 162
Moorman, C., 204
Morgan, D., 122, 123
Motivation
  intrinsic, 150
  rewards and, 203
  strategies for, 69–70
Muegge-Vaughan, Carolyn, 14, 15
Multimedia presentations, 80–81
Multiple-ability tasks, 153
Multiple intelligences, 70

National Commission on Excellence in Educa-
    tion, 24–25
Nation at Risk, A, 24–25
Native Americans
  cultural differences of, 198–199
  culturally sensitive instructional practices
    for, 166–167
  as percentage of population, 26
Natural approach to teaching cooperative
    skills, 76–78
Navarrete, C., 154, 155
Needs, of students, 99–100
Negative exemplars, 73
Nelson, D., 44
Networking, global, 80
Nevin, A., 157, 183
Noise monitor, 118
Noone, Karen, 183
Northwest Evaluation Association, 185
Numbered Heads Together, 141–142, 143

Oakes, J., 43
Objectives
   instructional, 57–58, 181–182
   learning, 158–159, 194–198
   unacceptable, 196
   unclear, 194–195
   unobtainable, 195–196
Observation
   of cooperative skills, 73–74
   forms for, 74, 192, 193
   by students, 108–109, 110, 118, 192, 193
Observer role, 118
Opportunities for success, 18, 32, 70, 183
Outcomes-based assessment, 180

Pairs Check, 143
Paradigm, new, 138
Paraphrase chips, 117–118
Paraphrasing, 194
PARC strategy, 104–107
Parental involvement, 7
   communication and, 126
   with diverse learners, 168–170
Parker, Francis, 30
Participation
   assessment of, 184–185
   behavior problems and, 116–118
   encouraging, 74, 75–76
   improving, 116–118
Peer acceptance
   between ethnic groups, 35–36
   of low-performing students, 37–39
   of students with disabilities, 36–37
Peer editing, 137–138, 188, 189
Peer evaluation, 179, 188–190, 191, 192, 193
Peer mediation, 6
Peer tutoring, 162
Pelas, Alicia, 162
Pepper, F., 119, 120
Perleman, L. J., 10
Petres, K., 25
Physical proximity, 17, 199
Planning
   for cooperative groups, 57–58
   Individualized Educational Plan (IEP), 6,
      183, 195
   of lessons, 81–93
   need for, 18
   for technology, 79–80

Portfolios, 6, 185–186
Positive behavior
   focusing on, 104–110
   rewarding, 107–110, 125–126
Positive feeling tone, 69–70
Positive interdependence, 11–12, 136
Poverty, 27–29
Power need, 99
Praise, 105
Praise chips, 117
Problem solving, 190–203
Procedures
   developing, 102–104
   examples of, 103
Processing, 136
Progress cards, 124–125
"Project method" of instruction, 30
Proximity, physical, 17, 199
Putnam, D., 166
Putnam, J. W., 27, 41, 159, 198

Raborn, D. T., 183
Reader role, 66
Reading specialist, 6
Recorder role, 66
Redl, F., 105
Reflection, 192
   in cooperative classroom management, 106
   on cooperative skills, 74–75, 76, 77
   group, 17
Regular Lives (film), 168
Resources, sharing, 67
Revenge-oriented students, 119, 121–122
Rewards
   extrinsic vs. intrinsic, 65, 187–188
   group, 32, 64–66
   motivation and, 203
   for positive behavior, 107–110, 125–126
Reynolds, Maynard, 31
Rhode, G., 122, 123
Roderick, T., 115
Role(s), in cooperative groups, 66–67, 78, 117,
   118
Role play, 78
Rolheiser-Bennett, C., 181
Rothstein, C., 126
Roundrobin, 143
Roundtable, 143
Routines, 102–103

Royte, E., 16*n*
Rubrics, 188
Rules, developing, 100–102, 103–104
Ryan, R., 105

Salend, S., 118
Sapon-Shevin, M., 168
Sautter, R. C., 28
Schools
    expectations for, 24–25
    integration of, 30
Schunert, J. R., 8*n*
Science, mixed ability pairs in, 38–39
Scoring. *See also* Grades
    equal opportunity, 32
    individual improvement, 146
Scott, L., 38
Second International Assessment of Educational Progress (IAEP-2), 25
Self-assessment abilities, 179
Self-esteem, 40
Self-monitoring, 123–124
Sharan, S., 28, 36, 148–149, 150, 151*n*, 152
Sharan, Y., 34, 148–149, 150, 151*n*, 152
Sharing, 67
Silberman, M., 121
Silence signal, 63
Simultaneity, 141
Skill(s). *See also* Cooperative skills
    communication, 72
    conflict resolution, 42, 72, 110–115
    group management, 72
    interpersonal, 33–34, 70–71, 72
    keyboarding, 79
    leadership, 72
    study, 162
    task assistance and, 69
Skill games, 77, 78
Skon, L., 44
Slavin, R. E., 5, 11, 18, 31–32, 33, 36, 37, 40, 41*n*, 43, 44, 144–148, 183, 187–188
Sleeter, C. E., 24
Small Group Teaching: A Trouble-Shooting Guide (Tiberius), 194
Smiley, F. M., 30
Smith, D., 122, 123
Social behaviors, 10
Social outcomes, 33–34, 42
Social skills, 33–34, 70–71, 181
Socioeconomic status, 27–29

Software, 79
Space, interpersonal, 17, 199
Special education consulting teacher, 7
Speech therapist, 6
Spenciner, L., 198
Spiegel, A., 27
STAD (Student Teams–Achievement Divisions), 146
Stainback, S., 117
Stainback, W., 117
Steinbrink, J. E., 30
Stevahn, L., 181
Stevens, R., 44, 147, 148
STL (Student Team Learning), 144–148
Stout, J. A., 43
Strain, P., 44
Strom, R. D., 42
Structural approach, 137–143
Structure, 140–141, 143
Students
    assigning to groups, 58–59
    autonomy of, 187
    in developing rules and procedures, 103–104
    interest level of, 70
    level of concern of, 69
    needs of, 99–100
    as observers, 108–109, 110, 118, 192, 193
Student Team Learning (STL), 144–148
Student Teams–Achievement Divisions (STAD), 146
Study skills, 162
Substitute teaching, 54–55
Success
    criteria for, 57–58, 62, 194
    opportunities for, 18, 32, 70, 183
Summarizer role, 66
Support
    climate of, 168
    individualized, 162
Swisher, K., 166

Tack-on skill games, 77
TAI (Team Assisted Individualization), 148
Talking chips, 117
Task assistance, 69
Task completion, 202
Task interdependence, 67
Taskmaster role, 118
Task-related problems, 199–203

Task restructuring, 77
Tateyama-Sniezek, K. M., 44
Taxonomy, Bloom's, 57
T-chart, 75–76
Teachers
    consulting, 7
    in cooperative classroom, 5–6, 7–8, 56–57
    substitute, 54–55
Teaching methods. *See* Methods
Team, 145
Team Assisted Individualization (TAI), 148
Team Learning, 144–148
Teams–Games–Tournaments (TGT), 146–147
Team Word-Webbing, 143
Technology. *See* Educational technology
Tejas, Vernon, 14, 15
Testing, 180–181. *See also* Assessment
TGT (Teams–Games–Tournaments), 146–147
Think–Pair–Share activity, 106, 143
Three-Step Interview, 141, 142, 143
Tiberius, R. G., 194, 196
Time keeper, 66
Torrey, R. D., 43

Training, in conflict resolution, 78, 114–115
Tutorials, 162

Udvari-Solner, A., 159, 162

Vaughan, Norman, 12, 14–16
Video feedback, 118
Violence, 28
Voice control technician, 66

Walberg, H. J., 169
West, R., 122, 123
Wheelan, S., 121
White, R., 109
Whittington, D., 25
Wiltsie, Gordon, 14, 15
"Wind Project, The," 160–161
Wineman, D., 105
Withdrawal, 119–120, 122
Wolfgang, C., 120
Worsham, M., 100, 102

Young, R., 122, 123